HOW SHALL I LIVE MY LIFE?

ON LIBERATING THE EARTH FROM CIVILIZATION

ALSO BY DERRICK JENSEN

HOW SHALL I LIVE MY LIFE?

ON LIBERATING THE EARTH FROM CIVILIZATION

DERRICK JENSEN

The following interviews appeared in slightly different form in *The SUN:*
Thomas Berry, Vine Deloria, George Draffan, David Edwards,
Jan Lundberg, Kathleen Dean Moore, and Carolyn Raffensperger.

Cover photograph by Anna Peters Wehking
Back cover photograph by Derrick Jensen
Cover design by John Yates, Tiiu Ruben and Aric McBay
Text design by Courtney Utt

Edited by Theresa Noll.

10 9 8 7 6 5 4 3

LCCN 2007906931
ISBN 978-1-60486-003-0

Published by:
PM Press
PO Box 23912
Oakland, CA 94623
www.pmpress.org

Printed in the USA on recycled paper.

TABLE OF CONTENTS

INTRODUCTION

We are in the midst of an apocalypse. This culture is killing the planet. Resistance must take many forms, from the physical to the emotional to the intellectual to the legal (and illegal) to the philosophical, and so on.

The people interviewed in this book have all made powerful contributions to helping us see our way toward resisting this deathly culture. David Edwards helps us disentangle ourselves from some of the illusions that keep us tied to the system. Thomas Berry helps us remember what it feels like to be connected to "the natural order of things." Carolyn Raffensperger turns this culture's use of science on its head. Kathleen Dean Moore asks that most central of all questions: How shall I live my life? And Vine Deloria talks about the fundamental difference between Western and indigenous ways of being.

I offer this book—these conversations with these and other authors—to strengthen readers' necessary and often desperate resistance to this culture's onslaught against all that is natural, all that is wild.

I interviewed the people in this book over several years. The interviews were mainly published in *The Sun*.

David Edwards

Interview Conducted
By Telephone
1.11.00

After climbing the business career ladder for most of his twenties, David Edwards left his management-level marketing job to become a writer. He had no idea how he was going to make a living, but the standard version of success had increasingly felt to him like a terrible, deadening failure. "Three things had become obvious to me," the English author says. "The misery of conventional 'success'; the vast and perhaps terminal havoc this 'success' was wreaking on the world; and the fact that no one was talking about either."

Leaving his apartment, his town, his girlfriend, and most of his friends, Edwards wrote until he ran out of money. Then he moved to a small seaside town and supported himself by teaching English as a second language. "Nine months earlier," he says, "I had been head of a marketing department, and now I was teaching the names of fruits to fourteen- and fifteen-year-old Thai kids: I was the happiest man alive!"

The problem in modern Western society, according to Edwards, remains the age-old one of struggling for freedom—but freedom from a very different set of chains. In his first book, *Burning All Illusions* (South End Press), Edwards writes, "we have been prisoners of tyrants and dictators, and consequently have needed to win our freedom in very concrete, physical terms. We now need to free ourselves not from a slave ship, a prison, or a concentration camp, but from many of the illusions fostered in our democratic society."

Edwards grew up in a little English village called Bearsted in the county of Kent, where he was known as "Eggy Edwards" and was infamous for playing practical jokes. His mother was from Sweden, and he spent summers in the country there, an experience he credits with having introduced him to a natural, uncomplicated alternative to modern living.

The boredom and sense of futility and emptiness we feel when working solely for our own benefit, Edwards says, is the first piece in the great puzzle of how best to live our lives. The second piece is the realization that, to escape this sense of futility and find happiness, we have to work to relieve the suffering and increase the happiness of others—not just the poor, or women, or animals, but all living beings. Most people are good, reasonable human beings, Edwards says, but they are prevented from doing good by the delusion that it involves a miserable sacrifice. In fact, he contends, the best way of looking after ourselves is to work for the benefit of everyone else.

Edwards lives in a one-room apartment on a quiet road with lots of trees, birds, and squirrels, just a twenty-minute walk from the English seaside. He works part time for the International Society for Ecology and Culture, writing and doing research on the impact of globalization and the need for localization. He also writes on environmental, political, and human-rights issues for the *Big Issue* (a British magazine sold by homeless people), *The Ecologist*, and *Z Magazine*.

▟▚▞▙

DJ: You have written that there are five things everyone ought to know.

DE: The first thing I believe everyone should know is that the planet is dying. To name one of endless examples, last year marine biologists found that between 70 and 90 percent of the coral reefs they surveyed in the Indian Ocean had just died as a result of global warming. This year, much of what remains is likely to follow. Even though reefs cover only 0.3 percent of the area of the oceans, they're home to one-fourth of all fish species. Not only is this loss tragic and inexcusable in itself, but millions of people depend on reefs and the fish which live there for their lives and livelihoods.

Coral reef ecosystems are probably the first major victims of global warming, with others lining up to follow. Scientists now predict that the polar bear will be extinct in the wild within twenty years. Once-great populations of other sea mammals and seabirds could die out as well.

My second point is that huge numbers of intelligent, motivated people are working all out to obstruct action to save the planet. Take the much-ballyhooed Rio Earth Summit in 1992, for example, and then the Kyoto Convention in 1997. How is it that no matter how clear the evidence nor how stern the scientific warnings, time and again effective action is stifled? What prevents it, and why? In the case of the Kyoto Convention, we have a clear answer. John Grasser, Vice-President of the National Mining Association, and a member of the Global Climate Coalition, an organization set up by over a hundred major corporations for the express purpose of combating efforts to limit greenhouse gas emissions, said, "We think we have raised enough questions among the American public to prevent any numbers, targets or timetables to achieve reductions in gas emissions being agreed here... What we are doing, and we think successfully, is buying time for our industries by holding up these talks."

And of course Grasser isn't alone. What we're seeing in the so-called debate over global warming is that the biggest enterprise in human history, which is the worldwide coal and oil industry, is at war with the ability of the planet to sustain life. And part of the battlefield over which the industry is fighting includes our hearts and minds.

The corporate press and politicians keep talking about global warming as if there's significant doubt about it, yet the debate is between perhaps half-a-dozen high-profile skeptics bankrolled by this trillion dollar industry against the consensus of fully 2,500 of the world's most qualified climate scientists working as part of the Intergovernmental Panel on Climate Change. How is it that these six—whose arguments are often shot full of illogic and absurdity—count the same as all other evidence?

That leads directly to my third point, which is that the death of the planet is symptomatic of a deeper, institutionalized subordination of all life—including human life—to profit. The world is chock-full of environmental and human rights catastrophes that are very real, but the world is just as full of people "buying time for our industries". The lack of discourse about the crucial question of valuing profits over life brings us to the fourth point, which is that the same economic and political forces that profit from these atrocities also profit from the suppression of truth. The defining political and economic truths about the world we live in are not very complicated or difficult to understand. We don't have to dig very deep before things become painfully obvious, but it's the role of the corporate mass media and politicians to prevent us from digging at all, to make sure that instead we spend all of our time thrashing around in the shallows.

DJ: Like by watching *Judge Judy* or *Entertainment Tonight*?

DE: If we can just stay distracted enough we'll leave the deep delusional supports of state and corporate power alone. And so we drown in superficiality.

Not only that, but we participate in our own mystification. Although the planet is being demolished before our eyes, the media remain content to artificially isolate each new disaster—the status quo is preserved by our playing with pieces of the jigsaw, but never being able to complete the picture—and we remain content to let them, believing all this nonsense about "developing nations," "progress," "sustainable growth" and Western leadership of the "free world". We steadfastly refuse to interpret events as symptomatic of the logic and overwhelming power of the corporate system. And while the notion that we have a free press seems superficially plausible, it only takes a moment of honest reflection to realize that when a world is being ravaged by corporations, a corporate media system is the last place to look for truth.

But it's important to be clear that our delusions are not the result of some conspiracy on the part of a few business moguls. It's much more structural, and psychological. Modern thought control is dependent not on crude conscious planning, but on the human capacity for self-deception. I think one of the central themes of my work is that one of the biggest obstacles to social change is the propaganda system working secretly and unsuspected inside of our own.

I'm not immune from this, even though I work on these issues all the time. I'll feel this strange internal conflict between what I know is true—what every cell in my body tells me is true—and what I am told is true from the outside. It's almost as though people become hypnotized, or hypnotize themselves, to believe these obvious absurdities. The key, I suspect, is that "the world" be made to appear to basically accept what might otherwise be considered absurd or outrageous, and then that small, lonely, insecure part of us that longs to belong, that is terrified of being alone, thinks "Oh yes, well that must be right," not as a matter of reason but out of fear of exclusion, isolation.

Erich Fromm said that if our greatest physical fear is death, our greatest psychological fear is total social exclusion, isolation, rejection, aloneness. So world leaders talk about freedom and democracy while supporting dictators with arms and money the world over. The right of the superpowers to kill people worldwide is rooted in nothing, certainly not in legality or justice—because if justice isn't rooted in compassion it's not rooted in anything—yet because "the world" is made to seem as if it agrees, even the victims may well have a sense that it is somehow just and right.

DJ: I think there's something else going on here, too. You've written about the work of Daniel Goleman.

DE: He cited a very interesting study done in the 1960s by a guy by the name of Lester Luborsky, who used a special camera to track the eye movements of people who'd been asked to look at a set of pictures. The people were supposed to tell which pictures they liked or disliked. Three pictures were sexual in content. One, for example, showed the outline of a woman's breast, beyond which a man could be seen reading a newspaper. The results were amazing. Many of the viewers were able to avoid letting their gaze stray even once to the sexually suggestive parts of the pictures, and later, when asked to describe the content of the pictures, they remembered little or nothing suggestive about them. Some people couldn't even recall seeing those pictures at all! The interesting thing is that in order to avoid looking at the parts of the pictures the person feared would be objectionable, some part of the mind had to know what the picture contained so that it could know what to avoid. Somehow the mind anticipates when something will be offensive or threatening to our worldview, and hurries to throw a protective filter in place to steer away our awareness. The avoidance is not at all random but incredibly efficient. We know exactly where not to look.

DJ: How does this play out in day-to-day living?

DE: I think it was Upton Sinclair who said, "It's difficult to get a man to understand something when his salary depends on his not understanding it."

We build our lives on foundations of ideational schemas, which we then spend much of our lives protecting from conflicting facts, experiences, and ideas. The self-deception is made easier for us by our society's cult of specialization. People have allowed themselves to be convinced that they're basically just journalists or arms salespeople or oil executives. Their jobs define their lives. And it is their job in each of these cases to make money for business. Anything going beyond that profession is rejected as 'nothing to do with me'. That's drilled into us all the way through school and into business. We see being professional and expert and talented and intelligent as a matter of being specialized. And of course the first thing that's lost when you specialize is your humanity. It's like Rousseau said: we've got lots of chemists, physicists, and so on, but there isn't a citizen among us.

DJ: Let's take this slowly.

DE: Say you've got an executive passionately committed to the idea of his own fundamental goodness. That person would have a terribly difficult time seriously entertaining the notion that the corporation for which he's worked over the course of a lifetime, and indeed the entire corporate system of which he's a part, is responsible for terrible destruction of humanity and in nature. To acknowledge that would be to acknowledge that he has in fact lent his talents to genocide and ecocide. But he can't do that—it's a very difficult thing to do. He's spent years building up a career. His prestige and sense of self-worth are closely tied to his success, to how much oil he has discovered or how many cars he has produced.

Given all this, serious consideration of the moral status of the work would create profound conflict between his morality and his financial as well as his emotional/social needs. The money, by the way, is no small matter. It may seem in a very real sense that he has everything to lose and nothing to gain from that sort of serious examination, and so his unconscious will protect his sense of self from a very painful conflict by dismissing or ignoring any evidence that he's participating in these atrocities. And it will do this in such a way that it never even occurs to him—even with the evidence staring him in the face, like the breast in the photo—that there's the slightest thing wrong with what he's doing. The same is true of journalists who know that their livelihoods and sense of social esteem are based on serving corporate power, and so who under no circumstances allow themselves to comprehend the true nature of the role they're playing.

R.D. Laing described this perfectly. He proposed that dysfunctional families—those with severe alcoholism and child abuse—are able to keep themselves unaware of their own problems, and agree to the delusion that they are a "happy family," if they follow a set of three rules, which are:

Rule A: Don't.

Rule A.1: Rule A does not exist.

Rule A.2: Do not discuss the existence or nonexistence of Rules A, A.1, or A.2.

That these rules apply not only to dysfunctional families should be obvious. One example from the media might concern Pinochet. Now, in the media, "Don't" as far as Pinochet was concerned, is "Don't discuss the fact that the CIA and U.S. business interests were behind the coup that put him in power and that it had nothing to do with the Cold War." And of course don't discuss the pattern of which Pinochet is only one little part, which is that the atrocities are repeated all over the Third World to protect profits, and have been for hundreds of years now. You can discuss the facts that he was a dictator and that he committed atrocities, but don't discuss the real issues.

Now, to Rule A.1: Rule A does not exist. People reject out of hand any conception that there's a ban on discussing stuff like that, and yet strangely that stuff never gets in. You see this time and again, no matter the topic. The mainstream is happy to discuss just about any weird and wonderful idea: UFOs, aliens, babyism, anything, but somehow these equally unusual and interesting ideas don't make it. And that leads to the third part of the rule, which is that in polite society you simply can't have the sort of conversation we're having right now, where you discuss the unspoken rules that govern essentially all of our discourse, and in fact much of our perception.

DJ: These rules seem to apply across the board, whether we're talking about (or rather, not talking about) a father raping his daughter or a culture destroying life on earth. We can't talk about the fact that we're going crazy because we're so unhappy with our jobs. It's a generic set of rules.

DE: It's like Harold Pinter said, about how the crimes of the U.S. throughout the world have been "systematic, constant, clinical, remorseless, and fully documented," yet nobody talks about them. Or, to use another example, children aren't forced to choose from a wide range of careers within the corporate system, by which I mean they aren't deliberately brainwashed into believing they have freedom. Instead they're convinced they're making a free choice because society functions in such a way that they're entirely unaware of alternatives.

DJ: As we talk I keep thinking about a series I saw in the regional paper on what life will be like in a hundred years, and it was all grossly positive. Nobody talked about the fact that we probably will not have a planet. How does that fit in?

DE: There's a strange split in the press. On the one hand, it's the press job to be extremely upbeat about the future, compared to what people actually feel about the future: "We've never had it so good, everybody's out shopping, isn't it wonderful?" At the same time they have to be extremely negative about human nature, about people's concern about the world and people's willingness to do anything. As John Pilger has said, it's a big part of the media's role to ridicule the notion that people are capable of organizing a better, more compassionate way of life. For example, the demonstrations against the WTO in Seattle were so large that the press really had no choice but to cover them (keeping in mind Laing's three rules, for example, making certain to not address the real issues), but since then the press has totally dropped it, and it's been amazing to see the newspapers once again back in the required groove: "Nobody cares about anything any more. Everybody's totally indifferent. We're all focused on ourselves. There are no big ideas. There's no belief in any sort of religious or moral principles." The point I'm really getting at is that I think these two—being positive about the future and negative about human nature—go together.

DJ: Why?

DE: They both serve the interests of power. On the one hand the utopian future is the same promise we've been handed since the start of civilization, that we'll go to heaven as long as we do what we're told. And for us heaven is a sort of technological materialist utopia.

Now, on the other hand, the reason we even need this utopia (and in fact need those in power in the first place) is because we're so 'flawed' and 'evil'. If we were satisfied—or god forbid, happy—with ourselves, maybe we wouldn't need, or be deceived by, a utopia that keeps us living in a way that actually makes us miserable. And if we allowed ourselves to believe that human nature was fundamentally good—that people could come together to solve their own problems—we might reject the authoritarian systems that keep us on our knees. We would also reject the forces of authority we've internalized.

This internalization is central to the maintenance of current power structures. Sheer force has many disadvantages as a means of social control, not the least of which is that it contains within it the obvious problem that people can easily see they are being oppressed and so may well seek freedom. It's much more powerful to get people to want and even need to obey, to get people to believe disobedience is sin and obedience is virtue.

All of that conditioning breaks down if you don't believe human beings are fundamentally evil. If people ever begin to believe they can manage their affairs without depending on the 'tough love' of these all-knowing, authoritarian leaders, the powerful few will have a real reason to be worried.

DJ: How did you get started thinking about all this?

DE: For me it really started in the mid-eighties when I began to be aware of environmental problems. The closer I looked, the worse the damage seemed. Yet there was next to nothing about it in the press. That dissonance pushed me in the direction of asking, Is the version of reality that I'm getting actually real? Or is it possible that somehow a whole false version of reality is being created and imposed on me? From there I began to ask, What are the consequences of that for me personally, and for other people personally? To what extent are these political issues personal? In other words, concern about global warming and the ozone layer, and the fact that we don't talk about these in any meaningful sense, led me to questions about the conduct of my own life.

I began to question what constitutes happiness. I had this idea that happiness would consist of falling in love. If I just met the right woman everything would be okay. And if I were just successful in my career, then I would be happy. On one level I already knew this wasn't true, because my own parents had money, and their friends were successful in conventional terms, but when you got past the false-fronts there were huge amounts of alcoholism, nervous breakdowns, and pills. So it began to dawn on me that the official version of success might actually be a sort of failure, another deception of the kind I was seeing with regards to the environment.

All that said, I tried to be a good businessperson, but the more successful I became, the less successful I felt. I was becoming more and more miserable. And then in 1987, there was this incredible storm, a hurricane across the UK, which knocked down hundreds of thousands of trees, and you couldn't walk against the wind. Something sort of snapped inside of me. There's a quote from Ovid that matches what I felt at the time, trying to walk against this wind: "I who pursue thee am no enemy. Thou knowest not whom thou fleeest, and for that reason dost thou flee. Run with less speed, I pray and hold thy flight." I began to think that I needed to not run away from the feelings I was having—the dissonance, the unhappiness, the doubts, the fears—and I also needed to not run away from my growing awareness of what we were doing to the planet, but that I needed to somehow learn the lessons that each of these areas I was trying to avoid could teach me. I realized that if you didn't run away from them—into more success, into more indulgence—and actually confronted them, these horrors could in a sense be transformed into fantastic lessons. And so I began to see all this sense of failure, this sense of the inadequacy of romantic love, and the inadequacy of career success, as a way of actually transforming my life, in terms of rejecting them, and looking for something else.

DJ: What happened then?

DE: Well, I became even more miserable! I continued to make quite good progress in my business career, but my doubts were starting to get in my way. As you know, in business you're supposed to be very aggressive, and you can't fight with one arm tied behind your back. So I continued to suppress my doubts.

DJ: Recognizing the significance of the violent language that you just used.

DE: Business is a form of warfare. No doubt about it. Profit is the primary goal, to which everything else must be subordinated. One of the most disturbing things about having to work in business—which most people are aware of but don't want to think about—is that everything you do has to reflect that ultimate goal. The way you smile, shake hands, your attitude, everything has to conform. And if you don't, you're seen as a kind of traitor, in the military sense. I found that any expressions of moral or compassionate concern were viewed with tremendous hostility, because they presented very real threats to the primary goal, ideas that cannot coexist in the business culture with that primary goal.

So for example when I was at British Telecom in the late 1980s I tried to set up a Green Initiatives group, and as a result my career was finished within that organization. Why? Because I had betrayed the fact that I didn't share the cynicism, ambition, and aggression required in this military style corporate campaign.

I was living a double life at the time, working as a manager, running a small business within a larger business, and at lunchtime reading these books on green issues. I had to keep my lunchtime self hidden from the people around me, for the reason I've just explained. It wasn't really a terrible crisis for me though because I never took business that seriously—I always saw it as a bit of a joke—so I wasn't really torn apart. But I never thought I would have the courage or motivation to abandon my career. And then I came across Joseph Campbell's book, *The Hero With A Thousand Faces*, which was able to strip me of my inertia. The basic message for me in that book was this: in mythology, as above, so below. That was it. The light bulb went on. What's happening inside of people in any society is also reflected outside. And when society and people go the wrong way, people and society end up in what Campbell called "The Wasteland," represented in the world by environmental destruction, chaos and war, and represented in society by a culture emptied of all real vitality and honesty.

Now, it's important to bring this out of the realm of philosophy and into the everyday world. On the most basic level, one of the worst parts for me of being in the business world was the utter boredom. I couldn't stand to do these bloody awful business reports, and have these interminable meetings about bullshit. By 1991 I was earning probably $50,000 a year, with three or four holidays, but I had a sense of my life ticking away.

DJ: The defining moment came for me sitting in front of a computer, wishing time would pass till 5:00 so I could go home, and realizing that I was wishing away the only thing I had. I remember holding my fingers in front of my face, and realizing that selling my hours is no different than selling my fingers: I've only so many of them, and when they're gone I've nothing left.

DE: I think that one of the reasons we're so profoundly lonely, bored, and stressed at work is that the manipulative logic of business is simply incompatible with our behaving as human beings in relation to each other. Another way to put this is that because the "answer" to life we have effectively been forced to choose—happiness through money and status—does not come close to answering our deepest needs but instead the deepest needs of the economic system into which we've been born, it's no wonder that we experience terrible boredom. The question becomes: what is that boredom telling us? And here's another: how can we respond to it?

Yet another way to say all this is that the cause of the Wastelands inside and out is, simply put, that individuals and society are motivated by greed. Money is dead, as Marx said. And if you're motivated by something dead, you become dead yourself, and you kill the world as well. What's wrong for me is wrong for the planet. Saving the planet isn't about trying to be nice and righteous and green. It's about saving your own life, and the life in the world in the process. And vice versa.

So what do you do? You change your motivation. You look for happiness by working for the forces promoting life not death. You try to build your life around reducing suffering, promoting happiness. As far as possible you try to find compassion and love as your motivators. And in the meantime, in my case, you quit your job. I just walked out one afternoon. I said, "People, I'm off."

They said, "Right. See you on Monday."

I said, "No, I'm off. That's it. I'm going."

People thought I was committing some kind of suicide. My sister thought I was going crazy. Maybe from a cultural perspective I was, but that's a good thing. It's not necessary, or possible, to abandon all work, but the idea I think is to begin to change your orientation away from doing things just for the money.

Even though I, too, sometimes thought I was crazy, I also really began to understand that we all have inside of us energies and desires and motivations that lead us into trouble if they're thwarted. If you try to deny and suppress the way you feel about the world, it can actually damage you. Fromm talked about how biophilia—a love of life—is a biologically normal principle, but that necrophilia—a love of death or destructiveness—grows as an alternative to biophilia, when biophilia is repressed. And of course ignoring the impulses to live your own life also makes you just plain miserable.

DJ: What are some of the illusions that force us to stay in our self-imposed prisons?

DE: I think romantic love is an important one, in terms of the idea of finding 'the one' who will make you perfectly happy. I've always thought that the song "All you need is love!" is the perfect message from the point of view of the status quo. Don't get me wrong: romantic love can be a tremendous thing. Unfortunately, no romance can ever provide an adequate answer to a life lived in a society of dramatically limited freedom. So I would say that romantic love, like green consumerism, corporate responsibility, and the Western "yearning for freedom and human rights", often serves to divert genuine concern and genuine searching into a harmless cul-de-sac while appearing to be a genuine message of hope for humanity.

I would say that another illusion is that we can trust our leaders.

DJ: You've written: "To expect our leaders to adhere to basic standards of rationality and morality in their public lives is to indulge in a kind of anthropomorphism: they will not, indeed cannot."

DE: A big part of the job of politicians and CEOs is to look very much like ordinary, reasonable human beings. But they are peculiarly constrained by their public roles. It doesn't really matter whether leaders are personally moral or not, because in their public lives they're constrained from acting with the kind of compassion and reason we associate with the idea of a fully human being. Their highest priority must at all times be the defense of profits, to which logic and morality are always without question subordinated. Where basic logic and reason threaten profits, leaders routinely resort to audacious extremes of illogic and unreason—often carefully wrapped in deliberate obfuscation—to hide the reality as far as possible. The same is true for morality: where decency threatens profits, our leaders have no choice but to put aside their humanity, or to risk disappearing from public view.

What this means in practice is that while all but the most depraved individuals would agree that it is wrong to steal from children, to torture and kill them, our leaders are required in effect to disagree, and to act accordingly, in Iraq, for example. Profit can never be satisfied, and stealing food from dying children to give to the wealthy is institutionalized within the capitalist system. Again, that's a good example of a truth that simply can't be true however true it actually is. In earlier societies it would have been the issue of whether God really existed and so on—it's a constraint we're always confronted with. It's incredibly naïve to imagine that we're finally free of such constraints.

To expect humanity from our leaders—both political and corporate— is anthropomorphism. Time and again our hopes will be raised and then dashed. Indeed, the aim of much of politics is to raise our hopes and then let them drift off into nothingness, into "business as usual."

It all comes back to an experiment I once saw on TV about how crystals are formed. If you put a square box on the floor, and you put a funnel over it, full of thousands of ping-pong balls, and you tip the balls into the square frame, the balls automatically build a pyramid. Nobody's consciously designing it. That's just the way the structure is built. I think it's vital to remember that politicians are like little balls falling into that system. And those who make it to the top fit the bill. The politician who succeeds represents the framing conditions. Politicians who don't fit into those framing conditions don't get to the top, they bounce out into obscurity.

DJ: What is it that causes some people to feel their own numbness, and do something about it?

DE: I don't know. It's certainly not intelligence. Maybe courage, being willing to face the possibility that what you've built your life on for many years has been a waste of time. Maybe faith in the idea that truth—however frightening it might seem—will always bring benefits. Thought itself is very scary. Bertrand Russell has a great line about this: "Men fear thought more than they fear anything else on earth—more than ruin, more even than death. Thought is subversive and revolutionary, destructive and terrible; thought is merciless to privilege, established institutions, and comfortable habits; thought is anarchic and lawless, indifferent to authority, careless of the well-tried wisdom of the ages..." And this is my favorite bit: "But if thought is to become the possession of many, not the privilege of the few, we must have done with fear. It is fear that holds men back—fear lest their cherished beliefs should prove delusions, fear lest the institutions by which they live should prove harmful, fear lest they themselves should prove less worthy of respect than they have supposed themselves to be."

DJ: Where do we go from here?

DE: We can begin by challenging the idea that a life motivated solely by desire for personal gain can lead to good things: point to the obvious, really clear, collapse of the environment, the terrible suffering of the Third World, alienation, the utter deadness of work life and much Western culture. Then when people have started to see that working for greed leads to all kinds of actual and metaphorical death in themselves and outside, then you can maybe begin to consider the remarkable argument proposed by Buddhists: that your life and happiness, all life and happiness, are best served by working for the benefit of others, not yourself. I can honestly say that mixing that idea with my own experience has been the most extraordinary revelation for me because I think it's true and yet it's an astonishing thing to even think about. The biggest obstacle though is getting people to recognise that there is any kind of fundamental problem—they think there's so much to lose from even thinking that way, for the reasons we've discussed.

DJ: You've written, "There is no greater obstacle to freedom than the assumption that it has already been attained."

DE: What prison could be more secure than that deemed to be "the world," where the boundaries of action and thought are assumed to be not the limits of the permissible, but rather the limits of the possible? "Democratic" society is based around sustaining that illusion. It's the ultimate prison, because nobody's going to try to escape from a situation of apparent freedom. Concomitant to that is that we must be happy, because if we're free, then we can do whatever makes us happy.

DJ: And if you're not happy, it's your own damn fault.

DE: If life is tough, it must be because life is dreadful—that's life! You're born, you suffer, and you die. That's deeply, deeply ingrained in people. I think our society doesn't really believe it's possible to be truly happy—but that actually reflects on our culture, not life.

DJ: Which is a self-fulfilling prophecy.

DE: It's certainly an odd way to organize a culture, but that's what we've got. We've got a system that's evolved over centuries—millennia really—to satisfy the requirements of power, becoming progressively more efficient. So, for example, totalitarian systems were also designed to satisfy the requirements of power. But because people knew they weren't free, and therefore knew they couldn't be happy, they sought to change it, which makes it a very unstable system. So systems of power have refined their strategies and tactics through a process of unnatural selection to produce a system that creates the illusion of freedom, but so powerfully that people actually believe in the illusion.

One of the things that breeds is pervasive cynicism, because on some deep, deep level—the level at which the mind saw the breast so that the picture could be avoided—we cannot ultimately lie to ourselves. We believe that life is awful, but our cynicism should be about the culture, not life. Yet because cynicism about the culture isn't allowed…

DJ: Because it would call into question all of the lies on which we base our lives.

DE: It gets transferred over to life itself.

DJ: I've always thought that the people who believe the world was created 6000 years ago were just ignorant, but I now understand the deep psychic need for that: they really are defining the beginning of this culture as the beginning of life. The alternatives simply do not exist. They've been defined away.

DE: I work with Helena Norberg-Hodge, who spent many years in Ladakh, the trans-Himalayan region of Kashmir. One of the things she said in her book *Ancient Futures* is that when she first got there she couldn't believe the people were really as happy as they seemed. She thought, "My god, how can they go around putting these smiles on? It's ridiculous, a social pathology." Suddenly it dawned on her that they really were that happy. You read that time and again in the accounts of the European explorers. The Tainos, for example, who were slaughtered by Columbus and the Spaniards. Columbus's primary impression of them was how happy they were.

DJ: What are we afraid of?

DE: Emotions, for one thing, kindness for another. We in the West seem to take it for granted that emotion and reason are conflicting. We think that to be rational is to be like Spock from Star Trek, and that to be unemotional gives you the capacity to see facts clearly. You find this often with business-people and scientists: when they want to be taken seriously they speak in a cold, unemotional manner.

I'm interested in the Eastern idea, which I think fits perfectly with what we've been saying about selective inattention, that some emotions actually help you to perceive the world more clearly. Others do not. Another way to say this is that if greed, ambition, and selfishness create blockages to perceiving the world as it is, to clear away those blockages would help you to perceive the world more accurately. That leads to the next question: How do you clear those blockages?

DJ: Can you please define compassion?

DE: Compassion is the desire to remove the suffering of others, and love is the desire to reinforce and preserve their happiness. So the two are related.

Anyway, by reinforcing our capacity for compassion and love, by concentrating on other people's needs rather than ourselves, we can remove this sort of energy system which creates this selective inattention, which creates this capacity for self-deception. This is what the Buddhists have been saying for some two and a half thousand years: compassion and kindness and love empower reason, because you're taking away the energy that drives the selective inattention. I think that's important not only personally, but especially for dissidents.

DJ: Compassion sometimes seems a fairly abstract word. What do you want people to do?

DE: It took me a long time to realize that compassion isn't passive, but active. As I said earlier, you need to begin by challenging the results of the self-serving life, after which you can maybe start to see the benefits from an other-serving life. How you actually work to help others is maybe less important. I think spreading ideas that challenge destructive illusions is important, but that's just one way. Activists always focus on the suffering caused by political injustice and so on, but actually life is full of suffering that is just the suffering of life: loss of loved ones, old age, sickness, death. Working to relieve that suffering is just as valid, just as important. For me, working for others in any way at all is a kind of political act because our political problems are rooted in a culture that has toxic levels of egotism and selfishness. We think of political action in terms of protesting, leafleting and so on—all very important—but when you think about it, to reorient your life away from happiness through selfishness to happiness through helping others, however you do it, if you're sincere about it, can mean changing all of your subsequent actions to work against the greed system that is destroying us.

I would say one of the first things is to simply try to increase awareness of the problems, and to ask yourself how you might deal with them. Then you might also ask how those problems might be dealt with from outside the Western tradition.

None of this is to say that you should just sit there and say, "I'm going to have compassionate thoughts" but then live exactly the same way you've always done—your compassionate thoughts need to be reflected in what you actually do, how you behave. How can you aspire to compassion and yet work for an arms manufacturer? You need to help other people, to experiment with working in that direction. You need to find out what the real problems are. And that for me means gaining some sort of awareness of compassionate movements and compassionate philosophies. I think we Westerners have got a lot to learn on this, we need to try hard to be humble—which is hard because we are very proud, very arrogant. I am, and I find reflecting on my ignorance helps.

The analogy I like is becoming a weightlifter. I know this sounds kind of trite, but I think one's ability to feel compassion and love has to be developed through learning and practice. And just as no one expects you to finish your first session of weightlifting and then go and lift up a car, there will be situations that if you try to be compassionate, it will be beyond you. Compassion also doesn't mean allowing yourself to be a punching bag, allowing yourself to be abused or destroyed. The point I'm trying to make is that while we should try to be more compassionate, that should include being so toward ourselves.

If you start to see through unrestrained hedonism—status, possessions, consumption, luxury—you will find that you begin to have all kinds of freedom and time to work on this stuff: it's a kind of deal you can make with the universe: I'll give up greed for freedom. Then you can start putting this time to good use.

One of the things I think that stops a lot of people from doing any of this work is a kind of helplessness: the problems are so big, what can one person do? I have two answers to that. The first is that once you realize that helping others is also helping yourself, the size of the overall problems becomes irrelevant. You're not doing it as a one-man, one-woman army to save the whole world, but simply because it's good for them and good for you, and it feels good. And incidentally it is good for your physical health. There are studies now that show that caring for others, even just having affectionate thoughts, is good for you in quite crude, measurable physical and mental health terms. It's no secret really: anyone who has watched their little two-year-old niece unselfconsciously absorbed in her games, and felt that wonderful warm affectionate sense that she's a wonderful, dear little thing who you would die for, knows that kindness and personal happiness go together, whereas grasping, hate and arrogance make us thoroughly frozen and miserable—it's clear but our values are often based on a very different view of happiness.

The second part of the answer is that actually one motivated person can accomplish a disproportionately large amount of good. Selfish illusions are based on nothing, just lies, and even one moment of honesty based on a desire to relieve suffering can destroy vast numbers of lies—that's why power is so paranoid about controlling what we know and believe.

The question becomes, how do we get there? If our culture is based on necessary illusions, then the first thing we need to do is expose those illusions. If the first rule of a dysfunctional system is "Don't," then the first thing we need to do is "Do": Speak!

There is a certain bliss that comes from telling the truth. And I think the real goal is to tell the truth, to be as honest as you can manage to be, in a way that you think will be helpful. Of course that will cost you publication opportunities, and probably money, but when you consider the real extent of the suffering in the world, it really isn't asking very much of us that we not write articles about bullshit for money.

I think that people underestimate the power of somebody willing to tell the truth, because in fact very few people are: How will I pay the rent? How will I eat? Where will I publish it? But the universe is more magical than that; it doesn't work like that. People think they have to identify a market, what people want—even radicals do this—but that's exactly wrong. What is true? What really inspires me, excites me? What will really help people, really take away their confusion and suffering? Write about those things and to hell with what people are supposed to want. It's sort of a funny, crazy, bloody-minded way, but I think it's the only way to bring water to the Wasteland we've talked about. When I read something truthful, something real, I breathe a deep sigh and say, "Thank you so much—I wasn't mad or alone in thinking that after all!" So often we are all left to our own devices, struggling in the dark with this whole external framing system and internalized propaganda system, and then for someone to tell us the truth is such a gift. In a world where people are bullshitting all around us, confusing us—and confusion is a cause of huge suffering—it's a great kindness to be honest.

Thomas Berry

Interview Conducted
at a hotel in Greensboro, North Carolina
11.16.00 – 11.17.00

T homas Berry doesn't fit the image of a typical environmentalist. A Catholic monk in his late eighties, he is a philosophical forebear to younger generations of activists. His main focus is not the immediate battles being fought, but the roots of the problem, which he traces back to the beginnings of Western civilization.

Berry wrote his book *The Dream of the Earth* (Sierra Club Books) beneath an ancient oak in New York City, on a slope overlooking the Hudson River. That tree, to which he dedicated his book, lived through many changes, beginning with the arrival of the Europeans and the end of traditional Native American ways. It lived through the disappearance of the wood bison, the passenger pigeon, the great American chestnuts, the wolverines who prowled the shores of the Hudson, the Atlantic salmon that were once so numerous they threatened to carry away fishermen's nets. It stood there as men cut down the neighboring trees, demolishing the forest where its life began. It lived through the pouring of billions of tons of concrete, the erection of brick buildings and rigid structures of steel.

Born in 1914, when there were fewer than 2 billion people in the world, Berry, too, has lived through many changes. He grew up in an undeveloped— read, undestroyed—area of the South. "I saw the beginnings of the automobile age," he says, "and, to some extent, the age of industrialization. I remember the discovery of the Arabian oil fields in the 1920s, and the development of the petrochemical age after the Second World War. By the time I was eight years old, I already saw something happening that I didn't like."

Berry has spent much of his life trying to understand why this culture is bent on destroying the natural world. When he was twenty, he entered a Passionist monastery, and for ten years, he got up at two every morning for liturgy. From 3 a.m. on he studied the foundations of Western thought. He discovered that environmental degradation is not a recent development: for example, by the time Plato wrote his Republic, the Greeks had already cut down the forests of their homeland.

At thirty, Berry went to the Catholic University of America, where he earned a doctoral degree in history. He also learned Chinese and Sanskrit, he says, "so I could find out how other cultures and religions dealt with the problems of human existence." Berry traveled to China to teach and later became director of the graduate program in the history of religions at Fordham University. In 1970, he founded the Riverdale Center of Religions Research in Riverdale, New York, and remained its director until 1995.

The fate of the next generation, which will live to see a world of 8 to 10 billion people, is often on Berry's mind. "They are going to be in a tragic situation," he says, "particularly in regard to petroleum. Our food depends on petroleum, and in a sense is transformed petroleum, just like our energy, transportation, clothing, utensils, and plastics. What are people going to do when the petroleum is gone?"

One of Berry's book titles is *The Great Work: Our Way into the Future* (Crown Publishing). The "great work" facing humanity, he says, is to move from mindlessly extracting and consuming the earth's resources to establishing a mutually beneficial relationship with nature. His other books include two academic works on religion, *Buddhism and Religions of India* (both Columbia University Press), and *The Universe Story* (Harper SanFrancisco), coauthored with cosmologist Brian Swimme.

The old oak tree under which Berry wrote is no more. It was cut down by a homeowner worried that its branches would fall on his roof. And Berry no longer lives in New York. He has returned to his place of birth in North Carolina, where he lives on a former farm that is now part of the city of Greensboro. I stayed there on a cool November night, talking with him until the small hours and starting up again the following frosty morning.

DJ: Do you think this culture will undergo a voluntary transformation to a sane and sustainable way of living?

TB: The first part of answering that question is to ask what kind of transformation we have to undergo. It seems to me that there are two dimensions to this transformation. The first is that we have to get beyond the artificial division we've created between the human community and the rest of planet. There is only one community, and it lives and dies as a unit. Any harm done to the natural world diminishes the human world, because the human world depends on the natural world not only for its physical supplies but for its psychic development and fulfillment. This is most important, because people talk about the need to destroy the natural world in order to advance the human world. Well, anything that diminishes the wonder and fulfillment we receive from the natural world spoils the human enterprise. We may get a pile of possessions, but it won't mean much if we can't go to the mountains or the seacoast, or enjoy the songs of birds or the sights and scents of flowers. What does it do to our children when they cannot enjoy such things?

The other dimension to this is that we have to somehow get beyond Western Civilization, which must be profoundly altered because it is so destructive in its present state. This alteration is so absolute and so deep in its implications that a person has to wonder about the continuity. In other words, Western Civilization itself is causing our difficulties, which makes this type of a change hard to really comprehend. Transformations of this magnitude are generally associated with some type of religious change.

It seems clear the mission of our times is to reinvent what it means to be human. One thing we know about human beings is that they invent themselves. As a species we are genetically coded toward a further transgenetic cultural coding through which we become fully human. We must be taught how to be human, through our parents, through our community, through rituals, through interactions with the natural world. This is why there is a diversity of ways to be human under different cultural contexts. The Western mode of being has developed into such a distortion that it is causing overwhelming impact not only on the human dimension of the planet but other dimensions as well. Civilized humans have become a planetary power, beyond what any species has been previously. Because language derives from experience, and ultimately from the natural world, we're in a situation that is hard to present in any kind of known language. All of this means that it can be hard even to imagine the type of transformation that is necessary. We need to imagine it before we can deal with the question of whether or not people will voluntarily accept it.

I suspect that when it happens it will not be so much voluntary or involuntary, but subconscious. In other words, I don't think we'll be entirely conscious of what's going on. Cultural formations don't happen consciously. For example, we surely did not intend to damage the continent to this extent, nor did we intend to establish a structure of human lives that would have these implications. There may be some people who understand the transformation—just as there are some people now who understand the culture's destructiveness—but for the society at large the actions of the culture are nearly always unconscious.

DJ: You've written about the role of Passover in the beginning of a process of separation…

TB: The beginning of Western Civilization. The spiritual structure of Western Civilization gets its start in a very profound way at the time of the Passover, when the Hebrew experience of the cosmological springtime festival was transformed into an historical event of liberation. This is a profound change: from the experience of the divine in the cosmological order—in the world around us—to the experience of the divine as manifested in the historical moments of particular communication between the divine and the human. It's profound because this then becomes the basic referent for what might be called reality and value; it changes the entire mode of human development.

DJ: I don't understand.

TB: Within the earlier perspective, communication between the cosmological and the human worlds generally took place through shamanic types. Within the newer worldview, divine/human communication takes place through prophetic types.

DJ: What's the difference?

TB: The prophetic type becomes the voice of the personal divine, or the medium whereby the divine communicates itself to the human and the human communicates itself to the divine. But the shamanic world is more cosmological, by which I mean that the shamanic personality is in relationship with the powers present throughout the universe.

In back of this, and really what I'm concerned with, is the question of how we experience the universe. My proposal—and this is why a cosmological worldview is so important—is that a cosmological order is what might be called the great liturgy. The human project is validated by ritual insertion into the cosmological order. Our job is to participate in the great hymn of praise that is existence.

We have lost touch with the natural order of things. For example, which day of the workweek it is may be more important to many of us than the great transition moments in the seasonal cycles, and which hour of the day it is—will I get to work on time? Will I avoid rush hour traffic? Will I get to watch my favorite television program—may be more important to us than the transitional moments in the diurnal cycles. We have forgotten the great spiritual import of these moments of transition. The dawn is mystical, a very special moment for the human to experience the wonder and depth of fulfillment in the sacred. The same is true of nightfall. And it's true when we pass from consciousness to sleep, where our subconscious comes forward. That this is a special moment of intimacy is particularly apparent to children. They often know that the moment of falling asleep is the magic or mystical moment when there is a presence. Parents talk to their children in a very special way at this time. It's very tender, sensitive, quiet. It's the great transitional moment in our day-night cycle.

There are magical moments in the yearly cycle, too. There is the winter solstice, the moment when the transformation takes place between a declining and ascending sun. It's a moment of death in nature, a moment when everything is reborn. We have lost touch with this intimate experience.

In the springtime, humans are meant to wonder and to ceremonially observe succession, leading to the fulfillment of summer, and the beginning of the movement again toward death. At the harvest there is another time of gratitude and celebration. I think the Iroquois thanksgiving ceremony is one of the greatest festivals in the religious traditions of humankind. Different elements are remembered and thanked: the water, the rain, the wind, the fruitfulness of the earth, the trees. The Iroquois articulate fifteen or more specialized powers that humans need to commune with and be grateful for.

All of this is cosmological. Such experience evokes a sense of wonder at the majesty of things. We participate in the world of the sacred, the world of mystery, the world of fulfillment. To recognize our fulfillment in these moments is to know what it is to be human.

We can say the same for places as for moments. To be fully human is to fully experience the spectacular formations of the planet: particular mountains, particular rivers, certain rock structures.

We no longer do this. We don't experience the natural world surrounding us. We deny ourselves our deepest delight by not participating in the dawn, the dusk, the solstice, the springtime.

I went to a monastery when I was twenty. The monastery rituals are based on cosmological processes. We get up at two in the morning to celebrate the liturgy of the night. At dawn we have the liturgy of the day, largely singing or chanting songs of the Bible or hymns written through the centuries to celebrate the dawn or the particular season of the year. Songs celebrating the summer are different from songs celebrating winter. The point is that all through the various moments of the day we celebrate the wonder of existence: the night, the dawn, midday, vespers, the evening, then the closing of the day.

But even with this basis, the sense of it being caught up in sacred cosmological liturgy escapes most people in monasteries. If it is difficult even for people performing these celebrations so many times each day, how much more so for those who do not often reflect on, much less sing to, the dawn?

We can't lay the blame for all of this on the Passover transition, or the movement from mythological to historical celebrations. That one incident didn't kill our sense of the cosmological. Our connection to the rest of the planet and the need to celebrate all life lives deep within our bodies, and has never been easily eradicated. Instead, it has slowly been eroded over the centuries and millennia of civilization.

DJ: Can you back up?

TB: After the Passover and with the rise of the Judaic tradition, we saw an increasing emphasis on the historical, the literal, the linear, as opposed to the mythological, the cosmological, the cyclical. Moses was a real person, who had a specific connection to God at that place and at that time…

DJ: And Moses or God were the points of the story, instead of the burning bush itself.

TB: Yes, and later Christianity followed this same path. Jesus was a historical figure, as opposed to a mythic one. Connection to the sacred or to God—who is distant from the earth and not of it—is reserved for a special few who exist in specific places at specific historical times, and everyone else must experience the sacred through these representatives. This experience of the sacred is not, within this perspective, something available to all through their participation in the greater whole.

This historical Christian world then bonded with Greek humanism to create the Western anthropocentrism with which we have unfortunately become all-too-familiar. Humans are the only creatures on the planet who matter. Everything else loses its sacrality, its wonder. All wonder and sacrality is, in fact, vested only in these prophetic figures. It is not vested in the natural world, according to this perspective, and does not surround us every day. All of those things—not beings—that surround us are here merely for us to use. They are not here, under this worldview, to fulfill their own destinies, to commune with each other and with us, and for us to commune with them.

Now, as I said, this perception of the sacred in the world is not easy to eliminate, and so the cosmological relationship did continue, up through the medieval period, until the plague, called the black death, that took place between 1347 and 1349, when a third of Europe died. In Florence, the population declined in six months from ninety thousand to forty-some thousand. In Sienna the population went from forty thousand to fifteen thousand in less than a year. Because part of what we do as human beings is discern meaning, these events had to be interpreted. Not having the slightest knowledge of germs, people didn't have the possibility to interpret all of this physically. They could only think of moral explanations; for example, the idea that God was punishing humans for becoming weak and sinful. The thing to do, then, was to become more spiritual, and to get redeemed out of a world increasingly seen as a vale of tears anyway. So over the next hundred years there was a big change in the spirituality of Europe. The art, for example, changed dramatically. When studying late fourteenth-century art from Florence, you keep encountering scenes of death, or last judgment scenes, where Christ with an upraised arm condemns the wicked into hell. You never saw these things before. The last judgment became a fearful thing, as did death. Before that, death had been more or less acceptable, simply part of life, something you dealt with through religion. But the people had been traumatized, and now death frightened them far more than it had before.

DJ: Let me get this straight...

TB: People lost touch with much of their participation in the great liturgy: the world instead became filled with manifestations of sin, became horrifying. The task of the spiritual person was to withdraw from the natural world as contamination, as seductive. This was articulated well by the great spiritual writer Thomas á Kempis. Then in the sixteenth century Protestant Puritanism overlaid this withdrawal with a certain sternness. In the seventeenth century you get Catholic Jansenism, a kind of Catholic puritanism, an aversion from the natural world. The Jansenists determined that the eucharist—the communion celebration with wine and bread in commemoration of the last supper of Jesus, making Christ present in a special way—was such a holy ritual, and humans were so wicked, that even those who went to mass were not considered worthy to receive the eucharist more than, say, once or a few times a year. Not only had one's direct access to the sacred been banished from the world, the faithful had been alienated from the church's own rituals. It was only after much soul searching and penitence that at the beginning of the twentieth century the custom was reasserted for common people to participate in communion each time they went to mass.

Things continued to get worse after the Jansenists. If you perceive the natural world as not sacred, and as composed of things put here for your use, you are going to exploit it. The church articulated the need to be redeemed from the earth, whereas science articulated the need and means to understand and control the earth. Thus really began the division between the sacred and the secular in the contemporary Western world, which made both the church and scientists happy. The religious people were happy because they didn't have to deal with the secular side of life, and the secular people were happy because they didn't have to deal with the spiritual. This latter has led directly to the aggressive commercialization of the planet. Because the natural world was ostracized from the world of the sacred, we have felt free to do with it anything we wanted.

DJ: Let's go at this from another direction. You've written how there are three fundamental types of relationships humans can enter into.

TB: From the beginning, Western Civilization has been very conscious of God-human relations as well as our intrahuman relationships. Think of the Bible. Much of it is concerned with how humans should relate to God, and how humans should relate to each other. What gets lost in all of this are intimate relations with the natural world.

What this means is that our theology has long been highly developed, and particularly in modern times our anthropology has become highly developed, as have our social studies, as part of anthropology. And of course we have the so-called life sciences, but we are still trying to figure out how nature works in order to control it, not how to regain our sense of the natural world as sacred, as fulfillment.

All that is left to most of us these days is the possibility of gaining a kind of romantic fulfillment in going to the seashore, the mountains, or traveling to wilderness areas. But this has progressively tended to become less meaningful, and more separated from our day-to-day existence. In our day-to-day existence, our workaday existence, we are no longer present to the natural world in any manner. We no longer see trees as other beings to be communed with. Nowhere are we taught how to do this. Nowhere is it encouraged for us to speak of this. That is why we live in this world of concrete and steel, of wires and wheels and mechanisms. That's the tragedy of our children. They don't see the stars because of light pollution, they play on grass poisoned with pesticides, they experience the world as circumscribed by so much human-made material. Our children have been taken away from any kind of normal human/earth relationship.

We maintain that disconnection as adults. At one time we depended directly on the earth for our life support. We recognized this dependency, gave praise and thanks for it, as do indigenous and agricultural peoples. By now most of us have no idea where our food comes from.

DJ: And we work a lot harder to get it, harder at least than hunter/gatherers.

TB: The way humans lived before civilization was a lot less work, because the planet naturally produces, naturally renews itself. It offers itself to us not only for food, but in the sense of offering wonders, and its presence. There's none of this separation of the sacred and the secular in the natural world, both spiritual and physical well-being are offered at the same time, because—and this is what is most important—the physical and the spiritual are two dimensions of the same thing.

If people would only pay proper attention, there are certain verifications that someone could receive even from within the scientific worldview. For instance, the fact that nothing is itself without everything else. The human story and the universe story are in reality a single story. The story of anything requires the telling of the story of everything. And each thing is so present to everything else in the universe that nothing is separated. Every atom influences every other atom without passing through the intervening space.

Many scientists understand this, but often they do not take the next step of understanding. Steven Weinberg, for example, wrote *The First Three Minutes*, a brilliant scientific study of the first three minutes of the universe, but then later in the book he says, "The more you know about the universe, the less point it seems to have." My response to that is, "Well, Steven, if there's no point to it, why do you study it so much? Why do you give your life to it?"

The answer is very simple. The point is the attraction of the Great Self and the small self. Every being has two dimensions: its individual dimension and its universal dimension. The universe is the Great Self of every part of the universe. Why are we so happy being with trees, other animals, hearing birdsongs, seeing the colors of flowers, the flow of rivers? Why do these inspire us so? Well, that is what might be called the large self, where we experience our fulfillment. We are not ourselves without it.

Imagine a drink of water when you are thirsty. It is as spiritual an experience as it is a physical one. You see a river. You drink from it. The river takes care of you physically, and spiritually. That is everything right there.

DJ: Different subject. I'd always thought traditional indigenous peoples lived in dynamic equilibrium with their surroundings, but you propose something else: creative disequilibrium.

TB: Well, there are two basic forces in the universe: differentiation and bonding. That is, pushing things apart, making them different, and bringing things together, making them present to each other. At the beginning of the universe, it had several options. If the differentiation overcomes the bonding, then the universe disperses, and nothing happens. If the bonding overcomes—is too strong for—the differentiation, then it collapses. If the bonding and the differentiation enter into equilibrium, everything becomes fixated. The only viable option of the universe is for it to be in a state of creative disequilibrium, holding together sufficiently to not fall apart, but open enough to be expanding.

DJ: How does that manifest in relations involving humans?

TB: Creativity. Play. I don't know if you've heard of Paul Winter, the musician. He asked me to write something he might read at his wedding. I wrote a verse he made into a bookmark. "Look up at the sky. The heavens so blue, the sun so radiant, the clouds so playful, soaring raptors, meadows in bloom, the woodland creatures, rivers singing their way to the sea, wolf song on the land, whale song on the sea, celebration everywhere, wild, riotous, immense as a monsoon lifting an ocean of joy and spilling it down over the Appalachian landscape, drenching us all with a deluge of delight as we open our arms and rush toward each other, Paul and Chez, and all of us, moved by that vast compassionate curve that brings all things together in intimate celebration, celebration that is the universe itself."

There is a difference between a philosopher and a poet. Philosophers look for equilibrium. Poets delight in a teasing disequilibrium, in the interplay and modes of tension of all beings with each other.

This is also the difference between Chinese and Japanese art. Chinese art, while it has its dynamism and interplay, looks for balance. Japanese art, on the other hand, always insists on a certain disequilibrium. That's why it is often more free than Chinese art.

DJ: Do you think we're in a state of destructive disequilibrium?

TB: I'd be more inclined to say we're collapsing from excessive equilibrium.

DJ: I don't understand. What's in equilibrium?

TB: We can't stand the wild. We can't stand the creative disequilibrium. Concrete and asphalt are flat. They're under control. That's a form of equilibrium. Probably the ultimate form. Stasis. Which is surely what Western Civilization aims for.

If we are to expect to survive, and to remember what it is to be human beings, we need to establish a pattern of viable activity for the whole earth community. This community should be ruled by the principles that every being has three rights: the right to be; the right to habitat; and the right to fulfill its role in the ever-renewing processes of nature.

DJ: How do we get there from here?

TB: I've always liked the title of Chellis Glendinning's book, *My Name Is Chellis & I'm in Recovery From Western Civilization*. What does it mean, and how far do you go? I said earlier that we have to terminate our present phase of Western Civilization…

DJ: And I agree with that.

TB: But how would we do that? People talk about reform, and they talk about revolution, but in either case, it's something that emerges from within the tradition itself. That the impulse for reform comes from within should be obvious. But revolutionary elements always emerge out of the same source as the tradition. Communism and capitalism derive from the same place: they're both driven by the millennial vision of promise at the end of the Bible, in the last chapters of the book of Revelations, seventeen through twenty-two.

DJ: How so?

TB: Many Christians were quite puzzled in the early stages of Christianity. The Messiah had supposedly come, and the promise was that when the Messiah came there would be peace, justice, and abundance. The Messiah was going to bring a healing of the nations. But it didn't happen. The Messiah apparently had come, the fulfillment had taken place, but there was no peace and no justice. Instead there was persecution, oppression, and rejection almost everywhere. The early Christians had difficulty making sense of this.

It was in this context that St. John went to the island of Patmos and wrote the visionary book of Revelations. Sometimes people put it aside as being filled with wisdom too esoteric to be understood. But that's not true. The symbols expressed simply need to be understood. The Book of Revelations is a marvelous document. In the last chapters there is a woman cloaked with the sun, with the moon under her feet, and a crown of twelve stars. A dragon is waiting to devour the child the woman is bringing forth. The woman can be interpreted here as the Christian community. A battle goes on until the end of time, but before the end comes, there is to be a thousand years when the dragon would be chained. This was how St. John helped the early Christians out of their puzzlement: it was only when the dragon had been chained that there would be peace, justice, and abundance in the world.

This promise has been in Western consciousness ever since. It's inescapable. Anything Westerners do will be driven by this millennial vision. The belief that someday there will be a communist workers state, and then we can have peace, justice, and abundance. Someday the riches of the capitalist system will trickle down to bring peace, justice, and abundance to those made poor by this same system. Someday modern science and technology will create some sort of heaven on earth. Someday, someday, someday.

DJ: And in the meantime this culture destroys the world.

TB: It's all based on a deep resentment of the human condition, of being born, of living, and of dying. Of being out of control. Of being dependent on the universe in ways we can never fully understand. Particularly after the Black Death, this resentment that the millennium had not come was very strong. Really, this resentment is what drives technological society. It drives communism. It drives capitalism. It drives our society. This quest for an abiding peace, justice and abundance.

DJ: So why shouldn't we just get rid of Western Civilization?

TB: When I say that the problem is within the Western world, the solution must be there also. You find the solution where the problem is. You can't avoid it.

This brings us back to where we started: to the notion of reinventing the human. I mentioned that humans need to be taught how to be human, probably more so than trees need to be taught how to be trees, and bears need to be taught how to be bears. But, as Carl Jung's work shows, there are archetypal forms present in all humans, though realized differently in different cultures. Cultures generally have some cosmic sense, and they have the great mother tradition, and so on. One of the most frequent archetypes is the performance of death and rebirth ceremonies. Humans are not fully human until they've gone through some ceremonial rebirth.

I think that an understanding of death and rebirth provides one clue to understanding our situation. We have believed for far too long that the natural world will take care of itself, no matter what we do to it. We could get by with this—at cost to our immediate surroundings and to our own humanity—when we did not have these current levels of technology. Our current worldview could continue to propagate itself. But our worldview does not protect us from the very real fact that all communities in the larger earth community benefit or diminish together. And so while we may feel that we are gaining an advantage, this advantage comes at the direct expense of other beings, and by now we are tearing the earth to pieces.

DJ: How does this relate to death and rebirth?

TB: The full flow of the Western relationship with the natural world could not be seen by so many until we got this power, which means that the Civilization's vulnerable side couldn't be fully seen until we actually have entered the process of killing the planet, and thereby of course ruining ourselves. But now, as we've begun to mature, there are millions of people awakening to this desperate situation. Despite this awakening, it's still very desperate, because we're so caught in this predatory basis of our existence that it's almost unthinkable to seriously diminish it.

That said, even within our own tradition there is a capacity for understanding that the small self cannot survive without the large self, and that the well-being of the universe is the primary value. Only in an integral planet Earth can we become integral humans.

DJ: I don't understand.

TB: The whole universe together participates in and manifests the divine more than any single being whatsoever.

If you're doing a painting, you don't just put this thing here or there. Everything must be seen in its relationship to everything else. It's the same in music. Or in building a house. The different components by themselves don't constitute the house. You see this everywhere: the principle of the integrity of the whole is the reason for the determination of the parts. The components make sense only together.

We see this even Biblically. In the story of creation, after each day God says, "It's good." After the last day He says, "It's very good." It's good in a special way. From this statement St. Thomas concludes that the purpose of creation was not one part, not even the humans, but the entire created universe.

Out of all of this a person could say that if there is such a thing as the divine coming to earth in human form, its purpose is not primarily the human, but the universe. If there is redemption, if there is a salvation experience, it's primarily for the benefit of the whole universe.

DJ: What do you see ahead?

TB: The decline of the West. Oswald Spengler published a book of that name in 1924. He believed a community goes through a lifespan just as any organism does. It moves through its origin, childhood, maturity, its full development, and then its decline and death. Once a culture starts to decline, it really can't be stopped. The culture will try to stabilize and prevent this, but the processes as a whole will consist of ossification. Recourse will be had to organizations, to institutions, but nothing will work.

The World Bank, the World Trade Organization, the International Monetary Fund, all these are efforts to stabilize an increasingly unstable and declining system. And one of the interesting things about these attempts to stave off the decline of the culture is that they actually tend to speed it up, because they end up choking us to death.

The extraordinary rate at which this culture is destroying the planet makes clear the unsustainability and undesirability of this culture. An impressive intellectual critique of civilization has been building now for many years. Organizations are rising up to fight the destructiveness of the culture, and millions of young people are acting on their knowledge that things just aren't right. Churches are putting out declarations now, as are universities.

Back to your first question. Do I think that our culture will undergo a voluntary transformation to a sane and sustainable way of living? I don't think the question is whether it will be done. The question is how well. And I think how well it will be done will depend on how well we're able to keep the changes authentic, to make certain we face the difficulties at the proper level, so that we are able to adequately respond to this most significant of all problems.

Jan Lundberg

Interview Conducted
at the office of the Alliance for a Paving Moratorium
Arcata, California
2.27.00

Anti-road activist and publisher Jan Lundberg hasn't owned a car in seventeen years. In 1997, he tore up his driveway and planted a garden on the spot—hardly the behavior one would expect from a former oil-industry insider who once drove a Mercedes.

For Lundberg, the convenience and freedom cars offer are just bribes that don't even come close to balancing the costs—not just in gas, service, and insurance, but in loss of life, damage to the environment, and enormous government subsidies to oil and automobile companies. One of the largest of these subsidies is the public expense of building roads. By calling for an end to new roadbuilding, Lundberg hopes to "[rip] the rug right out from under the car" and force people to explore other alternatives for getting around.

Lundberg grew up around the oil industry. His father ran Lundberg Survey, Inc., a company that collected statistics on gasoline prices and industry trends. In 1973, just before the oil crisis, father and son began publishing the Lundberg Letter, which became the number-one trade journal for the oil industry and went on to predict the second oil shock of 1979.

After his father's death in the mid-eighties, Lundberg quit the family business and directed his efforts toward energy conservation. (His sister Trilby now runs Lundberg Survey.) By that point, Jan had realized that our "waste economy," as he calls it, is unsustainable and the cause of massive environmental damage and species extinctions worldwide. We are laboring, he says, under the false impression that we can "have it all": the physical comfort of our current way of living and a livable planet.

In 1988, Lundberg founded the Fossil Fuels Policy Action Institute, which soon spawned the Alliance for a Paving Moratorium, a diverse movement of grass-roots community groups, individuals, and businesses with the common goal of halting roadbuilding. In the Alliance's view, a paving moratorium would limit the spread of population, redirect investment from suburbs to inner cities, and free up funding for mass transportation and maintenance of existing roads.

But for Lundberg, the battle against new roads is about more than just sprawl, traffic, pollution, and other car-related ills. Our entire economy is oil based, he points out, and oil is a limited resource—perhaps more limited than we realize. Phasing out massive fossil-fuel use, Lundberg says, is crucial not only to saving the earth's climate, but to lessening the impact of the crisis that will occur when the world's oil supply begins to run out. He writes that "The challenge before us all is to survive an ecological correction unprecedented for our species. The correction will likely include an economic collapse and a conversion to subsistence activities and trading."

I talked to Lundberg in a small downtown office, where the walls are covered with protest posters and broadsides. A middle-aged man with graying hair, dressed in a t-shirt, he displayed an impressive knowledge of the facts and figures and a passionate concern for the future of the planet and human society. When we took a break to go to the market, we walked.

DJ: What's wrong with cars?

JL: For one thing, the number of them. Right now there are about 130 million registered passenger cars in the United States, and about 486 million in the world. We can go through the litany of problems caused by our reliance on the car culture. First, each year more than 500,000 people die in road accidents. Two-thirds of these deaths involve pedestrians, of whom one-third are children. Just in the United States about 46,000 people die per year because of auto collisions, nearly as many as the total number of Americans killed in Vietnam. Everybody knows someone who has died or been seriously injured in a car crash, yet cars have insinuated themselves into our social life and our psyches so thoroughly that we somehow accept these deaths as inevitable, or not shocking, as opposed to perceiving them for what they are: a direct and predictable result of choosing to base our economic and social systems on this particular piece of technology.

Motor vehicles are the biggest single source of atmospheric pollution worldwide. Just in the United States about 30,000 people die each year from respiratory illness stemming from auto-related airborne toxins. Sixty-five percent of all carbon monoxide emitted into the environment is from road vehicles. Carbon monoxide, besides being fatal, contributes to global warming by removing hydroxyl radical from the air, allowing buildup of methane (a powerful greenhouse gas). Automotive fuels account for 17 percent of global carbon dioxide releases, two-thirds as much as rainforest destruction. Motor vehicle air conditioners in the U.S. are the world's single largest source of CFC leakage into the atmosphere, and subsequent destruction of the ozone layer.

Speaking of ozone, motor-vehicle-generated ozone costs an estimated $9 billion per year in health costs, lost labor hours, and reduced agricultural revenues.

DJ: Agricultural revenues?

JL: Automobile exhaust damages crops to the tune of $2 to 4 billion per year just for corn, wheat, soybeans, and peanuts.

If we open our vision beyond cash crops to generic damage from motor vehicle air pollution the price goes up to about $200 billion per year. That doesn't include global warming. Nor, of course, does that include deaths, on which you can't put a price.

Cars kill nonhumans, not only by paving over or fragmenting their habitat, giving industrialized humans access to their homes, and changing the weather, but also simply by running them down. Approximately one million animals per day are killed on U.S. roads, including endangered species like the Florida panther. In Southern California, cars are the leading cause of death of mountain lions. Add to this the countless small rodents and insects obliterated by cars. A moth fluttering into your windshield at sixty miles per hour may not seem like much of a tragedy to you, but I guarantee you the moth perceives it differently.

We have become slaves to these machines. If a group of aliens came to this planet and said they would bring us all sorts of goodies like jet skis, tomatoes in January, computers, and so on (or at least they would bring them to the richest of us), on the multiple conditions that we offer up to them a yearly sacrifice of a half-million human lives, change our planet's climate, individually spend increasing amounts of time serving them, and socially devote an ever-increasing amount of land and other resources to their service, we would rebel in a flash. Or at least I hope we would.

But that's the reality we face. And that's the reality we accept. It's a reality we don't even talk about. More teenagers are killed by oil-consuming cars across the U.S. every afternoon than the 14 highschoolers gunned down in Littleton. Everybody says that living in an inner city is dangerous, that you're going to get shot. But the truth is that because of car crashes, suburbs are statistically far more dangerous places to live. I've proven this to people, and they still refuse to walk with me in downtown Seattle, but they're perfectly happy to get in a car, just because it's normal. We don't talk about any of this because this violence—the violence of U.S. transportation policies—is so ingrained into our psyches that we believe it is inevitable, and not the result of policy decisions and subsidies.

In this country, close to half of all urban space goes to accommodate the automobile, leaving more land devoted to cars than to housing. Nearly 100,000 people a year are displaced in the U.S. by new highway construction. Every minute, the U.S. loses three acres of productive farmland to urban sprawl via roadbuilding and automobile dependence. That's 1.5 million acres per year. Since the first Earth Day in 1970, we've lost more than 40 million acres of farmland to so-called development. In Lodi, California, for example, rich soils forty feet deep were recently covered by a Wal-Mart parking lot. Pavement now covers over sixty thousand square miles in the United States. That's two percent of the surface area, and ten percent of the arable land.

And we pay for the privilege of destroying the continent. The United States spends nearly two hundred million dollars per day building and re-building roads. Total state and federal expenditures on highways and major roads are two hundred and fifty-five million per day. Even in purely fiscal terms, roads are monumentally expensive: the 4.5 mile Cyprus Freeway in Oakland, to choose just one example, cost taxpayers $3,500 per inch.

To simply maintain roads in their current poor state would cost U.S. tax-payers about $25 billion per year. Yet we spend typically $13 billion per year on maintenance, assuring existing roads will deteriorate. Meanwhile, the government spends $16 billion to widen existing roads and to build new ones. Setting aside for a moment all the deaths and pollution and global warming, it makes no sense, even when we confine ourselves to a strictly fiscal stand-point, to build more roads when we cannot maintain the ones we've got.

All told, the United States subsidizes roads and cars by more than $300 billion per year. This is in addition to annual outlays of tens of billions of dollars from dedicated gasoline tax receipts.

And things are only getting worse. Even though the United States popula-tion increased "only" about 40 percent between 1960 and 1990, the number of licensed drivers nearly doubled, the number of vehicles did double, fuel consumption more than doubled, and the number of miles driven almost tripled. The percentage of U.S. citizens who commuted by car went from about 70 to 87 percent. The percentage of people commuting by public transit dropped by far more than half. Walking to work decreased from 10 to 4 percent. Those working at home decreased by half. In the 1950s and 1960s, 60 percent of children walked or rode their bikes to school. Now it's down to 10 percent.

All of this adds up to more traffic jams. The way to measure road con-gestion is by figuring the percent of roads near or at capacity during rush hour. Between 1975 and 1993 that number went from about forty to seventy percent. This means that average vehicle speed for crosstown traffic in New York City, for example, is under six miles per hour, which is less, by the way, than it was in the days of horses and buggies.

The U.S. General Accounting Office predicts that even if this country's road capacity were to increase by 20 percent over the next fifteen years—a very unlikely goal—congestion will triple. Driving delays are expected to waste more than seven million gallons of fuel per year over the next two decades, increasing travelers' costs by $41 billion, and adding 73 million tons of carbon dioxide to the atmosphere. You think road rage is bad now, just wait a few years.

DJ: We've got a ton of disparate facts here. Bring them together for me.

JL: The car is an environmental problem to solve. It's too late to try to modify it or bring it somehow under control. For us to really reverse the trends, the car has got to be targeted for extinction. In a world being hit by global warming, and wracked by an epidemic of cancer, it's not enough at this point to declare progress when emissions go down. Pollution accumulates. We need to stop emitting pollution.

DJ: Can't we just make cars that pollute less?

JL: I see three problems with that. The first is that I just don't think it's going to happen. The power and size of the oil and auto industries guarantee that for the time being, any policies that curtail the massive subsidies handed over to these huge corporations by governments, or that in any way impede their profitability, will never be put into practice. Not only are these corporations larger than most governments, in many ways they already are the de facto governments. The second problem is that the question implies that we still want cars to do their basic function. We will come back to this problem later. And the third is that while most people think that the problem with cars—in terms of air pollution—is what we see coming out of the tailpipe, the German Environmental Forecasting Institute revealed that most of the air pollution associated with a car is not out of the tailpipe, but instead because of pollution caused by mining and manufacturing associated with cars. So, switching fuels? Sorry, doesn't do it. Similarly, it doesn't help matters much if a clean car runs over you. You won't be any less dead.

Our entire economy is based on petroleum. Cars are only the single biggest user, in this country anyway, and oil is used for asphalt in the roads, tires on the cars, plastic for the cars. The whole system is absurd.

DJ: I don't understand. Why is it absurd?

JL: All the reasons I gave a moment ago. Cars kill, they're stressful, and they're totally inefficient. They're a joke. Ivan Illich performed calculations revealing the absurdity of the whole car culture. If you divide the distance we travel by the number of hours we spend taking care of our cars, not just behind the wheel but in some way associated with the car and supporting it through our work and our time and our efforts, it comes to around five miles per hour. And that doesn't even include the environmental or social costs. That's just the time you spend earning money—the hours you sell—to buy the car, pay for insurance, buy tires, and so on.

As you know, we can walk about five miles per hour. But when you show this to people, they still say, "I've got to have a car, because I'm in a hurry." It's crazy. It's just cognitive dissonance.

Cars are absurd. We can't afford them, as a society, as a planet, as individuals. Ten to fifteen thousand dollars is the average cost of a registered vehicle. Why not save that money? Why not get your exercise? Why not live longer?

DJ: You mean by not getting in a car wreck.

JL: I mean by not leading a sedentary lifestyle. In a book called *The Right Medicine*, David Cundiff, MD, calculated the monumental cost to society and our health of our being so sedentary: it's higher even than tobacco. As he writes, "Out of the over one trillion dollar health care budget that people in the United States shouldered, two hundred billion dollars a year is from sitting in cars, that's from spending one hundred billion hours in cars, while not exercising our bodies, at two dollars per hour compensation." That is the cardiovascular-related cost of car-dependency. He continues, "An even greater cost comes from car crashes. Without pain-and-suffering, the medical costs of car crashes total about one hundred and sixty billion dollars per year. With the pain and suffering, which is a related medical cost of crashes, the total has been estimated at 300 billion dollars per year. As for pollution, the American Lung Association estimates the direct health cost is fifteen billion dollars per year."

I'm happy to walk. I'm happier walking than biking. Biking is sort of a stressful activity, when you're on pavement and you're dodging cars. And if we really care about sustainability we have to ask ourselves how many billions of bicycles made of fancy alloys can be produced efficiently, sustainably, forever. It's just not possible. It takes so much energy to create some of the more expensive, lightweight bikes, because of the alloys, that you could never pedal far enough in your lifetime to save the energy that was consumed in manufacturing.

DJ: You said driving is stressful, but think of the freedom of the open road, windows open, tunes blaring, wind in your hair…

JL: If driving weren't stressful, would we need laws against road rage? Also, there are some very interesting statistics about road noise. Studies have found that nighttime traffic noise deprives people of dream-rich REM (rapid eye movement) sleep, encourages psychosomatic illnesses, and may cause cardio-circulatory problems. It may also affect your social life: people living on streets with less traffic have been found by other studies to be more friendly, pleasant, and cooperative. And they hear better. A comparison of Sudanese tribesmen with Americans discovered that because they live in a naturally quieter environment, eighty-year-old Sudanese heard far better than thirty-year-old Americans. And I'm sure you've heard that in Europe many songbirds are not learning their songs because they cannot hear over the noise of the traffic.

Driving is violent, because of what the exhaust does to you and others, and because of running over creatures, and because you're burning oil that men are going to fight and die over in another part of the world.

But more fundamentally, driving is a kind of violation of the spirit. You're not connected to the earth, your feet aren't on the ground, you're going at inhuman speeds, and all the while you're not moving at all. If I run fast I at least have the physical sensation of everything whizzing by.

DJ: I got in the car this morning in Crescent City, and got out in Arcata. On the way I passed through several squalls. But I didn't experience any of them. There's something existentially odd about that...

JL: You weren't living, and you obtained something without earning it. You got somewhere with no energy expenditure of your own, and with no effort.

There is something strange about speed. The faster we go, or the more ground we cover, the more we lose time, and we shrink the universe. Whereas a long time ago the universe was incomprehensibly big, and filled in with all the stories just in your neighborhood, now that it's all connected with roads and oil-burning machines, we're destroying that previous perception and reality of the universe being such a huge place. We're destroying the largeness and the magic. Even though we say, "Oh, now I can go to London, and so I can 'experience' the whole world," the truth is that we're cheating ourselves out of the experience of whatever we would be doing at a natural speed. You see more stuff when you are sitting still, or when you are walking. And you can smell the flowers. You notice things that even with a bike you don't see. You've got to be going pretty slow and looking right down at the pavement in order to see a snake that has been smashed down and has become the color of the asphalt. You would never see that from a car.

DJ: I can almost hear someone saying, "Look, I need a car because I've got to get to work. The mass transit systems don't take me where I want to go…"

JL: Mass transit systems in most cities are as bad as they are because they were demolished by the auto industry. Back in the 1930s, the electric railway systems that served most big cities were a major threat to the profits of big oil and automobile companies. So General Motors, Firestone, Standard Oil of California, and others bought out more than one hundred systems in forty-five cities, then ripped up the tracks and paved them over. GM and these other companies were eventually convicted of criminal conspiracy. For this our stalwart government—"of the people, by the people, and for the people," as they say—fined these corporations $5,000, and the guilty individuals were fined a whole dollar each.

DJ: "Be that as it may," I can hear the person say, "I've still got to get to work."

JL: People make decisions every day of their lives. If they say they're stuck, they're admitting, ultimately, that they're prisoners or slaves. But if you're not a slave, you can make new and different decisions. You can decide that maybe you're not going to work for the rest of your life at one job, and if you switch jobs, you may consider finding one closer to where you live. Or you may consider changing homes. You don't have to move farther away from where you work—you can live closer, or you can change your career entirely. Some people work out of their homes.

Another thing people can do is try to relate more to what dollars are supposed to bring us, instead of orienting themselves toward the dollars themselves. What's the point of working and then of money? It's not to collect some green pieces of paper, or to shuffle electrons on a bank's hard drive. It's to get us things. But we need to ask ourselves what we really need. We need food, clothing, and housing. Can we get by more cheaply, so we don't have to sell so many hours? How much sense does it make to work extra hours to pay for a car that we use to drive us to where we work in order to pay for the car?

Or here's another thought: we all need love, which of course dollars don't buy. Maybe it's easier to find love—not just romantic love but love of ourselves and our communities—if we're not stuck all day in an automobile or in an office. So when people talk to me about needing a car to get to work, I urge them to change the terms of the debate: to think in terms of personal liberation, and maybe living better without so much money. Having more time. It's a real simple equation: if you don't have a car, you have more time. And you have better health, which means you're better able to enjoy the time you have. I've met so many people who live well and are happy without a lot of material possessions, without a lot of money. Now, by and large these people are young and free, but there are a lot of clever people who have learned how to benefit from intelligent choices. It all boils down to what you value.

This leads us directly to what is often called anarchy, which is really all about taking care of each other on a community basis, without the necessity of structured work or government regulation. We raise our kids communally. We take care of each other. We share. That's an alien concept in this materialistic culture. Why is it that when you go down any residential street in this country every family has its own separate oven? That's a terrible waste of energy. One oven could be baking a half-dozen loaves of bread, instead of one.

If happiness is what we really care about, we realize very quickly that we don't need money, we don't need cars, we don't need government. We don't need pollution.

But it's hard to achieve any of these—to get rid of money, cars, government, pollution—when we've got so many people. To be honest, the number of people, and the fact that our entire system is based on petroleum and automobiles, sometimes makes things seem hopelessly difficult, and leads to a conundrum for any activist trying to be honest yet trying to get a message out. The conundrum is this: How do you speak the truth while still seeming "realistic"? "Get rid of car culture?" the mainstream media says, "You must be joking." But we continue with our form of activism and our message because our hope is that when the big wrenching socioeconomic adjustment comes—and it will come—we may have helped to pass on some helpful concepts, a body of experience, and even some technical knowledge that will help the people who come after to rebuild some kind of human cultural system, and not make the same mistakes again. To help them to not start building new roads. In a sense we see ourselves as writing off the present culture as being unreachable, too tightly caught up in its materialistic death urge to salvage, and so we're looking past that to do what we can now to help the humans and nonhumans who come after.

DJ: Whenever my friends and I talk about the end of civilization, we search for some sort of marker, and what we've come up with is the end of car culture. How do you see the end of car culture playing out? Even before that, do you agree the car culture is in its endgame? What will cause it to end? And if you do think it's in its endgame, is that because you don't think we're smart enough to find new oil, or failing that, to figure out a new fuel system?

JL: A lot of these questions have to be gone over in basics because the mass media and the educational systems provide zero insight into them. They act as though how much oil there is and what it can be used for are of no concern to the public.

Probably the best place to start is by talking about Marion King Hubbert, a geologist who died several years ago who became famous for charting the life of an oil field. Extraction follows a bell curve—called the Hubbert Curve—in which production rises as new wells are put in, reaches a maximum when about half of the "Estimated Ultimately Recoverable" (EUR) oil has been extracted, and then tails off as wells begin to run dry. During the decline, technologies such as water flooding and gas injection may be introduced to slow the rate of depletion, but all they do is stave off the inevitable. The same pattern that is true for individual oil fields holds for geological basins as well: production rises as new fields are found and then tails off as the larger and more accessible fields are depleted. This pattern can be extended also to entire nations, and ultimately to the planet. The bottom line of all this—and this is so obvious we shouldn't need to say it, but we have to because there is so much ignorance and intentional deceit surrounding this subject—is that the production of any field starts at zero, rises to a peak, and then falls to zero.

For the United States, production in the lower-forty-eight peaked in about 1970—as predicted by Hubbert some forty years ago—and has been on the decline ever since.

DJ: When will world oil production peak?

JL: Before we can ask that—and that is the question, isn't it?—we need to ask another, which is, what is the world's volume of EUR oil? Once again, production will peak when half of this volume has been extracted.

One of the best figures I've seen for EUR is about 1,800 billion barrels, which would mean that global production would peak by the year 2007.

Even if EUR oil is as high as 2,600 billion barrels, that would move the peak back to only 2019. To be honest, both of these figures seem too far away, because I don't think they fully take into account that oil consumption continues to rise very quickly. I have seen other credible figures—and these seem far more feasible to me—suggesting that global oil production could peak as early as this year.

Now, when United States production peaked, that didn't mean the end of the oil age, since the U.S. could still import oil. But when global production peaks, as it will shortly, if it hasn't happened already, it means the beginning of the end of the economy as we know it. Five Middle East countries will regain control of world supply. This will make the oil shocks of the 1970s seem like nothing, because then there were plenty of new oil and gas finds to bring onstream. This time there are virtually no new prolific basins to yield a crop of giant fields sufficient to have a global impact. The growing Middle East control of the market is likely to lead to a radical and permanent increase in the price of oil long before physical shortages begin to appear, and they will appear within the next decade.

This will, of course, demolish the economy, which has been driven by an abundant supply of cheap energy for a century. We're going to live through an "economic and political discontinuity of historic proportions," as one analyst puts it, or the crash, as we more often refer to it. I like the language of oil industry geologist Dr Walter Youngquist: "My observations in some seventy countries over about fifty years of travel and work tell me that we are clearly already over the cliff. The momentum of population growth and resource consumption is so great that a collision course with disaster is inevitable. Large problems lie not very far ahead."

DJ: Wait a minute. I've seen industry and government figures showing that "proven reserves of oil are enough to supply the world for forty-three years at current rates of production."

JL: I see two immediate problems with this. The first is that these figures come from government and industry. You don't think that either of those groups would lie to the American public, do you? For political reasons, proved oil reserves are consistently substantially overstated. It is in the interest of both oil-producing nations and companies to overstate their remaining oil, because their business agreements limit them to pumping and selling a proportion of their remaining resources. For example, if contracts limit you to pumping 10 percent of your proven reserves per year, you'll make a lot more money, and you'll make it a lot more quickly, if you simply lie about your proven reserves. But in fact the rate of oil discovery is falling sharply. Discovery of oil and gas peaked in the 1960s, and the situation has deteriorated enough that by now the world consumes more than three times as much oil each year as is discovered. Do you think the oil industry is aware of oil field depletion? Of course. It's their business. Why do you think no new supertankers have been built for twenty years? A report written for oil industry insiders and priced at $32,000 per copy concludes that world oil production and supply will peak this year, and decline to half by 2025. The report predicts large and permanent increases in oil prices for the very near future.

The second problem with that argument—that oil reserves will last forty-three years—is that it is based on "current rates of production." Their use of that language should clue us to the fact that they are dissembling, because the truth is that production is skyrocketing. At one time I thought that the downslope of the Hubbert Curve might be at least slightly gradual, but because in recent years production has accelerated to unanticipatedly high levels, I've come to believe that the downslope of the curve will be extremely steep.

DJ: I don't understand what that means.

JL: It means we're using up the oil far faster than anyone anticipated, so the crash will be sooner and harder than even environmentalists predict.

DJ: But as oil becomes increasingly rare, it will become increasingly expensive, which will provide financial incentives to develop other forms of energy. Tar sands for example, or oil shale.

JL: Economists say this all the time. They like to argue that scarcity results in price increases, making it more profitable to access poorer deposits. It's too bad that economics and the real world so rarely intersect.

DJ: True. I took a year of graduate study in Mineral Economics back in the 1980s, and I remember informally renaming one of my classes "ME 514: Guessing at Things," and another "ME 525: Pretending to Have Answers."

JL: In this case the economists are confusing dollars with calories. The fact is that as an oil field ages, it takes increasing amounts of energy to pump out the remaining oil. You need to subtract that energy cost from the total value of the energy extracted. Even now, the average energy profit ratio for newly-discovered oil in the United States has fallen to 1:1, meaning the energy required to find and extract a barrel of oil increasingly exceeds the energy contained in the barrel. At some point it will no longer make sense to use oil for energy, no matter how much you can sell it for. Too often, both economists and engineers forget that they cannot repeal the laws of thermodynamics. They forget, to switch ways of speaking here, something known to every child: that an orange only has so much orange juice in it.

DJ: Energy profit ratio?

JL: That's a measure of how much energy must go into a process to get a certain amount of energy out. The early oil wells in Pennsylvania had a ridiculously high ratio because you had almost zero energy input. You just had to go scoop it up and burn it. But the ratios for all these other forms of energy are much lower. Ethanol, for example, has an energy profit ratio of less than 1:1, meaning it takes more energy to make it than you get out of it.

DJ: You make a great point, but I still have another concern. The government already subsidizes the oil industry, and subsidizes many other industries that make no fiscal, ecological, or economic sense. Why would we think that the same government wouldn't just continue with these subsidies, even when they make no sense from an energy perspective? Why wouldn't the government just use the full force and power of the state to hand over money and energy, so that from the perspective of the corporation the tar sands are profitable?

JL: That's a good question, especially because that's already happening. Our entire economic system is based on these subsidies, from agriculture to manufacturing to energy. Especially energy. That's why oil is so cheap right now. Just including the cost of the Persian Gulf military presence—for which we as taxpayers foot the bill—would at least double the price of oil.

The thing that scares me even more than monetary subsidies, however, are the hidden subsidies that can never be accounted for. Can you put a price on global warming? Can you put a price on a pristine lake or river? The so-called economic view of our planet and of life is anti-life.

So long as we cling to our economic view, we will be able to maintain the illusion of cheap oil for just a little bit longer, paying for the oil in ways that we don't know and don't necessarily feel.

But I'll tell you what scares me the most about all this: everything in our economy is based on petroleum. It's not just cars. It's the food we eat, fertilized with petroleum products, transported by petroleum. It's the plastics we surround ourselves with. It's everywhere. Everything is oil. People don't even know. They don't even think. And it wasn't very long ago that we supported ourselves on a plant-based economy. Canvas, for example, was from cannabis, and now it's from DuPont. One reason they outlawed hemp was that DuPont was able to make substitutes. Medicines, clothes, it's all there.

DJ: What about natural gas? Can the system keep going another couple of generations on natural gas and coal? Maybe coal gasification?

JL: There's not a lot of natural gas out there. And coal gasification is another one of those inefficient processes, in which you have to put in a lot of energy and to not get that much out. Now, there's a hell of a lot of coal, if you're willing to destroy the surface of the planet to get it out, and pump all the mine wastes into your rivers, and the soot into the air. I'm not certain that even our culture is crazy enough to do that.

DJ: Let's cut to the chase. Do you think we'll see the end of car culture in our lives?

JL: Yes. It may be because of running out of oil, or it may be because of economic collapse from which we do not get up, based on the demand for oil so greatly outstripping the supply that the price goes through the roof. And the end of car culture may ultimately be a liberating event, for those who survive, as we try to remember how to live with what the land will give us. But if the collapse is so pervasive that too many nuclear events occur, even the collapse may simply further the destruction that is the hallmark of our culture.

DJ: Let's take this step-by-step. When we talk about the end of car culture, we're not talking just about the end of traffic jams and commuting…

JL: Because our agricultural system is also petrochemically based, we're essentially eating oil. So we're really talking about the collapse of the agricultural infrastructure, and the associated transportation and distribution network, which goes beyond agriculture. It's the products, it's commuting, it's food.

We're essentially fucked, and we don't know it. It's like Youngquist said, we're already over the cliff, but we aren't paying attention.

Part of the problem is that our reliance on fossil fuels has allowed us to overshoot the planet's carrying capacity.

DJ: What's that?

JL: The book to read on all this is *Overshoot: The Ecological Basis of Revolutionary Change*, by William R. Catton, Jr. Any environment's carrying capacity is the number of creatures living a certain way that can be supported permanently, for example how many deer could live on a certain island without overgrazing and damaging the capacity of that island to grow food for them. Permanently really is the key word here, because it's possible to overshoot the carrying capacity—to temporarily have more creatures than the land can support— but doing so damages the land, and permanently lowers the future carrying capacity. Think about it this way: a few thousand people could probably live in the nearby forests forever, eating salmon and clams and crabs and deer. But if you have so many people—and so much technology—that you kill off the salmon and clams and crabs and deer, the land won't be able to support the same number as it did before.

And that's one of the problems: our dependence on oil has allowed us to grossly overshoot the earth's carrying capacity as a whole, and the capacity of every region on its own, but at what cost? We are grossly reducing the capacity of the earth to support human beings. And things will not be pretty for those who come after us.

DJ: Will the end of the oil age be slow-motion?

JL: I don't believe so, because people are going to panic. The particular reason for the crash will probably be debated in post-history, but we have examples to look at. I mean, the assassination of Archduke Ferdinand touched off World War I. But no one could have predicted the flashpoint, because Ferdinand didn't really have that much to do with it. If it hadn't been that assassination it would have been something else. So I don't know what the flashpoint will be: collapse of the socioeconomic system and the political system may be from a major petroleum supply interruption, or it may be financial meltdown, because the banking or insurance industries go belly up. The whole thing is a house of cards. We have an economy based not just on consuming but on growth and debt. Growth is not sustainable, and debt is unhealthy. Our whole economy is overbuilt.

The problem with the economy collapsing, as I see it, is that when the trucks don't pull into the co-op, we're not going to have food in reserve. And the realization that the trucks aren't coming in will cause a cascading effect whereby people are going to be looking out for themselves. And then at some point even the government won't be able to prop up the economy to make sure those trucks unload safely at Safeway and Wal-mart. So we'll have consumers who are hungry and panicking, and there will be riots, and there will be martial law.

People can only live thirty to sixty days without food. They don't know how to fast, and they don't know how to grow or gather their own food.

One of the things automobiles represent for me is the degree to which we've been cut off from the land. The land is literally paved over, and we're separated from it by this layer of asphalt, this layer of petroleum product. And when you don't have access to land, you've really got nothing. It's your food. It's your freedom. It provides you with the traditional ways of surviving.

Picture a supermarket. Are you free in a supermarket? There is a cost. You can only be in there if you've got the money. And when you leave the supermarket you've still got more costs. You've got to pay for the energy to prepare that food. It's not a pretty picture at all. It's really discouraging, and it's not getting any better because the so-called leaders are giving us nothing in the way of solutions or relief.

DJ: One of the things that amazes me is that the internal combustion engine is so recent. Whenever I'm on an airplane, I think about how we're among the very few generations of humans who will ever see the planet from twenty thousand feet. And we're among the very few who will ever hear the sound of internal combustion engines.

JL: Marion King Hubbert called fossil fuel production a "pip." You look at the human time scale—not even geological time—and it's just a snap of the finger. It's all so recent. But people get used to their conditions so quickly that after only fifty years of petroleum-based fertilizers and pesticides, organic food is considered weird.

Or buying water. You would think that people would rebel against that. But we're like sheep in pens. What's next after that?

As bad as cars are, I learned in my years serving the petroleum industry and the government that you cannot get the price of gasoline up with good faith legislation, or policy analysis and good ideas. The same is true for efforts to raise the price of gasoline through developments like road pricing, where a car pays its way through paying for roads. None of that is going to happen. The system is too corrupt.

You see, all along I wanted to see higher gasoline prices, because the low prices are subsidized by all the means we mentioned earlier. But I learned very quickly that while the oil companies wanted to see high prices, too—though obviously for different reasons—the oil industry didn't want to see super high prices. They wanted to keep the price low enough they could keep their huge volume, and especially low enough that alternatives couldn't make any inroads.

So, when I realized that the price of gasoline wasn't going to go up high enough to reflect anything resembling its real cost, no matter how strong a case could be made, I switched tactics. That's when I started talking about a national paving moratorium. At first I suggested this just as a way to put Amtrak on a slightly more level playing field, because I realized that every new freeway cuts into Amtrak, and I thought that Amtrak would be a far more efficient form of motorized transport.

I realized another problem with pushing for higher gasoline taxes when I looked at the European model. Even if we were able to get the price up, it wouldn't stop the degradation. They're still building roads over there, and they've still got loads of cars. The cars may be a little smaller, but that's about it.

So it seemed to me that since traffic is really generated by roads—if you build a road, people will drive on it—to stop roadbuilding is a much more basic level to work on. It rips the rug out from under the car.

DJ: So maybe my first question should have been, "What's wrong with roads?"

JL: An immediate problem, long before the invention of cars, is that a village loses its local self-sufficiency when it becomes dependent on trade and travel. And certainly now roads are the precursor to so-called development, leading to all the ills of the modern industrial economy, from oil and gas exploration to mining to ranchettes and gentlemen's farms. Time and again they trash the garden of Eden.

But they do other things people aren't aware of. They generate more traffic, they overpave the land, so that we lose farmland and wildlife habitat, we lose communities. Wider roads are worse than narrow roads because they cut right through communities. Kids can't play, the elderly can't cross, trees are taken out from front yards and lost to road widenings, property is taken by eminent domain.

DJ: What would you hope that those of us who care would do?

JL: Honestly, I think we all care. We care about our health, about our loved ones, and even those of us who are afraid of nature don't really hate nature.

We all like to see a seal pop up in the water. We all like trees. Perhaps what you mean is those of us who are not too deeply in denial.

What we can do is seek out the truth and be honest, and take action.

You see so many people who talk so eloquently about so many of the environmental problems we face, yet when it comes to solutions they will not come to grips with the fact that because our condition is dependent on finite resources, some sort of wrenching adjustment will occur.

There is no easy way out. There's not going to be a green consumer culture on this level with anywhere near this population. Yes, there will be a crash. Yes, there will be vastly different lifestyles to cope with. We must come to terms not only with the facts that that we're out on this limb overconsuming and that we've got to get back to carrying capacity, but also that we've trashed the land.

DJ: If the crash would have come a hundred years ago, people in the Pacific Northwest would still have had salmon to eat. I've got a salmon-bearing stream twenty yards from my house, and it holds maybe five salmon. A hundred years ago I wouldn't have cared about international trade because there would have been more salmon than I could ever have eaten.

JL: That means our carrying capacity is way below what we've got now. Maybe not even a tenth of the population. Maybe a tenth of a tenth. Because we're not talking about a healthy ecosystem. You can't go out and hunt and gather. The landscape has been denuded. And so many people don't want to look at it. They want to enjoy their vacations and keep driving their SUVs and feel good about recycling. The bad news scares them. But how can we ever hope to find solutions if we won't look the truth square in the face?

DJ: I think that one of the most important things we can do is eliminate false hopes, which blind us to real possibilities and bind us to unlivable situations. So long as we believe photovoltaics are the answer, we're doomed.

Sure, photovoltaics are a lot better than some things. But where do you get the silicon? How do you transport it? You still need roads, and the whole infrastructure.

JL: It's ironic that electronic cottage industries have resulted in more road-building and more commuting. Because now people can be further out. They don't stay there and grow all their own food. No, they go back and forth buying stuff. I recently gave a talk to people up at Yosemite. They were all concerned about roadbuilding. But they themselves don't give up their vehicles. They're dependent on outside resources, and the goodies consumer culture brings them. That doesn't say it's all hypocrisy. They're more aware, they're more self-sufficient. If you can grow 10 percent of your food, that's 10 percent better. But the fact remains that when these people do drive, they drive further than if they lived in urban situations.

Yet there are so many ways that people can help. And they don't need to go someplace else, to take on some big environmental cause far from home. They can be aware of projects in their area, because if you live in Pennsylvania, you can make a lot more difference there at home then you can worrying about punching roads into Amazonia or into the redwoods. Fight the destroyers locally, and promote alternatives.

We need to respect each other's roles, and we need to work together. Maybe right now it's hard to be together in this materialistic culture, and in any case we will not really be able to practice sustainability until the dust settles. But we can and must be part of massive change, which is not only about the end of civilization, but also about self-liberation. When the oil economy is no longer, we will have to work together. And that may turn out to be a wonderful experience. Let's hope that it will be a clean enough world that people will benefit from whatever the land and air and water can still provide.

Steven Wise

Interview Conducted
at his home, Boston, Massachusetts
11.13.00

For decades now Steven Wise has worked tirelessly to change this culture by changing how it treats nonhumans. His focus has been on gaining legal rights for nonhumans. He teaches classes on animal rights at Harvard Law School, the Vermont Law School, and the John Marshall Law School in Chicago, and through the Center for the Expansion of Fundamental Rights (CEFR), which he directs with his wife, Debi Slater-Wise, and Jane Goodall. CEFR, according to its mission statement, "seeks to expand such fundamental legal rights as bodily integrity and bodily liberty to nonhuman animals, beginning with chimpanzees and bonobos, through litigation and education."

Called by *USA Today* "the country's best known animal lawyer" and by the *Yale Law Review* "one of the pistons of the animal rights movement," Wise is the author of the books *Rattling the Cage: Toward Legal Rights for Animals,* and *Drawing the Line: Science and the Case for Animal Rights.* This book derives its title from the central question of Wise's work. As he states, "At the center of the fierce debates over legal rights for nonhuman animals sits an inevitable question: Where do we draw the line?"

I interviewed Steven at his home on a cool fall day in 2000.

DJ: You've written, "For four thousand years, a thick and impenetrable legal wall has separated all human from all non-human animals."

SW: That wall is central to all of my work, and it's central to how we conduct ourselves toward nonhumans. Being on the side of the wall we're on is very important, because that means we're legal persons. As legal persons we're entitled to a panoply of legal rights, from the fundamental down to the very small and unimportant. On the other side of that wall, however, one is not a legal person, but a legal thing, not entitled to any legal rights at all, even the most basic: the rights to bodily integrity, bodily liberty, or life itself.

That wall is thousands of years old, and was constructed when there were at least two major differences in the way we understood the universe in which we live and nonhuman animals. At the time this wall was being built people understood, at least in the West, that the universe had been designed by some designer, and constructed hierarchically. It was understood that within this hierarchy were those who were inferior and those who were superior, and that those who were inferior had been made for their betters. So Aristotle, for example, wrote that plants were made for animals and animals were made for human beings. Similarly, he wrote that women were made for men and slaves for their masters. The Greek Stoic Chrysippus wrote that horses and oxen existed so they could labor for us humans, and pigs existed so we could eat them. Fleas existed to wake human slumberers, and mice lived to teach us tidiness.

Now to the second major difference: how we perceive nonhuman animals. Many at that time (I'm referring to the ancient Greeks again) thought that nonhuman animals were unable to believe, desire, have a memory, think about the future or past, or for that matter think at all. Some thought they weren't even able to experience or perceive, that they were similar to what we would now consider to be robots. Most people didn't believe it to this extreme, at least not until the time of Descartes, in the seventeenth century. But a good portion of the people did believe that nonhuman animals had extremely limited, virtually absent consciousness.

Both ideas have changed. Very few reputable scientists think chimpanzees and bonobos (sometimes referred to as "pygmy chimpanzees")—to take two creatures on which much of my work has focused—function anything like robots. And virtually no respectable scientist sees the universe as having been designed by a divine being in a hierarchical way simply for use by human beings.

DJ: We all just act as though it was.

SW: But we do so without philosophical underpinnings. The Greeks and other progenitors of our civilization actually believed this. Many people still act as if a Great Chain of Being exists, and that we are the highest corporeal beings (ruled over by angels, gods, or God). At one time educated people thought that. But educated people don't think that anymore. That doesn't mean many people don't still feel or act that way. But if you sit them down, and ask, "How can you justify what you're doing?" they usually dissolve into incoherency or say something facile like, "Well, the Bible says the world was created for us."

DJ: It seems you're getting at the dissonance between beliefs on which the laws are based and what we know.

SW: Yes. These ideas—that nonhuman animals are almost like robots, and that the world is a hierarchy created for us—may not have been irrational at the time or demonstrably untrue. To incorporate those ideas into law may not have been irrational either, because that's what people reasonably thought. But now, we have twenty-first-century science, twenty-first-century ways of looking at nonhuman animals, and twenty-first-century ideas of how the universe holds together, our law still operates on the facts as they were understood twenty-four centuries ago. Our law is the same today as it was in Roman times. In fact, if a Roman lawyer sat in on an argument about non-human animals up in, say, the Massachusetts Supreme Judicial Court, he'd probably feel completely comfortable, because the law of today is essentially the law of Rome. And that's really terrible for nonhuman animals.

DJ: Laws codifying this perceived separation between humans and nonhu-mans go even farther back than Rome...

SW: Yes. The oldest Mesopotamian laws concern themselves with both human and nonhuman slavery. That was about 4,200 years ago.

DJ: You call it nonhuman slavery.

SW: Sometimes it irritates people when I make that comparison. But I don't think it's inappropriate. I've been encouraged in that direction lately, as more and more people are making that comparison.

DJ: I've seen some feminists make it...

SW: And it's entering the mainstream. Just last February I was giving a talk at the Harvard Law School with Laurence Tribe, probably the United States' foremost constitutional law expert. He agreed that what we do to nonhuman animals is slavery. Slavery is a reasonable way of describing it. In fact, one may note, as I do in *Rattling the Cage*, that human slavery was even modeled on nonhuman slavery. I make the parallel case that the abolition of nonhuman slavery can, and should be, modeled on its abolition among humans.

DJ: How did abolition work among humans?

SW: Well, it was a very complicated process and, to some degree, is still going on. The way France abolished slavery was different than the way England abolished it. The United States abolished it differently than did Brazil. For example, the United States ultimately abolished it by civil war, while in England the first real nail—and it was a very large nail—in the coffin of slavery was pounded because of a judicial challenge, through common law, in what's called the Somerset case.

In 1749 James Somerset was captured in Africa, thrust onto a slaving ship, and shipped to Virginia. There he was purchased by Charles Stewart, who brought him to Massachusetts. Twenty years later, Stewart went to

England, and took Somerset with him. There, Somerset ran away. Stewart's men recaptured him a month later, and chained him in the bowels of a ship about to head for Jamaica, where Somerset would be re-sold. A group of English citizens heard of this outrage and sued on Somerset's behalf. Fortunately for them, their case was heard before the greatest English judge, maybe the greatest judge who has ever existed in an English-speaking country, Lord Mansfield. Mansfield didn't really want to adjudicate, and urged both sides to settle. They refused. At trial Stewart's lawyer argued that slavery was legal in England because no law forbade it. Somerset's lawyer demanded to know "upon what Principle is it—can a Man become a Dog for another man?" Mansfield replied, in language that still gives me chills, "If the parties will have judgment, let justice be done though the heavens may fall."

DJ: You have to admire his courage.

SW: His judgment was that slavery was so odious that common law couldn't support it. It was a watershed in human rights, and a terrific model for trying to see how legal things can be transformed into legal persons, which is precisely what Mansfield did: transform James Somerset from a legal thing into a legal person.

I would contrast Mansfield's courage with many of the judges in the United States, whose hands, it must be admitted, were at least partly tied by the fact that because of the compromises that went into the forming of the United States Constitution, slavery was at least implicitly approved in that document. So there was never a question here of whether slavery was or wasn't legal—it was—as there had been in England.

DJ: So in some ways wouldn't the abolition of slavery in the U.S. make a good model, since nonhuman slavery is even more entrenched in our culture than human slavery?

SW: It's hard to be more entrenched than human slavery was in the United States, although they're in the same ballpark. A tremendous percentage of our gross national product was bound up in slavery or slave-economics in some way in the first half of the nineteenth century. And the first ten or twelve presidents were slave owners.

DJ: One argument against abolishing slavery was that it would consist of "taking" private property, and that this value was immense. One pro-slavery philosopher estimated that the value of slaves in Virginia in 1832 was one hundred million dollars, which equaled about half of the total assayed value of all land and houses in the state.

SW: One reason I don't get discouraged is that I can see how embedded human slavery was in the United States, yet I can also see that it wasn't that many years after 1832 that it was abolished. There are many reasons to believe that the abolition of nonhuman slavery won't go down the same track as human slavery, but there are many parallels.

DJ: We were talking about the difficulties faced by US abolitionists.

SW: There was the at-least-implicit chiseling of human slavery into the United States Constitution. And then you had the problem that the United States was bifurcated into slaveowning and non-slaveowning states. Because of this bifurcation, and because of the newness of the United States, policy questions loomed large in the minds of judges whenever they had to deal with slavery. They were always weighing principle versus policy, that is, the principle of the odiousness of slavery versus the belief that if they didn't confirm the legality of slavery, civil war might ensue, or the United States might disintegrate. Time after time judges said they thought slavery was abhorrent, but also that more important than this was the integrity of the United States. In order to keep the United

States expanding economically, and to keep the different sections of the country from being angry with each other, they'd rule in a way that made slave-owners happy, though they fully understood that because of their decisions millions of people would remain in bondage. What they did was terrible, unprincipled.

Yet one reason I don't get discouraged is that I can see how embedded human slavery was in the United States, yet I can also see that it wasn't that many years after 1832 that it was abolished.

There are many reasons to believe that the abolition of nonhuman slavery won't go down the same track as human slavery, but there are many parallels.

DJ: How is nonhuman slavery different?

SW: Well, for one thing, sectarianism is not an issue. Nonhumans are en-slaved everywhere. But more important is that there was really only one kind of human slave. There were different jobs in which slaves could be forced to work, but there wasn't the extreme variation of slavery under which we hold nonhuman animals, simply because humans aren't as varied as nonhumans. A turtle and a chicken and a pig and a chimpanzee are dramatically different creatures, with dramatically different cognitive abilities, way beyond what would have been found in human slavery.

DJ: And you didn't generally have human slaves grown for food, or grown to be vivisected, and so on.

SW: Right. That gives us a fingerhold into which we can pry our way into the issue. To a large extent the economy of the American South was founded on the labor of those slaves. Today there are some states with substantial parts of their economies built on exploiting nonhuman animals.

DJ: Certainly the agricultural states. But your primary focus really isn't on agriculture.

SW: No. One reason for that is that people's economic interest tends to cloud their moral judgments, and crowd out their ability to think about other things. One of the many reasons I chose to focus first on chimpanzees and bonobos was because their economic value is minimal in the United States. For the most part people's personal wealth will not be affected by what we do to chimpanzees and bonobos either way. They can begin to focus more clearly on whether we should be doing what we're doing to them.

DJ: What is happening to chimps and bonobos in the United States?

SW: There aren't that many. No one knows exactly how many, but there can't be more than three or four thousand in the United States.

DJ: Including zoos?

SW: Zoos, vivisection labs, pets in the garage, everything.

DJ: Is it significant that when you mention chimps and bonobos you don't include apes?

SW: It is intentional. In *Rattling the Cage* I don't argue that great apes should have legal rights. If you look closely, you'll see I don't argue that chimpanzees and bonobos should have rights either. The species of an individual should be utterly irrelevant to whether she or he has what it takes for basic legal rights. When we look at a representative of a species, your average human or your average chimpanzee, and we can show they have what it takes for fundamental legal rights, that probably means that most normal members of that species do. By the same token, if an individual doesn't have what it takes for fundamental legal rights, it seems very difficult to make the argument that the person deserves them just because he or she happens to be a member of a certain species.

DJ: I don't understand.

SW: I defy someone to argue that an encephalic human child should be entitled to basic legal rights, without resorting to platitudes like, "We're all human," or something else that sounds good, but doesn't make much sense. Why should being human, or being any species, be relevant to whether we should or shouldn't have fundamental legal rights?

DJ: What fundamental legal rights are you talking about?

SW: The one I talk about most often is bodily liberty. One can't be enslaved, can't be kept in small steel or concrete cages. The second is bodily integrity. One can't, if one is a human being, be the victim of a battery. One can't be killed, and one can't be eaten. One can't be vivisected for medical research.

DJ: And you're basing your claim for those fundamental rights on...

SW: Possession of common cognitive abilities.

DJ: Using human cognition as the standard.

SW: No, using existing legal standards. I'm not a philosopher, like Peter Singer or Tom Regan, who puts forward a philosophical theory, then spins out the implications. I'm a lawyer, and I attempt to make sense of, and work within, our legal system.

DJ: And within our system cognition is the basis for those fundamental legal rights.

SW: It is one basis.

DJ: Commonly accepted?

SW: A certain kind of cognition, as in autonomy, is sufficient for basic legal rights. There might be other sufficient bases as well. But autonomy is one of them.

DJ: By itself.

SW: Yes. Now, while autonomy is sufficient, it's not necessary. A baby might be born without a brain. She will not be autonomous. A court may still give her a lot of legal rights, though it's not really clear why. As I mentioned before, when judges talk about autonomy their reasons for giving autonomous humans basic legal rights at least make sense. When they start talking about giving children without brains—who can't feel or think, who are neither conscious nor sentient—legal rights, the judges may start to become fuzzy, and may retreat into circular platitudes.

The point is that something like humanity as a basis for rights is not easy to defend. But autonomy is very easy. Judges, I would argue, care a lot about autonomy.

DJ: What is autonomy?

SW: The autonomy that is sufficient for legal rights is what I call "practical autonomy." If a being can want things, and has the ability to act intentionally to get them, and a sense of self that has developed to the point that she understands it is her life that she's leading, and that things can go good or ill for her, judges will respect that autonomy. It will be sufficient for basic legal rights. My fundamental argument is that many humans have that, but non-humans have it, too, and so while it's almost impossible to make a reasoned defense for all humans—anyone who has donned the human form in some way—it's not hard at all to make an argument that all autonomous creatures should have basic legal rights.

DJ: This cat, who just walked in the room, came over and reached up to be petted. Clearly she has that intention.

SW: It's hard sometimes to tease out what's going on in the minds of any being who lacks language.

DJ: Or who may speak languages that we do not know, or do not bother to learn.

SW: There have been running fights about this for more than a century. It's hard enough to tell what's going on in another human's head, much moreso in a cat's. But we shouldn't make too much of that, for there there's oftentimes a double standard. We end up willing to take any kind of evidence that something is going on inside of a human head, but will ignore very strong evidence for what's going on in the heads of chimpanzees or cats.

DJ: I've seen the same arguments put forward for American Indians, whom the Spaniards said were born for forced labor because they were "ruled by their passions and not intellect," and for Africans, about whom one pro-slavery philosopher pointed out the "many points of resemblance Anatomists have established between the Negro and Ape."

SW: In the nineteenth century the California Supreme Court barred Chinese from testifying against whites in court because the Chinese were a race, they said, "whom nature has marked as inferior and who are incapable of progress or intellectual development beyond a certain point."

DJ: And didn't that prohibition extend to all nonwhites?

SW: It did.

One thing that concerns me is that even many scientists assign this same double standard to nonhumans. Dedicated behaviorists like B.F. Skinner didn't have double standards. They said nobody has a mind. Humans don't have minds. Nonhumans don't have minds. I don't agree: it seems to be really forced and exceedingly unlikely. But at least it was intellectually honest.

It all comes back to this wall, which is not only legal, but also perceptual: we perceive this wall separating us from all others. I've seen hundreds of articles and books where scientists have written: "We did this experiment on a chimpanzee and got these positive results." Someone always seems to respond, "Oh, but that can be explained at a behavioristic level." Yes, it probably can, but when you get right down to it, everything you do can be explained, if someone really wants to, at a behavioristic level. The problem is that eventually it becomes as ludicrous to try to explain the actions of a chimpanzee that way as it is to explain your actions that way.

DJ: That reminds me of the Clever Hans story. Hans was a horse who lived around the turn of the nineteenth and twentieth centuries. He was considered clever because he could multiply, divide, add, subtract, convert coins, tell what day of the week it would be anytime in the future, and so on. He would answer by pawing his hoof. Scientists eventually discovered that Hans wasn't actually finding the cube root of twenty-seven, but instead was very carefully watching the person who asked the questions to detect his almost imperceptible relaxation when Hans reached the right answer. All the versions of this I've seen have ended the same way: Hans really wasn't so clever. But the question I always ask is this: would you rather have a friend who can find the cube root of twenty-seven, or one who can read and respond to your slightest emotional and physical movements?

SW: He wasn't doing what they wanted him to do, but he was certainly doing something extraordinary.

I usually think about this inability to perceive in terms proposed by Thomas Kuhn, who talks about the structure of scientific revolutions and how difficult it is, once we've attained strong beliefs, to shift paradigms. If I'm trying to convince someone that a chimpanzee should have basic legal rights, and I'm talking to someone who believes that God said they shouldn't, even though they can't prove that—in fact they have no evidence of it at all—their belief in it is so strong that there's nothing I can say. I'm not trying to pick on religion here. Thomas Kuhn makes the same point about scientists. People hold tightly to their beliefs, even when an increasing amount of evidence begins to make it clear that indeed they're wrong.

There is the famous case of Galileo finding the first moons going around Jupiter, and attempting to show them to a meeting of Bolognese professors. They all looked through the telescope, then straightened up and said, "I don't see any moons." You can just imagine Galileo breathing on the telescope, looking in and saying, "There they are, what's the matter with these people?"

DJ: Wasn't it Max Planck who observed about scientific revolutions...

SW: Ah, yes, he has that wonderful line about how "a new scientific truth does not triumph by convincing its opponents and making them see the light, but rather because its opponents eventually die, and a new generation grows up that is familiar with it."

I think generally we only see what we're prepared to see, or at least what we believe it's possible to see. If we think something cannot be seen, then we will not see it.

DJ: So if you think a chimp is a beast-machine with fur, then what you'll see...

SW: According to this paradigm, nonhumans are like clocks. One of the stories goes that Cartesians would stab a dog, and when the dog would scream they'd say it's no different than striking a spring in a cuckoo clock.

You can't imagine what it was like for me to walk into a courtroom in 1980 and argue that the interests of nonhuman animals should be taken into consideration. It was like talking to a brick wall. Or worse, like talking to brick wall that laughed at you, ridiculed you. They said I was being absurd.

DJ: Let's go back to chimps and bonobos. You started to tell me the conditions under which they're kept in this country.

SW: They vary dramatically, from roadside zoos to people's backrooms to bare steel and concrete cages at infectious disease laboratories to places like Roger Fouts's colony at Central Washington University, where they're kept in decent conditions. But chimpanzees aren't indigenous to the United States, so there are very few places I can think of where they're kept in anything approaching a semi-wild condition. People are trying to think of ways to do that now, and there's a lot of talk about having chimpanzee sanctuaries, but all the chimpanzees and bonobos are kept in one form or another of imprisonment. Some of it is relatively benign, some of it is not.

DJ: I didn't know until I read your book that even some of the chimps whom they've taught American Sign Language have later been vivisected, infected with diseases, injected with pesticides, "sacrificed," to use the parlance of animal experimentation.

SW: This is the inevitable outcome of a system in which they're viewed as legal things. It's the exact outcome you'd expect in a slave society, in which human slaves were viewed as things, and in which people would break up families, in which they'd sell children and parents to different masters, or break up husbands and wives. That's what happens when you enslave: you do not take into consideration the interests of the thing. And the inevitable by-product is cruelty.

DJ: I guess the question now is: do you believe that chimpanzees and bonobos have cognition sufficient to form a basis for legal rights?

SW: Chimpanzees and bonobos have been the subjects of cognitive work both in the wild and in captivity now for at least forty years, since Jane Goodall went to Gombe. They seem to have some ability, if not to count, certainly to assess at least small quantities at relatively sophisticated levels.

DJ: And of course there are tribes of Indians who don't count, which does not mean they are stupid.

SW: True. And so far as speaking, if chimpanzees and bonobos don't use language, they do use something remarkably like language.

DJ: Europeans said Africans could be enslaved because they didn't really use language, but instead "fart[ed] with their tongues in their mouths."

SW: That's how the Greeks came up with the term barbarian: the Greeks couldn't understand their language, which sounded like nonsense, like "barbarbarbar," to them.

Sue Savage-Rumbaugh at Georgia State University says that Panbanisha, one of the bonobos there, understands three thousand English words.

DJ: And how much of the language of bonobos do most scientists understand?

SW: That's a good question.

We also know that chimpanzees and bonobos seem to be able to act intentionally. They can certainly suffer. They have societies so complex and fluid that some have dubbed them "Machiavellian." They can deceive. They empathize. They treat their illnesses with medicinal plants. They communicate with symbols. It seems highly unlikely that they're not conscious, that they're somehow acting entirely instinctively. I know of no one who works closely with their societies who thinks they're just acting instinctively. They certainly appear conscious. Chimpanzees pass mirror self-recognition tests, one gauge of self-consciousness. Two or three weeks ago I was in Atlanta, and saw Panbanisha walking about. I happened to see her sit, look in the mirror, and start fiddling with her hair. I'd read about mirror self-recognition before, but I realized, My God, I'm seeing it right here. She was looking in the mirror the way my thirteen-year-old daughter might. I don't know if it means the same thing, but they certainly appear the same.

DJ: When you make these legal arguments, and those who disagree with you don't laugh, what do they say?

SW: I haven't made these kinds of legal arguments, and in fact I urge other lawyers not to make them, because I think it's premature. One of the reasons I wrote *Rattling the Cage* is that there was nothing like it out there. Judges and lawyers are just beginning to realize these kinds of arguments exist. In *Rattling the Cage* I try to show how the argument for at least basic legal rights for chimpanzees and bonobos is in the mainstream of traditional legal thinking under the common law, that far from being arbitrary to give them these kinds of basic legal rights, it is arbitrary to deny them these basic legal rights simply because they're not human beings. I make the further argument that to deny them these kinds of basic legal rights actually undermines any sort of rational argument that we might have for giving each other basic legal rights.

While commonsensical, these arguments are new. Most judges are in their fifties, sixties, or seventies, and never took a class in environmental law. They certainly never took a class in animal rights law. They're only dimly aware of what's going on in these fields, if they're aware of it at all. People who think they're going to walk into a supreme court of the state and convince several judges to make chimpanzees legal persons are naïve. They'll run into the same stone wall I ran into when I began doing animal law twenty years ago. That wall has been there four thousand years, and it's not going to evaporate on its own. We have to make a concerted effort to knock it down. And we have to do that through education. My own focus is on judges and lawyers and law professors. And *Rattling the Cage* is getting out to a degree that I could only have imagined. It's been reviewed many places where lawyers go to look, such as in the Journal of the *American Bar Association*, *The American Lawyer*, *The Federal Lawyer*. This month it's being reviewed simultaneously in *The Harvard Law Review* and the *Yale Review Journal*.

DJ: How are the reviews?

SW: They've ranged from excellent to moderately favorable.

DJ: But nobody's laughing.

SW: Nobody's laughing, and that's a dramatic change. Martha Nussbaum, the philosopher, is reviewing it for the *Harvard Law Review*, and Judge Richard Possner is reviewing it for the *Yale Law Journal*.

DJ: Are they big deals?

SW: They are. If they thought these arguments were at the laughing stage, they wouldn't have bothered. So they're taking it seriously, and doing what I was hoping to do, which is to ignite a sophisticated discussion as to whether or not chimpanzees and bonobos should have legal rights. When I began teaching animal rights law at the Vermont Law School in 1990, I was the only person in the country, maybe the world, teaching it at the law school level. To my knowledge, as late as 1995 there weren't any other law school classes in animal rights law being taught. By now probably fifteen to twenty law schools in the United States—including some of the best: Harvard, Yale, Boston College, Georgetown, George Washington, UCLA, Northwestern, Cardozo—have recently offered, are offering, or will soon offer classes in animal rights law. For the first time someone—me—lectured on animal rights law at Lincon's Inn in London, one of the four main Inns of Court.

This is what judges look to when deciding whether they're dealing with something frivolous. Law schools are also where the next generations of judges come from. Having taken animal rights law doesn't mean that students will believe everything they've learned. But they will no longer view it as something absurd, and I think they'll be more open to these kinds of arguments.

This is all a long way of saying I don't think we're ready to litigate now, because there's a lot of education to be done and a lot of intellectual foundations to be laid. But we're beginning the process. So I encourage lawyers to write about it, teach about it, lecture about it, but to not yet get it to court.

DJ: So you'd hope for litigation in twenty, thirty, forty years…?

SW: I think the earliest successful suits could come as early as ten years. Even five years ago I wouldn't have thought it would come in my lifetime, but things are moving much more quickly than I could even have hoped. If you'd have told me five years ago that earlier this spring I'd teach animal rights law at the Harvard Law School I would have said, "Not likely." Just the fact that I did, and that reviews are coming, and classes are being taught, and books are coming out makes me think that momentum is building.

DJ: Okay, so outside of litigation, how would someone who disagreed with you respond?

SW: One of my favorite things that any reviewer said was that I had reversed the normal mode of argumentation about animal rights. Critics find it hard to attack me with the standard anti-animal-rights lines—overemotional is a word that often comes up. Now the opponents make irrational or nonrational arguments.

The point, really, is that I've yet to hear any reasoned disagreements with the idea of extending basic legal rights to others who have practical autonomy, whether or not they're human. One argument I did hear was that to give legal rights to nonhuman animals would be the end of civilization.

DJ: Not necessarily a bad thing.

SW: But I don't think it's true. Similar arguments were made against ending slavery. Get rid of slavery and Virginia will be a howling wasteland. England will be a howling wasteland. The South will be a howling wasteland. The lawyer who said the bit about ending civilization also said, "The essence of property law is that whomever first occupies something—land or anything else—is entitled to it, which means we'd have to give up all of our land to woodchucks and deer." This may or may not be a good idea.

DJ: That lawyer is ignorant. We don't even have to talk about nonhumans. In 1820 Supreme Court Chief Justice John Marshall rationalized the U.S.

conquest of the continent from Indians, saying "if the property of the great mass of the community originates in it [conquest], it becomes the law of the land, and cannot be questioned."

SW: Be that as it may, giving land back to woodchucks doesn't inevitably follow from the arguments I'm making. Instead it creates a straw man, and allows him to rebut an argument I didn't make.

In order to rebut the arguments I do make, you have to argue that: a) chimpanzees and bonobos really are like robots; b) autonomy is not a sufficient basis for basic legal rights; or c) words like bodily integrity, bodily liberty, life, or equality are not important. There are legal and scientific arguments that one can try to make, but they're certainly not open and shut.

Double standards are unacceptable. One must use the same arguments you're making for nonhuman animal rights as for human rights. And one cannot permit lousy arguments to be made on behalf of humans and not allow better arguments to be made on behalf of nonhuman animals, or have good arguments be made on behalf of nonhuman animals, and then just say, "We're going to ignore them simply and solely because they're nonhuman animals."

Judges are in the business of drawing lines. And where you're finally going to draw the line throughout the nonhuman animal kingdom is not clear. It's a very difficult question. But I know that the line we draw at the human species is arbitrary, irrational, and just plain wrong. The lines need to be redrawn in a consistent, nonarbitrary, fair, and equal way. Judges have that responsibility.

DJ: It seems pretty clear to me that insofar as there is a relationship between law and rationality...

SW: There is a relationship. Irrational law tends to be eroded, because people don't like it.

DJ: Well, as slavery shows, it can take a while...

SW: That's true. But people value equality. They value liberty. They value fairness. They value nonarbitrariness. And they do have this sense of justice that eventually can get plucked.

DJ: What I was going to say is that insofar as that connection is there, it seems that what must inevitably happen is that the line will keep getting drawn further and further out over time.

SW: It may.

DJ: Once you've made the case for chimps and bonobos, I'd think it wouldn't be hard to make the case for the rest of the apes.

SW: I have a second book now in which I'm looking at how strong the arguments are for orangutans, gorillas, dolphins, elephants, African grey parrots, dogs, and honeybees. What do we know about them? Do they have minds? How confident are we they do or don't? And this raises the next important question: what happens when we simply don't know? Do we apply a precautionary principle? When we don't know, who has the burden of proof? How strong should the burden of proof be? I think it's likely that the arguments I make on behalf of chimpanzees and bonobos go beyond them, but how far beyond they go will be a matter of fact of the sort that judges are used to adjudicating.

One of the beauties of this approach, I think, is that I understand that the law is a conservative profession, and I think that we can change things without having to change the law. The major principles can remain the same. All we need to do is begin to act the way we say we believe.

This consonance between actions and words is crucial, not only to stopping the atrocities we commit upon nonhuman others, but to protecting our own basic rights. Our society and our judicial system are organized upon certain fundamental principles, and these principles must be applied in a nonarbitrary manner. By arbitrarily excluding nonhuman animals we undermine our own fundamental principles.

George Draffan

Interview Conducted
at his home, Seattle, Washington
5.27.00

E very day, George Draffan receives calls requesting information on corporate activity around the globe. On Tuesday, an environmental group in Indonesia might call to say that Weyerhaeuser is moving into their area and they want to know the company's history. The next day it could be someone from Washington, D.C., wanting to know which corporations are behind a phony nonprofit. Ask Draffan to trace the connections between fruit transnationals and Central American political unrest, and in a few days or weeks, you can expect a full explanation, complete with complex yet readable graphics.

Draffan has had a greater influence on my thinking than any other single person. For more than a decade, he and I have been having long conversations about our culture's destructiveness and what it will take for us to find—or remember—a more sane way to live. And for more than a decade, his stubborn insistence on pursuing these arguments to their logical conclusions has inspired me to move forward, or prodded me when my reasoning is faulty.

George and I met in 1990, when we came together with activist and physician John Osborn to write a book on how timber companies in the Pacific Northwest illegally obtain land that is part of the public domain. I was the lead writer and George the lead researcher. For several years, we worked together on that slim volume, sometimes churning out thirty pages in a weekend, other times spending several days fighting over a word. The book came out in 1995 and is now the centerpiece of a national effort to take back public land illegally held by timber transnationals. George and I have written several books together since then.

George was born in 1954 and raised in Wisconsin. He discovered activism in the summer of his fifteenth year, when his uncle in Washington State took him to see a clearcut. Looking at the ravaged, treeless mountainside,

George knew what he had to do with his life. Around the same time, he first learned about Buddhism, which helped him make sense of the chaos of his teenage years. He studied Buddhism and history at the University of Wisconsin and received a Master's degree in librarianship from the University of Washington. In the early 1980s, George joined Earth First! and helped found that organization's first Washington State chapter. He is still a practicing Buddhist, and that spiritual tradition informs his understanding of the economic and political realities in today's world.

These days, George runs the Public Information Network, an organization providing research services and training to citizens working for corporate and governmental accountability (P.O. Box 95316, Seattle, WA 98145-2316, (206)723-4276). The Network's Web site, www.endgame.org, is one of the best activism sites I've seen, full of useful, shocking, enlightening, and entertaining information.

In a sense, I've been interviewing George for ten years, but this particular discussion took place on a beautiful afternoon in May in the sunny dining room of his home in south Seattle, where he lives with his partner, Julene Schlack. We were sitting downwind of a Boeing manufacturing plant, and although we could not see the plant's toxic emissions, we were absorbing them into our bodies as surely as we took in the air, the sunlight, and each other's conversation.

DJ: I've got two questions. First, you've said if you could change just one thing to slow environmental destruction, you'd stop international trade. Why? Second, I once asked you, "What will it take for us to survive?" You responded, "Democracy." Is that still your answer?

GD: Maybe this is the same question looked at from different levels. On the economic level, international trade is the mechanism or engine for a lot of social and environmental destruction. But what would it take to stop international trade? The politicians of the world aren't about to ban international trade. So what would make a difference in the global economy? On the political level it would take a certain amount of democracy, defined perhaps as everybody having equal access to resources. You can't have a huge difference in wealth or power—as we have now—and have a democracy. Democracy is economic as much as political.

But there are spiritual and psychological levels as well. What is it that prevents us from having a democracy? How do greed, aggression, and other behavior come out our fundamental psychological delusions? Is "the problem" operating on all of these levels at once?

DJ: We keep hearing that international trade is good, and we want it to keep expanding. But you disagree. What's wrong with people being able to get cheap cassettes from Taiwan, for example?

GD: It's only a very small elite of the world's population that can afford the latest electronics equipment. The U.S. has 5 percent of the world population but consumes the majority of the world's resources, so again, how broadly you look determines your answer. Most people in the world don't benefit from international trade. The people at the top of the pyramid benefit (if you equate benefit with consumption), and seem to assume that everyone enjoys the same. But the rest of the world gets a lot of sacrifice and deprivation and destruction, even if you're just looking at humans. If you're also looking at nonhuman species and the ecological capacity of the earth, it's even more lopsided. The people who tell you international trade is good are the people who benefit from it. But they're a very small minority.

It's maybe not so obvious to those of us on the top of the global heap, but the statistics on the gap between the rich and the poor are sobering. In 1960, U.S. corporate CEOs received forty times the average worker's salary; today they receive over 300 times what the average worker does. The economic "boom" the politicians talk about has benefited the already-wealthy at the expense of everyone else: between 1983 and 1995, the bottom 40 percent of U.S. households lost 80 percent of their wealth; the top 1 percent of U.S. households now owns 40 percent of all wealth. The optimist points out that most Americans now own some stock, but the fact remains that most households are in debt. Ten percent of the U.S. population owns more than three-fourths of all real estate, corporate stock, and bonds. What's wrong with that? Ask a poor person.

DJ: We always hear that international trade is good for "development" of the nonindustrialized nations. The only way they can "join us," we're told, is if we "liberalize" trade.

GD: That's what we hear, but the more international trade there is, the higher the third world debt. Mexico, Brazil, and Indonesia have been paying off hundreds of billions of dollars of debt over the last couple of generations, yet they're farther in debt all the time. The wealth gap between North and South is even worse than the U.S. wealth gap. And wherever there's been economic "restructuring" to join the new world order, unemployment and income disparity increases. Once again, it's good for the elite at the top—that is, if you consider consuming more than your share a good thing!

We hear over and over that development—or industrialization, whatever you want to call it—and trade are good, but I see it as destruction. "Development" is a euphemism, much like the word "efficiency." Efficiency within the current system is really about how fast you can turn forests and mountains into wastepaper and soda pop cans. Is that good? If the purpose of life is to consume and destroy, then international trade and industrial civilization are definitely proven ways to speed that up. International trade is the ultimate institutional and economic tool for leveraging our ability to consume, destroy, and work our will on the world.

International trade and the whole corporate state are based on a set of delusions that have been institutionalizing and hemming us in for 6,000 years. We weren't always so destructive. Maybe we started out as animals whose sense of self began to get reified. We began to see ourselves as separate from the world. How you behave depends on how you see and feel your self. Once we see ourselves as separate from the rest of the world, we start to see every other being as a mere thing, and we begin to believe that we can get away with working our will on the world, that there wouldn't be negative consequences for attempting to do so, for pretending we're separate. But as you once wrote, Derrick, ignorance or denial of ecological law in no way exempts us from the consequences of our actions.

Our power to work our will upon the world has far outstripped our ability to distinguish what's sustainable. The international trade system is clearly beyond our capacity to control or use in a sustainable or democratic way. Any economy that's beyond the community level, where there's immediate and face-to-face feedback about what you do, is going to cause problems. How can I still be a citizen yet be in an international economy? I can't even know what injustice or ecological destruction the purchase of my computer has had. I had no contact with the women in Thailand who've gotten cancer from putting hard drives and computer chips together. Even if my intent is "good," I can have only the slightest understanding of the impacts of my consumption. It is impossible to understand all the social and environmental impacts of a computer or a car made in a dozen different countries. That's why consumers and industry are so enamored with the idea of certifying products so that the consumer can just walk into the store and buy the computer with a green star on the box. No thinking, no feeling, just confident consuming. "More of everything."

DJ: You've said one of the problems is that our economy fragments us into many parts, two of which would be, for example, consumer and citizen, and these fragments are pitted against each other. It's clearly in your best interest as a consumer…

GD: …to have my computer made by a woman who doesn't get paid enough, and who isn't protected by health and safety regulations. And who is thousands of miles away, and I will never meet. It's nearly irresistible to me as a consumer to buy the cheapest products. Even as someone who spends the majority of his working life examining the impacts and trying to change the system, I still drive a car, and I still buy computers assembled by underpaid people in the South. No matter how clear my perception or how pure my intent, as a consumer in the global economy I'm still drawn into situations that as a human I find abhorrent. It's an impossible situation. Look. I live a mile downwind from a Boeing airplane plant that produces toxic waste. The fact that I know about it, and that I have certain feelings and motivations around toxics, wasn't a strong enough deterrent to keep me from living here. I can live with those contradictions, and I may well die from the cancer that results. Polls indicate that most of us consider ourselves environmentalists— yet we're killing ourselves and destroying the ability of ecosystems to function. We're eating ourselves to death. Is anybody home?

Our economic activities are out of scale. Nobody would argue you don't need warmth to live. Some people would argue that electricity is not the most efficient way to produce that warmth. But even if you assume the need for electricity, how do you end up with nuclear power, with radioactive wastes that last for tens of thousands of years? It's absurd, and hardly commensurate with the need for warmth. International trade is likewise completely out of proportion to the needs for food, clothing, and shelter. It's not about survival. It's about death.

I don't want to focus too much on international trade, though. It's a human tendency, I think, to want to pick out the problem. It's too simplistic to say that if we could stop international trade then ecological sustainability would be possible, or if we could stop nuclear power then we wouldn't get cancer. Nuclear power, the institution of the limited liability corporation, international trade and globalization, the World Bank: all these things are just tools. They are not the causes of the problem, any more than a hammer is a cause of a murder. A hammer could be the tool of a murder, but the motivation and the behavior come from something much deeper. You take a hammer or a gun away from a psychotic, because he's not to be trusted with those tools. I would take international trade and nuclear power away from humans for the same reason. We're apparently not capable of having a global economy. We're not capable of controlling ourselves with that magnitude of a tool. Well-intentioned people say we need to have cultural exchange and we need to feed people, and we need to have a global economy to do that, but the evidence is that the more global we get, the more dysfunctional things get.

DJ: And the problem isn't just computers or cars or other obviously destructive things. You and I once traced the origin of everything in a dinner we shared.

GD: I remember. It was at that great Vietnamese restaurant in Spokane. You had lemongrass chicken with chile, and I had stir-fried vegetables. If I recollect, here's the scenario we concocted afterwards: the chicken was raised on a factory farm in Arkansas, owned by Tyson Foods, which supplies one-quarter of America's chickens and sends them as far away as Japan. The chicken was fed corn from Nebraska and grain from Kansas, and was one of about 17 million chickens processed by Tyson that week. The bird was frozen and put onto a truck made by PACCAR. The truck was made from plastics manufactured in Texas, steel milled in Japan from ore mined in Australia and chromium from South Africa, and aluminum processed in the United States from bauxite mined in Jamaica. The parts were assembled in Mexico. As the truck brought the frozen chickens to Spokane, it burned fuel refined in Texas, Oklahoma, California, and Washington from oil originating beneath Saudi Arabia, Venezuela, Mexico, Texas, and Alaska. All this, and you used to raise chickens yourself. I remember you always had baby chicks in your bathtub.

So far as my dish, the broccoli was grown in Mexico in a field fertilized with, among other things, ammonium nitrate from the United States, phosphorous mined and processed by Freeport McMoRan from deposits in Florida, and potassium from potash deposits in Saskatchewan. The potash was processed by one of the multinational mining, oil, and chemical companies Texasgulf, Swift, PPG Industries, RTZ, or Noranda. The pesticides we ingested were equally cosmopolitan.

Another company associated with nearly every facet of that meal was AKZO, with 350 facilities in fifty countries. The meal utilized many of their 10,000 chemical products: chicken vaccines that allow Tyson to keep their operations relatively disease-free; automobile coatings; chemicals used in many steps of the agricultural and manufacturing processes, and so on.

The point is that within the global economy the simple pleasure of eating a fine meal in a local restaurant depends upon thousands of underpaid people working in dangerous workplaces, and is tied just as inescapably to pernicious activities across the globe: monopoly and union busting, the cruelty and debasement of factory farming, and water pollution in Arkansas; loss of topsoil and the depletion of the Oglala aquifer in Nebraska and Kansas; the immiseration and debasement of labor exploitation in Mexico; air pollution in Japan; toxic mining wastes in Australia, South Africa, and Jamaica; chemical pollution from refineries in four states, and degradation from oil exploration and extraction in four countries; soil toxification, the poisoning of ground water, more labor exploitation, and the poisoning of agricultural workers in Mexico; air, water, and ground pollution in the United States and Canada, and so on.

The same exercise could be performed for the clothes we wear (sweat shops run by Burma's military dictatorship, cotton pesticides, polypropylene petrochemicals), the houses we live in (formaldehyde in plywood, deforestation, the extinction of fish and wildlife), other consumer products (40,000 American workers killed on the job each year), or any other activity that calls for participation in the global economy. The consumer products, the cruelty, the pollution, the exploitation, the debasement—all are tied together in this convoluted web that is the modern economy.

DJ: Part of the problem seems that the global economy is a parody of Indra's web.

GD: It's not a parody. It is Indra's web. Indra's web is an ancient metaphor from India that's been used by to illustrate the interdependence of the universe. A Buddhist teacher once created a model of Indra's net for a Chinese emperor—a net with a jewel in each of the knots, set up such that in the sunlight each jewel reflected all the other jewels, and also such that if you touched one part of the web, the entire web shimmered. It illustrates that each person and thing in the universe is in relation to everything else: everything is completely interdependent, and everything is reflected in everything else. You can't touch one part of the web without moving the whole thing. A simple idea intellectually, but it has enormous implications if you try to live as if everything you did mattered. No more denial—or at least no more excuses for it. Denial has consequences too.

I can keep flying in jets and buying computers and pretending that I'm not part of the global economy. But despite my denial, I'm smack in the middle of the web, and I'm going to get cancer from the toxics, and the laborers who put my consumer goods together are going to get cancer because I buy those products, and to believe otherwise is to fall into delusion. It's a convenient belief for the corporations that profit, and it's a convenient belief for me as a consumer, but it's simply not true.

If you think about it on a logical level, you can only go so far with it, because your imagination is only so large. But if you start to jump levels with it, and consider that your imagination is one of the jewels that reflects everything else, and is completely dependent on everything else, you begin to get a sense of its vastness. It's humbling, to realize that everything matters.

DJ: Let's go a different direction for a moment. Can you talk about subsidies?

GD: Subsidy was originally defined as a public expenditure for a social good. But nowadays subsidies are usually an unfair advantage for a corporation or an industry, at someone else's expense. Subsidies now are really about privatization and externalization—the two-sided foundation of the modern economy. The system is now based on corporations privatizing the commonwealth (the water, the forests, the labor) for profit, and externalizing as many of the costs as possible onto communities, workers, and other species.

Nuclear power provides one of the best examples of an externality, an incredibly inefficient, absurd, and expensive way of producing some usable energy. So inefficient, that even once you've built a nuclear power plant, the most efficient thing you can do is shut it down. From almost any perspective—economic, toxics, even energy production—they should never be built. And in fact they wouldn't be built without massive influxes of public money. After World War II, Bechtel and Westinghouse and the other energy and engineering corporations went to the government and said they simply couldn't and wouldn't do it unless the government took care of uranium enrichment and a bunch of the other costs. And the government obliged, pushing the costs (money, cancer, and all the rest) onto the public.

Nuclear energy is a glaring example, but in fact the entire economy depends on externalizing the true costs. Total U.S. corporate profits are about five hundred billion dollars a year, but even Ralph Estes' conservative accounting of the externalized costs of the American economy—pollution, health and safety, acid rain loss to buildings and crops, crime, and so on—comes to about $2.5 trillion a year. So profits are about a fifth of the costs. Clearly we're mining the earth, mining the human resources, and foisting off huge costs onto the environment and onto future generations. We're destroying not only economic productivity, as it takes greater and greater subsidies to produce the goods and services to which we're addicted. We are also destroying the functioning of the ecosystems on which we ultimately depend.

The economy as a whole is subsidized, and you can take any industry or any sector of the economy and see it operating. The public's forests are being sold below cost to multinational corporations like Boise Cascade and Louisiana Pacific. Electricity is sold at a discount to the aluminum industry in the Pacific Northwest—electricity coming from dams built at public expense, dams which wiped out the salmon and destroyed native human cultures.

Manufacturers dump their toxic waste in the drinking water system, and pump it into the aquifers, and leave it to the taxpayer to clean up. There are thousands of "brownfields," former manufacturing sites in cities across the country, abandoned, toxic, being cleaned up at public expense one by one.

Billions of dollars are spent taking care of people who've become sick because of automobile pollution. That's a subsidy not only to the automobile industry, but to the automobile culture. We think a car costs $20,000, but it's subsidized thousands of dollars each year by publicly-maintained streets and highways, health and disposal.

The military is a giant subsidy, both in terms of direct cash payments to Rockwell or Boeing, and in terms of the use of military and police enforcement of "favorable business climates." As Secretary of Defense William Cohen said to a group of Fortune 500 leaders, "Business follows the flag... We provide the security. You provide the investment." I'd say he's being generous. The public provides the subsidy for the security, and the public generally provides the subsidy for the investment as well. Other subsidies include oil company tax breaks, below-cost grazing on public lands, giving the public airwaves to media corporations, giving away money for research and development. When a corporation dumps toxic waste, people not only subsidize the industry with their lives, but when the community sues, the corporation gets to deduct the cost of its legal defense from its taxes.

Our corporate culture has institutionalized these subsidies. We have created permanent or semi-permanent economic institutions called corporations that pay certain taxes which are completely inadequate to mitigate their impacts. That's only the direct subsidies. But the subsidies shimmer out across the web. Our whole political process has been warped until it serves institutions which are really nothing more than a legal and economic tool to facilitate externalizing costs and privatizing profits. The costs of lobbying, for example, where corporations act like citizens and influence the political process, are also tax deductible. So taxpayers actually subsidize corporate interference with their political processes. It's completely counterproductive, except again for the few people at the top who benefit from the system. And we all operate under the delusion that we all benefit from it. I can get a car for $20,000, or a computer for $2000, so I think I'm getting away with something. We're buying ourselves off.

Ever since the beginning of the agricultural age we've been funneling resources away from the ground and away from communities and toward an elite.

That's the flip side of externalization, privatization. Obviously, at some point in the distant past everything was public. There was no private property. Then tribes began to mark off territory, had certain seasonal rights to salmon streams, certain rights to areas where wild plants grew. This really took off with the rise of civilization, as property no longer became even communal but individual, belonging to the rich, and defended by property law.

The philosopher Voltaire said "the art of government consists in taking as much money as possible from one class of the citizens to give to another." The economist Adam Smith wrote that "Civil government, so far as it is instituted for the security of property, is in reality instituted for the defense of the rich against the poor, or of those who have some property against those who have none at all." The political economist John Locke wrote that "government has no other end but the preservation of property." We've built our system on the ideas of these idiots. The basis of law today is property law, protecting one person's rights to the other person's fair share, and it's so embedded in our culture that we see nothing wrong with it.

DJ: The word private comes from the same root as deprive, because wealthy Roman citizens walled off public spaces for private gardens, depriving the poor of their use.

GD: Wow. Language doesn't lie. We just forget where it comes from. How convenient. The culmination of it is that today we have very little public property, and that which we have has been consciously set aside, usually at huge controversy, and is constantly being chipped away at. Almost everything is private, controlled by a person or a group of people with exclusive legal and physical rights.

DJ: Increasingly including the privatization of our own genetic material.

GD: Everything. Air, water, our own bodies. And depending on how you define privatization, the fact that half of the water in the United States is carcinogenic can be seen as privatization. Only rich people can afford pure water. We've externalized the toxics from the industrial processes that have primarily benefited the elite onto the poor people in the cities who drink carcinogenic tap water. You can look at this from the externalization point of view—poor people are having toxics externalized onto them—or you can look at it from the privatization point of view—wealthier people can move to the suburbs and drink clean water.

DJ: You mentioned tribes marking off hunting territory as a form of privatization. I don't see the shift taking place there so much as with the rise of civilization. I mean, the Indians of the Northwest may have marked off salmon streams, but they didn't kill off the salmon. And I don't believe the reason the Hopi didn't pave over Arizona is because they weren't smart enough to build backhoes.

GD: No, although when you bring backhoes and whiskey and guns to indigenous peoples now, most of them adopt those tools readily. There seems to be no inherent resistance to taking on new tools once they're offered…

DJ: That's only after existing social structures have been destroyed. It's as Michel Guillaume Jean de Crevecoeur noted in *Letters From An American Farmer*, "There must be in the Indians' social bond something singularly captivating, and far superior to be boasted of among us; for thousands of Europeans are Indians, and we have no examples of even one of those Aborigines having from choice become Europeans." Benjamin Franklin was even more to the point: "No European who has tasted Savage Life can afterwards bear to live in our societies."

GD: Social life, economic life, technological culture, they all arise together. Once again, we catch ourselves trying to reify life into separate compartments as if social structures were separate from technological ones. If you bring guns and snowmobiles to an Inuit group, and give them those, then their social relationships are instantly changed. Maybe the manifestation takes five years or a generation, but it's inescapable that the effects of the new technology will radiate out to all parts of the web.

We start using technology, which can be defined as something which separates us from nature, and gives us the ability to work our will upon nature, and pretty soon we can only see ourselves as separate from nature. Perhaps that's the source of traditional peoples not seeing themselves as separate from nature.

You can't add more knots to the web without everything being affected everywhere else. Nor can you cut knots away and hope to not feel the effects. It's a question of how perceptive you are, and how long it takes for you to notice damage to the web, and whether you care enough to take care of the whole web, or just run amok ripping out the parts you happen to want to rip out. Every species we drive extinct results in other species going extinct. That feedback, or those indications, are not immediately apparent. That's part of the problem. Once again, we're not perceptive enough to see what's happening.

Most of what we see is layer after layer of projection, and most of what we do is based on our inability to understand that fact. Everybody does what they think is going to make them happy, yet hardly any of us are. Somehow, though, we never make that connection, and so we keep doing this thing that isn't making us happy, we just do it harder, faster, more. Isn't that the classic definition of insanity, doing the same thing over and over, and expecting different results?

If what we see is accurate, and what we're doing is actually going to make us happy, then let's go for it, we should have even more international trade, more development, more industry. Cheaper prices. More consumption. But if you can extricate yourself from that even a little bit, you begin to see that it isn't making us happy. It becomes quite horrifying, actually, and for most of us, for all of us sometimes, the horror is just too much. We immediately go into denial again. If we even glimpse the reality of how we're completely interdependent on everything else, the impacts of our behavior become so shocking and horrifying that we immediately have to numb ourselves.

It operates on a personal level, when we turn away from a homeless person—or never even see them at all, standing there dying. It operates on the economic level, when we buy and consume vegetables with pesticides because they're cheaper.

We're stuck in our habitual ways of seeing and thinking and doing, and it's resulting in suffering. There's a great quote from a Canadian lumberman who said, "When I look at trees I see dollar bills." Before we can deforest the planet, we have had to change the way we perceive it. Picture a forest that had been on this continent thousands of years. The forest was a complex and interdependent web of trees and bugs and fungus and animals and water, and all the energy and genetic material that goes round and round. Up until five hundred years ago the people in what we now call North America lived in basic equilibrium with the forest, as part of the web. Then another culture and the beginnings of the industrial system were brought in from "outside." Before the trees could be cut, they had to be redefined as private or public property. But even before that they had to be redefined as property at all. If I see a woman on the street, and I perceive her as another being with wants and desires all her own, I will treat her differently than if I perceive her as a worker or as property or as an object for my personal enjoyment. It is the same with trees, mountains, the hours of my own life. Are they alive, or are they mere objects for my consumption?

Once that projection and objectification takes place, from living being to property—from trees to dollar bills—everything else falls into place. The forest has been privatized, and the clearcuts, landslides, and species extinctions are all externalized.

DJ: What is the relationship between privatization and history?

GD: History is the objectification of time and events. Time becomes linear, and we become obsessed with progress, and getting somewhere. And if you're not destroying the world around you, if you're not creating markers that way, there's no reason for there to be history; there is simply living in cycles. History and linear time are by definition marked by change. So, prior to the massive ecological degradation that characterizes our way of living, there wasn't history. Nothing happened. We call it "prehistory." Individuals were born, they lived, and they died, of course, but communal life wasn't based on the emotional need to build and acquire and make progress. It just moved with the rhythms of nature. The quarters marked the seasons rather than the quarterly stock dividend. Same time scale, but vastly different experience and consequences.

On a social level, history is objectifying events, storytelling, eventually monopolizing the storytelling, and creating a worldview to which other people begin to subscribe. Group projection. History is always told by the people in control. The lower classes—and other species—may or may not deliberately subscribe to an academic or upper class description of events, but to some degree most of us do buy into it. It holds sway whether we consciously subscribe to it or not.

I really like the social and political model called "the three faces of power." The first face is the myth of American democracy, that everyone has equal power, and society or politics is just the give and take of different interest groups that come together and participate and the best ideas and the most active participants win. The losers are lazy, basically. The second face says it's more complex than that, that some groups have more power than others, and actually control the agenda, so that some things never get discussed, like the distribution of property.

The third face of power is operating when we stop noticing that some things aren't on the agenda, and start believing that unequal power and starvation and certain economic and social decisions aren't actually decisions, they're "just the way things are." Even the powerless see things as being the natural order of things. Conspiracy's unnecessary when everyone thinks the same.

The three faces of power were developed as conflicting descriptions of reality but I'm starting to see them as a progression over time, as the story of history.

At some point we were all equal. In hunting and gathering times, everyone was five to six feet tall and had two arms and legs, and basically had the same amount of power. The social structures of many indigenous cultures were set up to guarantee that power remained fluid. At some point, as power began to be centralized, the powerful created a discourse—in religion, philosophy, science, economics—that rationalized injustice and institutionalized it into a group projection. At first the powerless might not have believed in this discourse, but by now, some 10,000 years later, we're all deluded to some extent and believe that these differentials in power are natural. Some of us may want to change the agenda a little bit, but there's no seeing through the whole matrix. Power, like property, like land and water, has become privatized and concentrated. And it's been that way for so long and we believe it to such an extent that we think that's the natural order of things.

There's a box full of salmon, and a man sits atop the box. Long ago this man hired armed guards to keep anyone from eating his private fish. Once in a while some of the people without any fish decide to rebel, and they rush for the box, but they don't get very far, and the majority of the people just continue to sit by the empty river, and eventually they die. But they don't die of starvation. They die of a belief. Everyone believes that the man atop the box owns the fish. The soldiers believe it, and they will kill to protect the illusion. The others believe it enough that they are willing to starve. Even revolutionaries believe in the man's ownership, storming the box out of righteous rage without changing people's minds, or without sufficient organizing, and getting themselves killed because they, too, believe in the system's power, and know only to throw themselves against the soldiers, like salmon against a dam. They believe the system's wrong, but they still believe in it. And the truth is that there is a box full of fish, and there is a river without salmon, and there is a man sitting atop the box, and he controls some soldiers with guns, and there are starving people.

It's hard to acknowledge that we all helped build that box and we all put the salmon in it, and that we all support the soldiers as they kill those who try to put the salmon back in the river, and that it's our way of seeing things and not the guns that hold us back. As an activist who understands the evils of the corporate economy, I don't like to admit that.

DJ: Years ago I asked what level of technology you'd like to live at...

GD: What did I say?

DJ: You said, "We can fantasize about whatever we want, but the truth is that sooner or later we'll be back in the stone age—it's inescapable—and the only questions will be 1) what's left of the natural world? and 2) will we still know how to feed, clothe, and shelter ourselves?"

GD: I guess trying to predict when we'll run out of oil or when civilization will collapse seems less relevant than asking the question: what do I want? It implies being able to imagine something different than what I have.

I think in asking or answering that question we need to keep in mind that the tools we use are a reflection of our mental state. And the tools I use shape the way I see things, too. Tools are not value-free, as much as the engineers and corporate executives (who have a vested interest in selling tools) would like us to believe. Maybe every day as we pick up our tools we need to ask: What level of technology will I use today to live in this world? The answer to that question will be reflected in how I see my internal and external worlds. If I want something do I have to get in a car and go get it, or can I watch the desire come and go? If I'm afraid of facing something inside or outside, will I turn on the television and watch it for five hours in order to distract myself? Will I use this or that technology in order to avoid facing something more basic?

I don't use a chainsaw. And when my neighbor gets his out, I shake my head and get irritated that someone is cutting down the few trees that are left around here. But as always, it's more complicated than it seems. I use paper, so I guess I've been letting somebody else wield the chainsaw. I use computers and autos and airplanes. My sister's an environmentalist, but she lives in a city where some of the electricity comes from a nuclear plant. Left to her own devices she would never invent, construct, and operate a nuclear power plant, but there she is, using nuclear energy.

The group projection has become mass psychosis. As a society, we buy into these things. But where do those technologies come from, and what levels of collective projection and organization are necessary to keep the system going?

Back to your question, which in some ways maybe is kind of silly: If I could snap my fingers would I still have my computer and electricity, or would I be in a cabin in the woods? If I could snap my fingers would I get rid of nuclear power, limited liability corporations, and international trade?

DJ: Not to mention the designated hitter rule.

GD: We get what we project, and to change the world we need to dismantle those projections. We need to shut down the nuclear power plants and take down the dams, too, but we'll never do that until we really feel the suffering they cause and understand the illusion they are based on.

Now I'm going to come back around again, and say that as a society, if we don't ask that question—what do we really want?—then we're just being pushed around by our impulses, whims, and our ability to work our twisted will on the world with what are really crude and toxic technologies. We like to think of ourselves as being sophisticated, but we really don't have a very elegant way of life, as Gary Snyder pointed out. Nuclear energy to warm up our living rooms and toast our bread?

Part of our mass delusion is the belief that we can talk about technology without talking about the internal world, the external world, the social world, the economic world, the world of physics, the world of ecosystems, and the emotional world. I have a real problem with our typical engineering approach. Engineers use technologies to extract "resources" from the world and then we consume it and dispose of it without an honest regard for what it's achieving or what its impacts are. And we hire them to do that for us.

Clearly a very dangerous thing. It's useful to have an engineer, if you are sure you want something. But you don't want engineers deciding what to make, and how to rearrange the world. If you're sure you want a highway built, and you (and all the other species) are truly willing to accept the consequences, call a transportation engineer. But you don't want an engineer designing your transportation system. That's a social and political decision, not a technological one. That's a major mistake we've made all along. We've put politicians in charge of policy. If you do that, you get what we've got.

DJ: It's dangerous to ask how without asking why.

GD: Or even asking what. We can, therefore we will. That's the external equivalent of going with whatever impulse arises. But based on what? I don't know and I don't care. The impulse comes up so I've got to have it. It treats others as objects, and it may kill me, but gimme it.

DJ: Why and how did you switch from being a frontline activist to a researcher?

GD: I was drawn to activism on an emotional level. I lived in the West and I saw clearcuts. They bothered me and I felt like doing something about it. But after a while I began to see I wasn't effective, and neither was anybody else. I began to see there was a much deeper problem than clearcutting, that clearcutting really isn't an environmental problem so much as it's an economic and political problem, and ultimately a spiritual and psychological problem—although the environmental impacts are very real. So I started questioning our tactics. What are we doing? What are we trying to achieve? Why are we pursuing certain organizing and political tactics that don't seem commensurate with the problem, that aren't effective?

Research is just re-searching, looking again at the problem and what the options are and what we're trying to achieve. The root of the word research is recherche, to travel through, it means taking the time to travel through the problem, and not rush to some apparent conclusion. I try to help environmental and community groups, labor unions, and so on take another look at problems, in terms of what's actually happening, and what they actually want, and how best to achieve it. And I try to tie the different issues together, to help myself and other people work on multiple levels at once. Even environmentalists, if they believe they can attack clearcutting without addressing other issues, are not very ecological thinkers.

DJ: This reminds me of the classic military mistake of attacking piecemeal.

GD: Absolutely. And so long as we only work on one level, even the most complex of us are at best going to make little adjustments on that level, reforms that will quickly get undone by the larger tide that's washing over everything.

DJ: So what do we do?

GD: As a researcher I would step back at least one level. Before we can ask "What do we do," we need to ask, "What do we want?" And before that, "What's actually going on here?"

DJ: I want a world that has salmon, and that has community control over economic systems that are not based on the belief that atomized individuals pulling in selfish directions can form any community at all. And I want a world in which men do not beat on women.

GD: Salmon is pretty specific. It's real. An "equitable" or "sustainable world" is abstract.

DJ: But it's like Indra's web. It doesn't matter where I start, because it's all going to be reflected back...

GD: Well, it does matter when it goes from the seeing and the thinking to the saying and the doing. Lots of activists run around working for a sustainable world, but never actually do anything but consume paper and petroleum. Some activists are just hyperactive Type A personalities who disdain making money. They let someone else do it, and get their funding from the foundations set up by the corporations they are fighting, and spend it on the same things the corporate offices are spending money on. How tidy.

If you want salmon on the stream you live on, then you do habitat restoration. If you want to restore salmon on a continental or global level, you have to go up against the factory trawlers and their lobbyists who get the bureaucrats to set the fishing quotas too high. If you have a toxic dump on your hands, find out who dumped the stuff and call them on it.

DJ: The whole time recognizing my contribution in the right direction is part of a larger stew.

GD: And the whole time being realistic, understanding that the damage is severe enough that we're not going to see our way through in this lifetime.

It seems the most important thing is to be able to re-search, to look again, and to ask yourself every day as you think or speak or act: what is happening, what does the best in me actually want, and what is the most effective way of getting it? And after you act, maintain that openness: what did I just do? What are the actual effects of what I just did? If something in you decides that violent resistance to tyranny is the way to go, and then you never re-examine that, then you're going to go around yelling at (or shooting) people and never look back. What are the effects of your actions? Are things becoming less tyrannical because of what you're doing? If you decide to restore a salmon stream and you spend your whole life working on a quarter-mile stretch, and never look beyond that quarter-mile to see the dam that's blocking the fish, what have you accomplished?

It's not that one tactic is right or wrong. What counts is the ability to slow down and act from clarity and compassion rather than projection and selfishness. To discover whether your actions are achieving the desired results, and adjust your goals or tactics, being able to perceive impacts which might be very subtle, very delayed, and to let that discovery actually inform your behavior. Any behavior we get stuck with won't be commensurate or suitable to the conditions. Most political movements aren't actually reforming society by pursuing an open course of action. They're mostly trying to defend a certain way of looking at things, another certain set of projections and behaviors, and a whole territory of funding and a nice seat at the decision-making table.

I guess if you were to ask me now the question you asked at the beginning—what will it take for us to survive?—I would answer that it will take attention and care for the world. No matter where you are, where you're coming from, what you're trying to do, whether it's in your personal life or you have some political ambitions or a desire to restore a natural forest—whatever realm you find yourself in, slow down, pay attention, and take care.

Carolyn Raffensperger

❖

Interview Conducted
at her home, Ames, Iowa
4.20.02

A few years ago, Carolyn Raffensperger invited me to a gathering of twenty environmental, social-justice, and community-health activists. We were there to discuss the precautionary principle, which holds that when a substance or activity raises threats to human health, you take preventive or precautionary measures. Although the principle seems to be common sense, our culture often encourages us to proceed despite the risks. For example, a potential toxin is considered innocent until proven guilty, even when human or environmental health is at stake. The burden of proving that pesticide use or genetic engineering is harmful falls to the public. The precautionary principle shifts the burden of proof, and thus stops potentially damaging practices before they are implemented.

At the end of the discussion, Raffensperger walked around the room and thanked all of us publicly for our contributions. She spoke for several minutes about each person, expressing her gratitude and praising what was unique about that individual. I've seen Raffensperger in enough situations to know that this is the type of person she is. The Dutch theologian G.C. Berkouwer could have been talking about her when he said, "Gratitude is the essence of ethics."

The precautionary principle is part of the foundation of a larger movement to democratize science. Raffensperger believes that the best way to protect public health is to take the power to make environment-altering decisions out of the hands of scientists and their employers and give it back to the people whose lives stand to be affected. Her ideas are catching on: in the past year and a half alone, Raffensperger and the precautionary principle have been featured in *Utne Reader*, *Scientific American*, and even *Gourmet* magazine.

Though her first love is archaeology, she went to law school to be able to fight for the natural world in court. As an attorney, she is an avid defender of the land and all its inhabitants. Until recently, she and her husband, Fred Kirschenmann, lived on and ran a large organic farm in North Dakota. They now live in Iowa, in a big house filled with books—about fifteen thousand of them. Their large plot of land is also inhabited by hummingbirds, deer, and foxes, which she loves, if possible, even more than the books. Raffensperger is always careful to include her nonhuman neighbors in her calculations. "We are the land," she says, "and the water, and the grizzly bears, and the soil microbes. This is not a New Age statement. It is a medical statement, a scientific statement."

Raffensperger is executive director of the Science and Environmental Health Network, a consortium of organizations promoting safe scientific practices. She coedited the book *Protecting Public Health and the Environment: Implementing the Precautionary Principle* (Island Press) and writes the "Science for Lawyers" column for the Environmental Law Institute journal *Environmental Forum*. Over the past fifteen years she has served on various U.S. government committees on risk assessment, pesticides, radioactive waste, and cleanup of Department of Energy facilities.

Raffensperger is an animated speaker, using her whole body to get her point across. This conversation is a continuation of a much longer one that she and I have had at conferences, in cars, and elsewhere. For the interview, I traveled to her home in Ames, Iowa, where we sat across a kitchen table that a few hours later would be covered with organic food from a farm in North Dakota.

DJ: What is the precautionary principle?

CR: The precautionary principle is a revolutionary idea that turns our culture's use of science on its head. It does this by saying a very simple thing, which is that when you have scientific uncertainty and the likelihood of harm, you take preventive or precautionary action. On the most basic level, there's nothing more to it.

But when you dig a little deeper, you find that something else is happening: the precautionary principle couples ethics with the questions of how and what we know. This is the opposite of how we currently approach environmental decision-making, which with its mantra of "wait for certainty" pretends to be devoid of all ethics, pretends to be neutral. It pretends that decimal points are more real than values, more real than love. This is, of course, nonsense.

There's currently nothing in the way we approach science—and business—that says we should prevent harm. It's all about managing risk. But that's just crazy. Why should we think about prostate cancer or learning disabilities—both of which have imminently preventable causes—only by thinking about how many there are, and by making sure we've got all the causes in line before we act to stop the damage?

DJ: What's wrong with trying to find cause and effect?

CR: Nothing, except that we've separated things like emotion, values, and ethics from most of our decision-making. We think science can make all of our decisions. That's bad enough. But who then makes these scientific decisions for us? Do you believe scientists at Monsanto or the USDA have your best interests at heart? Or the interests of your community? If not, why should you surrender the responsibility for decisions that affect your health, the health of your loved ones, the health of your community—human and nonhuman—to these distant others? Even if those scientists did have your best interests at heart, decisions that affect you and your health need to be made by you and your community.

Another problem is that cause and effect is so difficult to precisely define. Maybe we could figure out cause and effect in the old horse and buggy days. If I hit you with my horse and buggy and broke your leg, we knew what happened. But now that we've filled our world with toxic chemicals and are fraying the very latticework of life, science is not going to be as effective in proving cause and effect, particularly if they're separated over large periods of time or large areas of space. It's just not reasonable—nor very smart—to expect that sort of precision before we act to protect ourselves.

DJ: It seems to me that the precautionary principle is already in place. It's just that what's protected is different. It's not that we mustn't harm human beings or the environment, but that we mustn't harm profits and the processes of production. If it's possible something may harm people or the environment, cause and effect must be scientifically established. If it's possible something may cut profits, it ain't gonna happen.

CR: Strange isn't it? The precautionary principle in your formulation applies to this imaginary set of transactions we carry out with green paper. And admittedly that does guide much decision-making. But the principle as it has been codified in international law has an underlying ethic that turns the prevailing notion of protecting profits above all else on its head, saying that some things are more important than money.

DJ: What are some of the primary criticisms thrown at you and/or the organizations with which you work?

CR: The first line of defense—and sometimes the only line of defense—has been to call us names; for example, I've been called a Safety Nazi. That's because we want to take action before we've proved with 100 percent certainty that something causes a particular harm. But how much sense does it make to wait until your son has a learning disability or your daughter has breast cancer before taking action?

There are also those, especially within industry, who have twisted our position around to suggest that the precautionary principle is not compassionate.

DJ: How could they possibly say that?

CR: Because we want, for example, to make sure that a drug is safe for those taking it and for the larger community before it is put into general use. But the great compassion is that we will bear witness to the suffering, including the cause of the suffering, and that we will act to prevent any more damage and injury. We will work to protect a person even if it is late for her.

When name-calling doesn't work, we're told we want to make decisions based on personal opinion or politics, rather than on the sound foundations of science. But the precautionary principle calls for changing the kinds of questions we ask, and in the face of uncertainty gives the benefit of the doubt to the environment, public health, and community health, meaning the community of all the beings with whom we share this earth. And this actually requires more science.

When we make a mistake in science and miss a connection between cause and effect, we allow more harm to happen to the environment. But imagine turning that on its head and requiring a different approach to science, where we protect ourselves more against false negatives (not seeing a connection where there is one) than against false positives (seeing a connection where none exists). That actually required better science and more information. For instance, if you take a water sample that shows the presence of pfisteria, you go back and take another sample—more information. But if you take a water sample and miss the pfisteria, that's it: you've stopped the scientific investigation. You've stopped any more research in that particular area.

So the precautionary principle not only requires better science, it provokes different kinds of questions. Instead of asking, "How safe is this? Is this harm acceptable?" it asks, "How does nature work? Are there alternatives that are less harmful? How do we know that?" It uses science to serve goals like protecting public health and the environment, rather than serving some of its old goals. It asks that we make a new social contract for science.

DJ: You've been accused of attempting to shut down the entire economy. Not that, from my perspective, that would be a bad thing.

CR: We've been told we're going to stop civilization as we know it, or we're going to ask everybody to go back to horse and buggy days, or we're going to stop all technology. What's interesting about the accusation that the principle will stop all progress is that the precautionary principle actually calls for action, precautionary action. What a wonderful paradox.

DJ: But if the precautionary principle had been in place a hundred years ago there would be no automobiles.

CR: Probably. But that doesn't mean we wouldn't have a transportation system. It means we might not have used fossil fuels. It means we might have actually used human ingenuity and creativity to create a transportation system that honored our place on earth, that didn't fundamentally pollute the planet. Maybe we wouldn't have this technology, but that doesn't mean we wouldn't have any technology. We just wouldn't have one that is so overwhelmingly destructive.

DJ: Is it even possible to predict what future harm a new technology might cause?

CR: Surprise is the rule rather than the exception in ecosystems, particularly when we employ technology on a global scale rather than tailor it to local scales. Yet it is possible to scan the horizon for problems using ecological and evolutionary biology principles.

Our culture has used toxicology instead of evolutionary biology as our touchstone, asking, "Is it good for the 150 lb male"? That's precisely the wrong question. Instead we should be asking, "How does nature work?" All of this makes the case for basing more science on the precautionary principle rather than less. We need to monitor, monitor, monitor. As it stands now, we make decisions to do things like using Bt corn on millions of acres, and then we are caught by surprise when we've asked the wrong questions. Right now we don't have systems in place to catch our mistakes and short circuit them before they become global problems. We can change that.

DJ: I really want to hammer this notion of prediction for a moment. Could anyone, for example, have foreseen global warming when Henry Ford began selling the Model-T?

CR: Maybe not. But the Model-T is a scale issue. Some problems would have been predictable if we'd thought about billions of cars using fossil fuels. Big scale production always has some problems attached.

DJ: What about computers? Many people argue over whether personal computers are harmful, and they've been around for twenty-five years. If that question cannot be answered definitively now, how could the matter have been decided when they were just starting?

CR: The issue is that we haven't established goals for computers, which are systems that affect our lives in complex ways. We can't decide whether computers help us meet our goals, because we don't know what those collective goals might be. Harm always carries with it some notion of a goal and what is good, and we'll keep producing computers, even if they're harmful, until we figure out whether they are ultimately good.

DJ: And is it the job of scientists to decide? Most scientists aren't inventors. They develop new technologies without even knowing what they will be used for. How can they predict this? What if a new technology is only harmful if overused? Should we assume that people will abuse it? Is there any technology that literally does no harm? Isn't it the best we can do to simply weigh the potential for harm vs. the potential for good and make an educated guess?

CR: Scientists are not trained in methods for evaluating technologies except a rudimentary cost benefit analysis. Why aren't we grounding our scientists in ethics? Why aren't we requiring that they take evolutionary biology—a far better way of evaluating technology that some kind of pie in the sky cost benefit analysis?

DJ: Who decides?

CR: Right now we have ceded our decision-making authority to corporations in the guise of the "market."

The way this issue is handled in other countries—particularly Germany, which is most like the United States in its love for technology and its acceptance of risk—is interesting. In the United States we're all expected to be cowboys on some level: What, you're not going to let your kids climb up in the apple tree? What's your problem? We believe it's kind of neurotic and un-American to not like risk. But even with its love for technology and acceptance of risk, Germany has used the precautionary principle as a wonderful tool to force technological innovation, to clean up the most damaging and destructive technologies. This has worked extremely well internally. Unfortunately, it's proven to be an economic problem in international trade because some of those new technologies that cause less environmental damage cost a bit more. The reason, of course, is that the cheaper products externalize environmental costs, so that the companies that produce them don't have to pay for damage to a river, or the dead zone in the Gulf, or whatever else it might be.

DJ: Wouldn't the precautionary principle then destroy competitive advantage?

CR: I want to turn that sentence around and suggest that competitive advantage destroys. The idea that we can outcompete, that we can compete by lowering dollar costs, destroys. The idea that we measure goods in dollars destroys. How many of the world's goods are measured in U.S. dollars, and not, for example, in the number of bird's nests? If we measured all of our economy in the number of hatchlings of migratory birds, we would figure competitive advantage in an entirely different way. But competitive advantage drives lower and lower dollar costs on things, and increases the probability that we're going to externalize costs.

As Janine Benyus has pointed out, nature favors cooperation over competition. And that sense of mutualism and reciprocity is undermined with competitive advantage.

The whole question of competitive advantage leads to some absurdities. There are some things that are just plain stupid to trade. Why are we moving water around the planet using fossil fuels? Why does France have a competitive advantage with Perrier over some other bottled water in the United States, or over drinking your tap water? This is not rational.

So to worry that the precautionary principle is going to destroy competitive advantage is to worry about precisely the wrong thing.

DJ: You've said that the precautionary principle is one of six linked principles you'd like to see practiced more.

CR: Yes. The precautionary principle's fundamental idea is that we prevent harm rather than clean it up or fix it afterwards. There are a lot of places where people understand that at a common sense level, and even have some legal mechanisms for enforcing precautionary behavior. Although we have some laws that attempt to prevent messes and damage before they happen, quite often we find ourselves in a place where we have to have laws like Superfund, which at least ostensibly attempt to clean up problems after the fact.

That leads to the second linked notion: restoration. Heaven knows we've got many messes, and we need to do something about them. We need to restore the environment. We've developed some wonderful approaches for things like restoring tallgrass prairie to a condition where natural processes can flourish. But there is so much left to restore. For example, we need to clean up breast milk. Human breast milk is now one of the most contaminated food sources on the planet. We need to remove the flame retardants and DDT. DDT is just one of many chemicals which is persistent, biocumulative, bioactive, and is moving all over the globe on wind currents, being deposited in places where it's not used. Breast milk has to be restored to the condition that was meant for human babies. And we need to restore the breast milk of all species, not just humans.

On a larger scale, we need to fundamentally reverse all kinds of damage we've created through our "prove harm before we take any action" policies. I've been asked how the precautionary principle helps those for whom it is too late. For most of the earth, it's too late. But we have to restore what we can—tallgrass prairies, marine fisheries, breast milk—to save what we have left. That's how the precautionary principle and restoration are connected.

The next linked idea is called the public trust doctrine. Underlying the public trust doctrine is the value that you can't privatize everything. Some things belong to all of us. You cannot own the bed of a river or Lake Michigan and then withhold a person's access to it. The public trust doctrine's place in water law is very useful, and needs to be expanded to the land. Unfortunately, there's a move by governments worldwide to privatize water and air. It's truly frightening to think that people will have the power to withhold access to water or air. We as a society need to stop that.

DJ: What other areas would you like to see fall under the public trust doctrine?

CR: A healthy, clean environment. Several states have that provision in their constitutions. It means you cannot privatize your ability to pollute, and you cannot privatize access to resources.

DJ: What about food? The privatization of food has been central to civilization because it's been central to the regulation of the work force: if you have access to food, you don't have to work for someone else, so those in power can control or privatize the food supply, they can force people to work for them. Those in power have always been aware of that, and have used it to gain and maintain a work force.

CR: Wouldn't it be interesting if we treated agriculture and food like we do public education, so farmers were paid like teachers, and we made sure food was available to everyone? Even better, what if we guaranteed access to land to grow your own food as a basic right? Note that I don't say "human right" because access to food is all creatures' "right." I am interested in a food policy that actually feeds the world, not just one species. Even just for humans, access to land would be far better than a centralized bureaucracy growing all the food, then distributing it through a central warehouse. How much sense does it make to use herbicides on public lands to keep them a grassy monocrop, when that land could be used for community gardens and other methods for people to have access to land and seeds to raise food? The answer to why we don't do that, of course, is that the system we have makes corporations rich. We have this whole system built on competitive advantage, on economic competitiveness, even for something so fundamental as food. We should instead look at food cooperatively. We should separate food from the for-profit world. This would be a fundamentally different way to do our business.

DJ: You were listing off six…

CR: The fourth idea, one that I use as a fulcrum for these six, has to do with democracy, with the questions of how we decide, and who decides. Right now we take dictates from corporations, and we take dictates from governments that are not elected. We then have all of our life decisions prescribed—whether or not these prescriptions come in the form of "scientific certainty," judicial decisions, economic decisions, or at the point of a gun—and we have to check all the things we love and value at the door, so those in power can make decisions based on their financial ledgers or where they've decided to put their decimal point.

Democracy is fundamental to the precautionary principle. All of our work has emphasized that affected stakeholders need to have a voice. Allowing affected stakeholders a voice changes how we do science. For instance, members of a community are more likely than scientists who don't live there to have observed changes over time that can guide hypothesis formation and data collection. Democracy is a central idea to public trust, restoration, and to the precautionary principle. And this democracy extends to nonhumans. We need to remember, as Janine Benyus also said, that we're one vote in a parliament of millions.

All of those ideas lead to the consideration of my fifth principle, the idea of community well-being. By community I mean this web of relationships that sustains life, and that includes the geosphere. We're oxygen, and we're other gases and metals and chemicals that are not necessarily just living things. As Wes Jackson says, we have a bias toward the biosphere because we're living, breathing things. Rocks may have another opinion. So, community wellbeing speaks to the health the integrity of the relationships in that community. And in communities, plural.

And the last principle is an idea that undergirds much environmental work: future generations. There is some reference to future generations built into laws like the Endangered Species Act and the mandates for National Parks and Wilderness Areas. These places are being set aside not just for current generations to use up, but also for future generations of humans and other species, for their own reasons and their own purposes.

What good are these linked ideas of precaution, restoration, public trust, democracy, community well-being and future generations? Our scientific and political choices—and of course scientific choices ARE political choices—are of necessity be guided by principles. The principles that currently guide those choices are leading us to our own destruction and the destruction of much that we love. Different principles will lead to different decisions.

For too long the environmental community has shied away from discussing ethics, bringing ethics and values and what we love to the table. The precautionary principle is a way for us to begin talking meaningfully about these things.

DJ: Are you and other people fringe players at the edge of debate, or has there been much movement toward normalizing the precautionary principle?

CR: First, I want to bracket the word normalizing. The process by which those in power currently make environmental decisions, where they have to be certain about cause and effect and then they manage risk rather than prevent it, has been to normalize the massive damage they've created. So I hope we overturn the notion—and the reality—that this kind of damage is normal. I don't know whether that means we're normalizing the precautionary principle, but I do know the destruction has to be de-normalized.

And I don't think I'd call the precautionary principle a fringe idea. Fringe sounds like something that hangs off the tablecloth and hence is off the table. I'd rather use a microbial analogy, and suggest that the precautionary principle is like yeast. I hope it's rising and leavening and growing in the culture, and that you see evidence of it in many places. And that is happening. *The New York Times Magazine* said it was one of the important new ideas of the past year. And they didn't attach any names to it, which is good: you can't point to one person as being the guru of the precautionary principle. The precautionary principle is appearing in codes of ethics for professional societies like the International Society for Ethnobiology. And it has recently been moved from the preamble of treaties, where it functions symbolically, to the main body, where it is legally binding. It's in the body of the Persistent Organic Pollutant Treaty—the POPS Treaty—and in the body of the Biosafety Protocol, which more or less governs genetically modified organisms used for food.

One reason the precautionary principle is moving so quickly—and in a sense so microbially—through culture is that it's based on very simple understandings we all have and that are embedded in folk wisdom. Look before you leap. A stitch in time saves nine. These may seem trite, but they have a deep resonance. We understand them. To go contrary to what we know at that deep and profound level actually takes more work than it does to honor the precautionary principle.

DJ: All of this ties to something you've written about in many places, and that's ecological medicine.

CR: Ecological medicine attempts to look at our health care in ways that make ecological sense. There is an organization, for example, called Health Care Without Harm, which is fundamentally organized around the question: "What are we going to do with the irony that health care is such a toxic industry?" Or at least that's true of western conventional medicine.

DJ: For example...

CR: We incinerate PVC medical devices that have been used to treat your cancer, sending the toxic residue out to cause someone else's disease. What sense does that make? We use mercury in thermometers in hospitals, then send that up the incinerator to be deposited in fish and eventually to give your children brain damage. Again, what sense does that make?

I need to say, by the way, that medical care is only one component of ecological medicine. The idea of health as part of the natural world has much broader implications than just your chemotherapy, obviously. We know that health—both mental and physical—is enhanced when you can see a tree outside your hospital window. All of that goes well beyond whether PCV bags are causing disease.

Ecological medicine has many facets. One is environmental medicine, which has been used primarily to address multiple chemical sensitivity and a set of diseases primarily related to toxic chemicals. Another is called conservation medicine, which looks at some of the crossover diseases in wildlife and humans.

What we really want to do is rethink medicine with the understanding that you are the air and water. We want to look at the flow of medicine and health and the environment. Ecological medicine certainly comes out of the precautionary principle, which says we should prevent diseases we can prevent. But it's far more than that. We need to understand that health itself is an ecological process.

DJ: I don't understand.

CR: Ecological medicine is a field of inquiry and action that seeks to reconcile individual care and community well-being, as well as ecological wholeness. And we understand there are times when these cause difficult choices, which is why the word reconcile is in there. When you have a cancer or some other problem, how do you decide whether to use a treatment that can cause environmental damage down the road?

DJ: You and your husband have faced that question...

CR: My husband has metastatic prostate cancer. The decisions we had to make about his treatment were for me personally the genesis of many of these ideas.

I don't think most people face their own medical care or their own death with the same ferocious intensity with which they face those of their dearest and most beloved. When we talk about ecological medicine and what it might mean in terms of medical care, many people say, "That would be okay to limit my medical care." Fewer say that about their loved ones.

So I came at my husband's cancer with an almost desperate, I-would-do-anything-to-save-his-life attitude. I didn't care what it would take.

Early on we made choices that, fortunately, were based on how we understood our organic farm. How do we deal with nonnative species and noxious weeds, which by law we have to eradicate on our farm? How do we think about cancer? Is there any hope in those analogs?

DJ: Was there?

CR: Well, before I say anything else I need to say I'm not prescribing medical care. People need to use their own best wisdom to approach their own medical issues. And I trust people's wisdom and intuition to ask the right questions. I also know that it's much harder to make these decisions in the emergency of the moment, faced with a catastrophic illness, so I only say this in the spirit of understanding that it can be helpful beforehand to have at least a vague idea of the questions you might ask. That said, here goes. We knew that poisoning those plants hadn't worked as well as taking them out, and so we chose surgery as our first option, to take out the cancer rather than treat it with chemicals or radiation. Now, certainly radiation has been useful in some prostate and other cancers. But we made the choice from our understanding, and the best medical advice we could get.

A year later, after we thought a lot about this, we were sitting in the oncologist's office for the very first time. We hadn't seen an oncologist until that moment. We knew there were a lot of experimental protocols underway for prostate cancer. One of those protocols was thalidomide.

Now, thalidomide has had huge repercussions for humans. It causes serious birth defects when used by pregnant women. Are you familiar with how thalidomide came to be banned for use by pregnant women in the United States? It's an extraordinary story. It was because one woman at the FDA noticed something alarming in the trials: there was numbing and tingling of the extremities of people who had taken thalidomide. On that basis alone she said, "We're not going to have it in the United States." That's the reason we don't have a large cohort of thalidomide babies in this country. That is the precautionary principle in action. We didn't have good information about birth defects, but we had some information that something wasn't right.

DJ: It's extraordinary that people listened to her.

CR: Especially because she's a woman.

But thalidomide is now being recommended and used in the United States for cancers. There are some famous former politicians who now use thalidomide in their treatment.

Here's the point. My husband and I didn't know what happens to thalidomide in the body, how the body processes it. So we asked the oncologist what Fred would metabolize, what he would excrete, and what would be the environmental effect of thalidomide. The oncologist had never thought of any of those questions. We said, "We don't think we'll use this until we know." Because we could not put something into the environment that was going to give birth defects to the frogs, deer, muskrats, and others. We couldn't do it.

We know that personal care products, a number of drugs, and caffeine are now showing up in much of the surface water of the United States because we excrete these things.

DJ: Fish are changing gender in about half the streams in England because of hormones from birth control pills.

CR: It may be menopausal drugs—premarin and other estrogens—as well as birth control pills. And in the United States it may also be growth-promoting hormones used in the livestock industry. There may be multiple sources.

What you take in comes out in some form or another. I subsequently got more information about thalidomide. It lasts about half an hour outside the body. But if a big population begins taking thalidomide, suddenly it will be in the water. What do we think about that? How do we address that? You might not be directly exposed to thalidomide, but what if it or other drugs becomes present in water? The USGS is putting out preliminary information about the presence of many of these chemicals in the waters of the United States, including drinking water. What are we going to do about that? I don't have a great answer for that. But isn't it crazy that we're hurdling down this decision train, treating cancers that might have been caused by toxic chemicals in the environment with more chemicals, and then attempting to deal with the effects these chemicals have on water? That's just not a logical approach.

When my mother got married, one woman in twenty-five could expect to get breast cancer. Now it's one woman in eight. And when my nine-year-old niece gets married, it's probably going to be one woman in three. The change in genetics is not all that significant between my mother's and niece's generations. So something else is going on. We're seeing an increase in some brain cancers, and some kinds of children's cancers. This is not just because we've got better detection methods. There are changing patterns in the number of people with Parkinson's, learning disabilities, and other neurological problems. The same is true for reproductive problems and immune function diseases. There are indications that sperm counts among human men are declining in some parts of the world.

DJ: Crohn's disease, which I have, is a great example of that. It's probably an autoimmune disorder. It's almost nonexistent in nonindustrialized nations. As they industrialize, Crohn's disease increases. Nobody knows whether that's caused by the industrialized diet, industrialized chemicals, or something else.

CR: If we examine the western diet and the whole chain, from how we raise industrial commodities to how we move them around the world, it's no wonder we're seeing strange things. In our country we eat old food from far away. You see that even in the color of food. When I raise food in my garden, the jewel-like colors sing. And when I look at produce in the grocery store, where everything's been imported from Mexico and Chile and Australia, I see that the grocery store does not have a competitive advantage in color.

DJ: Nor taste.

CR: If you examine any one of the places in the commodity chain, from the agricultural commodities produced in monocultures using heavy doses of fossil fuel inputs, to the fossil fuel energy for tractors and plows and combines, to the nitrates that run off into the water, to genetic engineering, one of the many strange things you find is that the major commodities are priced below production costs. Corn, soybeans, wheat, rice—all of these cost more to produce than the farmer gets per bushel. This is not a good system. It's not sustainable on any level. And we have highly processed food, or we've got food that's been brought in from far away.

DJ: You've brought up food a couple of times. I know also that you've talked about the importance of gaining food locally.

CR: When I married Fred, I moved to North Dakota. We have a 3,500 acre organic farm, where we raised cattle, wheat, rye, buckwheat, sunflowers, and sometimes lentils. Lots and lots of food. But we weren't eating much of it. We ate our own beef, and like everybody else we put a couple of tomatoes in the ground, but that was it. One day I looked at our diet, and I was spooked by what I saw: we were eating, like everyone else does, old food from far away. I started counting the cost of our food based on the miles it had traveled rather than the dollars it cost, and we were eating very expensive food that had the mask of cheapness under the dollar guise. So I decided to raise our own food in North Dakota. Everybody said it couldn't be done. What about oranges and bananas? Well, what's the point of eating those? Is it vitamin C and potassium? So I set out to solve that problem in North Dakota. I had a garden that was just under an acre, not counting our orchard, and not counting the six three-quarter-mile rows of sweet corn. I had the best time producing food. I raised the most beautiful food I'd ever seen.

There were problems I had to solve. How do you get leafy greens in February in North Dakota? At first we figured we had to grow iceberg lettuce, just because that's what we were used to. But instead I froze about sixty quarts of kale, collards, beet greens and wild mustard—which was one of the weeds we had to get rid of anyway, so we might as well eat it. I told

Fred we were becoming wild mustard. And you always need the feeling of fresh in your mouth, so how do you solve that in March? We kept carrots and apples. I canned a magnificent corn/cabbage relish, and froze watermelon and cantaloupe. We had smoothies, and we had canned beets. We had salads, even though they weren't iceberg or romaine lettuce. It was a wonderful experience.

DJ: Not that long ago, the experience of growing one's own food would not have been foreign to many.

CR: No question.

So my husband was sixty-five, and I thought I was a farmer's wife. Then four days after his surgery for cancer, he accepted a job as a professor at Iowa State University, and as Director of the Leopold Center for Sustainable Agriculture. That was a major upheaval for a lot of reasons. I wanted to garden, and our whole food system was set for North Dakota. For example, we were raising squash that had been bred for over forty years for North Dakota. We had Hutterite soup beans and chokecherry wine.

The question of food systems being based on a locality raises complements our ecological medicine discussion: what if we considered ourselves creatures of local ecosystems? What if we considered ourselves adapted to the microflora as well as the macroflora and fauna of a specific region? The fungi on my apple, the microorganisms you can't even see, the whole community in my area: that's what I'm adapted to. The soil and the minerals in that soil: that's what I know. That's what my body knows. That's what the e coli in my stomach know. That's where we are happy, and by we I mean all of these wonderful creatures that coinhabit this body with me. And what does this mean for the global transport of foods? We know that there have been pests that have been brought in that have devastated trees and waterways and animals. But what about us? What is the response of the community in my body to microorganisms brought in from New Zealand? I'm not adapted to New Zealand. I'm adapted to the grasslands of the Midwest. This is all about knowing your body well enough to know that your immune system has worked out its agreement, its contract, with the world around you. And that world is local. People with allergies know this.

What does it do when we homogenize everything, from the landscape to the food we eat? I'm not saying we're not adaptable. Of course we are, or we wouldn't be found from the Arctic to sub-Saharan Africa. But as a matter of health, we may want to pay more attention to the fact that we're creatures of local ecosystems.

DJ: So you moved to Iowa.

CR: I moved to Iowa. The first thing we did was buy a big house with a big yard. We accepted the house because we wanted the yard. A very wise friend came by and said, "Well, who owns this?"

I was irritated because I thought it should be clear: "What do you mean? We own it!"

It was clear this wasn't the right answer. It finally dawned on me what he meant: who thinks they own it in a non-monetary sense? And then it was obvious who owns it, and it isn't us. It's the deer and woodchucks and raccoons and lots of other creatures. If I wanted to garden here, we could put up big fences and use all sorts of deterrents—basically declare war—but that wasn't the way I wanted to do it. Also because my husband's job is sustainable agriculture, we thought we had a different role here than proving we could feed ourselves, which is to go beyond self sufficiency to community sufficiency.I intentionally use sufficiency rather than efficiency or other words. One lesson taught by Mary Poppins and Laura Ingalls Wilder is that "enough is as good as a feast." So when I talk about community sufficiency, I talk about enoughness.

That all led to the question: how do we engage in community sufficiency here? We'd worked out self-sufficiency in North Dakota, although we shared our food with lots of people and lots of other beings; it was a pretty big network out there.

But here in Iowa we discovered that there are community-supported agriculture (CSA) farms, and I set out to see if we could get our food year round from within the state. My preferred distance would be within thirty miles, and my real preference would be within ten. All of this took a different method of planning than I used in North Dakota. The bad news was that I soon realized CSAs are set up, for obvious reasons, to provide food just for the summer. If you look at architecture archaeologically, our homes are set up the same way; we've lost our winter storage capacity. So we don't have room for canning. We don't have cold storage in cellars, nor do we have big freezers. The good news is that there are a couple of CSA farmers who live very close to Ames and together we are figuring out how to create a local food system year round. One farmer delivers a box of food filled with my preferences once a week. At another CSA all of us go and pick up our food one day a week. We've turned that into sort of a community gathering.

DJ: How has this all worked out?

CR: Great. We've had a little bit of reduction in diversity, because I planted much more—we didn't have the insect problems in North Dakota that we do in Iowa. It's all about figuring out this place, this climate, this community, and our sufficiency. And it has been more than sufficient. It's been wonderful.

DJ: If everyone ate like you did…

CR: We'd need thousands more farmers. I gave a talk recently, and the person who introduced me talked about being my personal farmer. You have your personal dentist and your personal doctor, and you don't use those services nearly as much as you use the services of a farmer. So it really is in our best interest to make sure they thrive economically.

DJ: Can readers of this interview put what you're saying into practice?

CR: Sure. It's an art form to think about your food. It takes planning, the same way you plan your winter or summer vacations. And you can set goals. What are the local sources for cheese and meat? What are the local sources for vegetables? Can you store them through the winter? For instance, we bought potatoes in the fall. We still have potatoes left in April. They're starting to sprout, but they're fine. Sweet potatoes last a long time. If you just start with a food you love, then eating becomes a story. You know the weather conditions that produced it. You know the travails and joys of the farmer that year. You know about that food. You have a relationship with what you eat.

DJ: And it tastes better.

CR: Oh my yes. Because it's not old food from far away.

DJ: I buy meat from a local rancher. Not only am I not supporting factory farming, and not only does it taste better, but it's much cheaper.

CR: The fiscal issue is complicated. My husband asks whether these CSAs are really sustainable economically. One of our farmers is a war tax resistor and so wants to keep his taxes below a certain level, and chooses voluntary simplicity. Do we adequately compensate our farmers to produce food so they can live in a way they can buy their children's eyeglasses, and go to a concert, and do things that the rest of us like to do? I don't think we've got a food policy in the country fiscally responsible for our farmers.

Another way the fiscal matter is complicated is that there have been accusations that rich people can afford organic, CSA produced vegetables, while poor people cannot.

DJ: Which is why, by the way, I'm against the labeling of genetically-engineered foods (I'm for their prohibition), because that will just turn it into a two-class system, where the rich get to eat non-genetically engineered food, and the poor don't.

CR: We've got to rethink the economics of this. I'm conscious all the time of how I'm participating in the larger economic system. As far as I know, food has always fallen in the for-profit category within our culture. Sure, there are a few not-for-profit charities for the poor. But we haven't thought about the for-profit and not-for-profit models. We have two complete economies set up side by side in the United States. For-profit, and not-for-profit. Harvard's endowment, the Catholic Church, the Women's Center down the street, and my own organization are not-for-profit. We have different laws that govern us, and we are a fully functioning economic system in this country. So one of my pieces of advice is to move over to the not-for-profit economy as often as you can. The more we can do that the better.

This all ties to what the sociologist Marcel Mauss called the gift economy, which is built on reciprocity. That's the way you maintain peace in stateless societies. You give a gift to the other tribe, and they gave a gift back. If you didn't reciprocate, war broke out. We need a gift economy with the earth. Right now we've got an extraction/growth economy, the cancer model, rather than a gift economy of reciprocity, both with each other and with the earth. So I want a gift economy with the farmers; I want to give and receive in equal measure. I want to make sure that the dollar, which is what we understand as part of that transaction, is enough, is right. But then we have other transactions going on. My farmer brought me some manure for my lawn. That's part of our exchange. It's not monetary. It's in the barter, nonprofit domain.

There are so many areas of our life that are within the nonprofit realm—education, many hospitals—and food has been left out of that. But food is too important to be left to competitive advantage, to make into the cheapest commodity from anyplace in the world, using the cheapest labor that we can possibly get, and causing the disruption of local ecosystems and local economies.

DJ: How does this tie back to the concern that only rich people can buy at CSAs?

CR: As long as food is part of the for-profit economy, we're going to have a system where rich people get the best and poor people are left to an impoverished diet. This all comes back to ecological medicine, and to the precautionary principle. We know that the health implications of diet will come back to haunt us. We now pay more than 10 percent of our earned income in medical care, and a little less than ten percent on food. Those two figures seem pretty clearly linked to me. It doesn't have to be that way.

All across the economy, whether we're talking about the toxification of our food, water, and air, or our diet, or almost anything else, we're building in things we're going to have to pay for down the road. Our food, medical, and other systems—built on this least-cost for-profit model—are bound to fail.

DJ: I want to go back to where we started with the precautionary principle. Because the system is founded on injustices and is manifestly nonrational, it seems to me that if we were to institute the precautionary principle on a massive scale, that it really would be the end of industrial civilization as we know it. Of course that's not a bad thing, but from the perspective of those in power, it is a really revolutionary idea.

CR: It is revolutionary to reevaluate who gets to define what progress is. One of the built-in notions of the way we do business now is that you can't stand in the way of progress. But we don't get to define progress. It's not in our hands. We have no control over it.

We're told, for example, that our goal is to feed the world, and so we have to have genetic engineering. What if instead we began by saying that our goal is a healthy food policy for the world built on justice, built on beauty? What if we laid out the goal? We would identify alternatives to all of our practices that are harmful, asking, "Do we really want to export all this food from the United States all over the world? Or do we want a different kind of food system?" In that sense the precautionary principle really is revolutionary. Because it says we do get to decide. We have the capacity and the duty to speak about our goals and to make them into reality.

I think about a different role for science than just proving cause and effect. The scientists I work with do a couple of things. One is they bear witness to and help alleviate suffering. And they bear witness to beauty. They do this instead of dissecting frogs and then dithering at just how much atrazine it takes to feminize their larynx so they can't call to each other in the spring. Instead they see healthy frogs as part of ecological medicine – a healthy world, a healthy humanity. The precautionary principle invites this better way of looking at goals. It values democracy, not corporations, not these faceless entities we've given personhood to. And it calls for us to act, not dither.

I'm sure you're aware of the "reasonable person" standard in the law: would a reasonable person act in this way? Well, if so, the behavior is sometimes legally excused. I'd like to change that to the "respectful person" standard. There are some places where reason doesn't work. Sexual harassment. The underlying notion is that sexual harassment is an offense against dignity. What does reason have to do with that? Not a whole lot. A much better criterion is: have you been respectful? In this big vast wonderful earth, with all of the complexity, all of its beauty, all of its wonder, wouldn't it be a better idea to be respectful? The precautionary principle opens up room for ideas like respect, and says, Yeah, we want to use all of the powers of humanity. And we are a lovely species with some interesting capacities. Not the only ones on the planet who are beautiful and interesting with wonderful gifts and skills, but amazing nonetheless. So, wouldn't it be good to be respectful? Not just rational, reasonable people who ignore the enormous love and connection that most of us feel for this world?

DJ: What can people do?

CR: I've talked here a little bit about food, mostly because I've thought about it, living on a farm. But if you want to go beyond not driving an SUV and beyond recycling, there are actually some things you can do. One of the most important is to help young people find their way to be in service to something larger than themselves. Normally the only reason kids go to college or graduate school—and, in Wes Jackson's words, the only real major offered—is upward mobility. But we fail to teach our children that service to something greater than themselves is far more likely to lead to a joyful and satisfying life, and one that is environmentally rich.

It all starts with the question: "What's the biggest and most important problem I can solve with my unique gifts and skills?" Even to form a preliminary answer to that question is to begin to define an appropriate—and fun—path.

After college and graduate school I didn't know what else to do with my life, so I thought I'd go to law school. Basically more upward mobility. I took the LSAT, and scored in at rock bottom. That's probably a good thing, because if I'd have gone I probably would've been a perfect subject for lawyer jokes. But later I got this sense that I had to go to law school so I could work for environmental protection. This time I scored in the upper few percent of the LSAT. I was the same person, but now it was the right thing for me to do. I had the right motivation. When people know what problem they can solve using the gifts that are unique to them in all the world, they often know what they need to do next.

Another option for action is what I mentioned earlier about choosing the nonprofit over the profit world. Why not purchase your clothes and furniture at Salvation Army or Goodwill instead of a department store? Lately I've been buying things at estate auctions, things that have been used by a family here in Iowa and that aren't newly shipped in from Taiwan or some other country where they were made with impoverished labor. If you want a finer tune on that, do the companies you buy from have shareholders that have no role in the company itself? If they do, the goal of the company is to make shareholders rich, and not to provide you with goods and services which protect the earth. Staying away from those sorts of corporations is a useful step to do.

Another thing people can do is to redefine property rights. Allowing property rights to be defined widely leads to big problems. Those in power are now privatizing genetic information, and privatizing water. This will lead to more haves and have nots. Defining things as property limits what we can do. We have built an entire legal system—the entire legal system of the United States, with a few footnotes and exceptions, with the exceptions in the footnotes—on property rights. There are other ways of constructing a legal system. I had a friend once tell me that we could have constructed the legal system based on making peace. What a fundamentally different idea.

The law is a set of rules by which a community agrees to be bound. I don't know about you, but I haven't agreed to be bound by a number of things. As a lawyer I want to promote a set of rules that will help our community flourish, and will foster health and goodness, and so my role as a lawyer is entirely different than if I'm defending your property rights. I'm making peace within that community. With all of these creatures that we see and with whom share this world. What a different world! What a different role for law!

There's something else I would like to say about the courts. So often the precautionary principle has been conceived of as a regulatory device. We've turned over environmental protection to administrative agencies. We somehow think that the EPA can solve most of these environmental problems if they just come up with the right rules. Following this line of reasoning, if a pesticide is labeled safe, that must certainly be the case. But there's something in all of this that we've neglected: by the time a pesticide or a medicine gets to where the EPA or FDA will make a regulatory decision, millions of dollars have already been spent on researching the thing. That's money that the government and industry won't want to have thrown away if the chemical is declared unsafe: they have a huge vested interest in making certain the chemical is approved, whatever its safety. Billions of dollars are spent at the National Institutes of Health, the USDA, NSF, and other agencies. We need to build the precautionary principle into the research agenda, so we ask the right questions up front instead of spending $26 million on some new widget that the EPA will never then be able to say, "We don't like it."

DJ: How does this relate to the courts?

CR: We need to move as far upstream as we can. The courts provide a great example of that.

If you've got a very conservative agenda—and I don't mean conservative in terms of conservation, but in terms using up and destroying the earth— you take on the courts. If you want to do something with school prayer you have to go to one agency, and if you want to deal with the environment you have to go to another. If you want to deal with all of those, go to the courts. In the past couple of decades we've seen essentially a conservative takeover of the courts.

DJ: What do you mean?

CR: We all know campaign finance reform is important because corporations dominate the agenda in Congress. But we haven't looked at what campaign financing does to the courts. Forty-two states elect their judges. And we're seeing an organized takeover of the courts by people who don't like the environment, who think we have a right to use up and destroy the earth. One of the dangers of this is that when judges make decisions, those decisions can set precedents that last for a very long time. For example, the original judge who determined that corporations are people, with the legal rights of people...

DJ: ...That judge owned stock in the corporation he declared a person, by the way...

CR: ...set a precedent that has had horrendous human and environmental consequences. The consequences for democracy have been ugly. And we are currently seeing the stage set for any number of decisions that are just as bad, with consequences just as far-reaching.

DJ: How does this relate to the precautionary principle?

CR: It becomes extremely difficult to prove that one particular chemical caused one particular cancer. Now, in 1993 a Supreme Court decision set in motion a whole new approach to science so by now you have to prove cause and effect even almost before the trial.

Increasingly the questions that should be up to juries to decide are never even being presented to them. The American Association for the Advancement of Science, the organization that puts out *Science Magazine*, wrote a letter to the federal courts recommending science masters to help judges make decisions. For example, scientists who would advise the judges on silicon breast implants, or pesticides, or whatever. This strips away the democratic component of the courts. The jury should get to decide about scientific uncertainty, and cause and effect. Not some behind-the-doors scientist appointed by the judge who has who-knows-what-kind of conflicts of interest.

But it gets worse. Say you've got a corporation being sued by someone who's been terribly injured. We all know what happens next. The corporation buries the injured person's attorneys under mounds of paper, frivolous motions, and so on. Well, let's just say that the plaintiffs persevere, and that they're able to prove cause and effect even to a degree undeniable to the judge, and the corporation has to pay something to the person who has been injured. At that point, all of this information that was entered into essentially a public record—that has been brought in through the whole court process—can be sealed through protective orders. This evidence, this science, cannot be used and cannot be disclosed for the next case, so the next lawyer has to go through the exact same process of discovery, and can have a very hard time getting access to the very same evidence that demonstrated harm in this earlier case. It's crazy. Clearly there are cases in which you want to seal the records to protect people. But when a case concerns public health and safety, you don't want to protect a perpetrator or defendant and seal that evidence. We want that evidence to be available so you can protect public health and the environment.

DJ: You were talking earlier about things people can do.

CR: Well here's a wild idea—whenever possible reject the copy. The copy is the hallmark of industrialization. We have become a culture of the copy, rather than a culture of the original, rather than a culture of the masterpiece or mistresspiece. We no longer deal with original ideas. We now deal with the regurgitated sitcom. We have taken this to ridiculous extremes. Does anyone believe that you can have a livable world based on the copy? Contrast cloning with sex. A clone is a copy. Sex, on the other hand, breeds originality. You get something entirely new.

Rejecting the copy will do interesting things to your purchasing habits, and to your experience of beauty, to your experience of what feels integral, to what has integrity and what is whole.

We can protect the things we love. We have the tools to do it. We can prevent this terrible damage, and we can restore the damage that we've already done.

We need to put love back at the center of our decision-making. We have allowed science to take over in a way that has displaced the things we love, the central feeling of love, love for our children and for our children's health and future, love for the natural world, love for the places we live. Somehow we think science is going to be able to give us answers, when our instincts, when our guts, tell us it can't. Science can tell us many things, but we cannot use it to make our decisions in place of love.

Kathleen Dean Moore

Interview Conducted
in the philosophy department
Oregon State University, Corvallis, Oregon
4.20.02

I've always felt a strong dissatisfaction with Western philosophy. It seems to promise answers to life's most important questions, but delivers little more than impenetrable prose. When I taught writing at Eastern Washington University, my office was next door to a philosophy professor's. I wandered in sometimes to chat but was quickly repelled by his relentless illogic. I remember his insisting, week after week, that because human beings are the sole assigners of value, everything else in the world has value only if we decide it does. Each time, I fled the room in dismay.

Kathleen Dean Moore is that rarest of creatures, a grounded philosopher; a philosopher who makes sense, a philosopher who works with the material of real life. And she is a superb writer. In her most recent book, *Holdfast: At Home in the Natural World* (Lyons Press), she writes:

"Last week a student who had studied metaphysics and epistemology and Soren Kierkegaard, the student who read Immanuel Kant and brought fresh fruit to class, killed herself with a single gunshot to the head, sitting at home, at the kitchen table. She left no note, no explanation, and no one can make any sense of it. Her professors lean heavily against the classroom walls and cannot speak. We realize too late that we never taught our students what ducks know without knowing, that 'we must love life before loving its meaning,' as Dostoevsky told us. We must love life, and some meaning may grow from that love. But 'if love of life disappears, no meaning can console us.'"

This is philosophy.

It's hard to say how Moore has been able to chart the terrain of Western philosophy without losing her grounding in the real world. Perhaps she learned the way on the walks she took as a child with her father, a weekend park naturalist, along the Rocky River south of Cleveland, Ohio. It was this sort of immersion, she says—both literal and figurative—in the geography of her childhood that has allowed her, as an adult, to remain fully and consistently a part of the natural world. That's not to say she never got lost or separated from the places that grounded her. But she always found her way back. She writes: "Philosophers fretted that the world would disappear if they turned their backs, but when I closed their finely argued books and switched off the light, it was their worries that disappeared, not the world."

Moore's first book, *Pardons: Justice, Mercy, and the Public Interest* (Oxford University Press), explores deeply and movingly the intertwined relationships among forgiveness, clemency, and personal and political power. In her second book, *Riverwalking: Reflections on Moving Water* (Harcourt Brace), she uses essays on different bodies of water to elegantly discuss notions of home, stillness, and movement. Her most recent book, *Holdfast*, is an examination of our connections to what we hold most dear: family, friends, memories, and the places we call home.

Moore is a professor of philosophy at Oregon State University, and her husband is a biology professor there. She and I talked on a warm May afternoon in the philosophy-department library, where we were occasionally interrupted by other philosophers coming in for coffee. The conversation flowed from philosophy to family to forgiveness to the destruction of the natural world.

★◨

DJ: In *Riverwalking*, you wrote, "I have come to believe that all essays walk in rivers. Essays ask the philosophical question that flows through time—How shall I live my life?"

KM: When you put on a pair of old tennis shoes and walk into a river, you move through a reflection of the landscape, upside down and shattered and put together again in the quiet eddies. You have to grope upstream through a world you can only barely make out, feeling with your feet, stirring up the mud. It can be slippery, and you have to move ahead on trust. An essay is made of surfaces and reflections, too, pieces of experience broken apart and converging—memories, facts, visions, smells, speculations. And the territory a writer travels is deeper than she can see, and riskier.

DJ: That seems true as well for life.

KM: Walking in rivers is a useful metaphor for a way of approaching the world that's full of risk and trust. You can walk alongside your life, going from point to point, living out your little time-line. Or you can plunge right in, immerse yourself.

One of my colleagues believes that if there is eternal life, it won't be in the length of her life, but in its depth. This makes sense to me. I have no doubt that each life has a definite limit, an end point. But I don't think there is any limit to the depth of each moment, and I have resolved to try to live in a way that reaches into those depths. I want to live thickly, in layers of ideas and emotions and sensory experience. What I'm recommending is a way of life that is rich with noticing. Caring. Remembering. Embracing. Rejoicing in... what... in the smell of a child's hair, or the color of storm light.

What resonance is lost—because we don't allow ourselves to respond to weather, for example, thinking we have to maintain a constant 72 degree emotional state throughout the entire day? Or because we have jobs that require us to be precisely intellectual, poor climate-controlled souls never looking out the window? Or because we live so separated from nature? I live in a house where hardwood floors, acoustical tile, eight feet of damp basement air, a layer of concrete, and a six-inch footer of gravel fence me off from the earth. If I dug under all that, under the philosophical, emotional, and physical house I live in, I would find myself—literally—in an ancient riverbed of round boulders, and below that, among sea animals so old they've turned to stone, all floating on a lake of molten rocks. Astounding facts we never think to wonder about.

DJ: How did you come to pay such close attention to rivers?

KM: My father worked as weekend park naturalist at Rocky River, which is a shallow, shale-banked stream fed by runoff from the suburbs south of Cleveland. My sisters and I spent every Sunday in that little river. In the summer, the E. coli count was terrifying, so we weren't allowed to swim. But we waded in and walked upstream, looking for fossils, trying to catch minnows, watching teenagers wash their cars by driving them right onto gravel bars in the river. This was years ago—they sudsed their Buicks up and sloshed them down with big buckets of water. In the winter, the river would flood and turn cold. If it had ever stopped moving, it would have frozen, I'm sure. I remember jumping off a wall onto what I thought was a pile of snow-covered leaves but discovered was a deep eddy with leaves floating on it. I still remember the look on my father's face as he inched his way down a log to where I was bobbing, up to my ears in ice water.

So the answer to your question, I guess, has to do with immersion, with the geography in which you were immersed as a child.

DJ: I've been thinking lately that immersion doesn't usually occur overnight, that it takes a long time to get to know a place, and for it to get to know you.

KM: That's especially true, given separations that characterize contemporary western lives. We don't lead lives of quiet desperation, Thoreau to the contrary. We lead lives of relentless separation—comings and goings, airport embraces, loneliness, locked doors, notes left by the phone—and the deepest of all those divides is the one that separates us from the places we inhabit. My work takes me from place to place and everywhere I go, I pass people who came from someplace else and left their knowledge of the land behind. Universities, which should be studying connections, specialize in distinctions instead. Biologists in their laboratories forget that they are natural philosophers. Philosophers pluck ideas out of contexts like worms out of holes, and hold them dangling and drying in bright light. We lock ourselves in our houses, in our cars, and seal the windows and watch nature shows on TV. We don't go out at night, or in the rain. Unless we have Goretex jackets. And mace. No wonder we forget that human beings are part of the natural world, members of a natural community. I think we are only reminded, if we are reminded at all, by a sense of dislocation and a sadness we can't easily explain.

DJ: How did we come to think of ourselves as so much apart from the other-than-human world?

KM: Where did it start? I don't know. But Genesis is probably as good a place as any to start looking. The story of creation itself is a matter of separation. At first you have only the spirit of God moving over the face of the waters. I love that image. But then God separates the light from the darkness, separates the heavens from the waters, separates the seas from the dry land, and the day from the night. (Never mind magical, mixed things like dusk and fog and marshland and mudflats and dawn). Then by creating humans in His own image and giving them dominion over the fish of the sea...

DJ: ...and the birds of the air and everything that creeps on the earth...

KM: ...another great separation is created—humans from the natural world. And everything non-human is reduced to nothing more than means to human ends.

Then we can fast-forward to Rene Descartes. Imagine Descartes (born and raised in an age of faith) sitting in his dressing gown, determined to doubt everything that could be doubted. And the evidence of his senses? Of course we can doubt our senses, because they deceive us all the time. Think of dreams. How about a priori knowledge?—Can we trust that two and three make five? Nope, because God could be putting false ideas into our minds or (if you don't think God would stoop to dirty tricks), maybe an Evil Genius spends his life planting false ideas in our unsuspecting brains.

DJ: There are also powerful assumptions behind even something so simple as counting, which presumes identity: if you put one person in a room, and then another, you don't have two people, you have this individual and that individual. One could be nice, the other horrid, one old, one young. So we can't trust arithmetic.

KM: Fair enough. But Descartes' problem was even deeper, because he realized we can't even be sure that we exist.

DJ: Ah, but…

KM: The famous "ah, but…" If I think I might not exist, he thought, then surely I exist—if only as a thinking thing. Cogito, ergo sum. Notice that he said, "I think, therefore I am." Not "I feel, or eat, or love, therefore I am." I like to speculate on how life would be different if Descartes had said, Amo, ergo sum. I love, therefore I am. Humans as loving substance.

DJ: But he didn't.

KM: What Descartes did do is immense. Now we have thinking substance— res cogitans—spirit, consciousness, human thought. This we know for sure. And we have everything outside the mind—res extensa—matter, physical things, plants and planets, animals and ancient forests. These we know uncertainly. We have thinking self (meaningful, knowable, subject) and unthinking other (nonrational, material, knowable only as object).

About the same time, the early 1600's, came Francis Bacon, who encouraged us to think of knowledge as a means to power. Not knowledge as a means to happiness or enlightenment or peace, as you would have in other parts of the world, but this great western celebration of the ability of the human mind—the thinking substance—to control the external world.

Put these two together—Cartesian dualism and Baconian knowledge—and what do you get? The great divide. On the one hand, you get human mind set apart from, against, in control of, and definitely over everything else. And on the other hand, you have everything else—objects understood in mechanistic terms, means to human ends, meaningful only as humans give them meaning. All the meaning is stripped from the physical world; the only meaning in the universe is inside our minds. No wonder we're lonely.

DJ: When Western philosophy is not outright damaging, like Descartes' separations, it's obscure. At a talk I gave recently, someone brought up a point about Hegel, and I said, incredulous, "You've actually read Hegel?" Everyone laughed, and then the guy admitted, sheepishly, that he'd only been able to make it through the introduction.

KM: You have to be careful when you ask what's wrong with Western philosophy, because there are so many different kinds of Western philosophy, and whatever is true of one may not be true of another.

That said, I think Socrates put his finger on the problem when he wrote that philosophy seeks "the true nature of everything as a whole, never sinking to what lies close at hand." A philosopher, Socrates went on, may not even know "what his next-door neighbor is doing, hardly knows, indeed, whether the creature is a man at all; he spends all his pains on the question, what man is…" The inference is that if philosophy is about abstract ideas, then it must be divorced from the details of our lives.

That is a huge mistake, a terrible inference. I believe that philosophy is about big ideas, and therefore, it must also be about how we live our lives. If I know what a human being is, to take Socrates' example, then I will know what makes a human life worth living.

DJ: The Christian scholar Marcus Borg wrote, "Ideas matter."

KM: And great ideas matter a great deal. What we fundamentally believe shapes how we live our lives. And so philosophy is—must be—the most practical of all the professions.

Philosophers are the plumbers of the intellectual world. They work with things everybody else takes for granted. Non-philosophers ask, "What time is it?" assuming that the concept of time, like a toilet, will be there when they need it. A philosopher asks, "What is time?" Is time circular or linear? Does it have direction? Is it one or many? What you fundamentally believe about the answers to those questions will determine how you will live your life, plant your crops, dispose of your sewage, treat your grandparents.

DJ: So what needs to change?

KM: A great deal is already changing. A few decades ago, medical ethics showed how abstract philosophical ideas can help decide terrible real-life dilemmas. The result was a great blossoming of practical philosophy. Now some professional philosophers are even hanging out shingles on the street, helping people think their way through confused lives. Environmental ethicists are starting to understand that they need to get neck-deep in the marshes.

But there's a long way to go. I don't think it's an overstatement to say that when they ignore the practical implications of their ideas, professional philosophers betray the public trust, just when we need them the most. They work in isolation on little intellectual islands, and when inhabitants live in isolation for a few generations, they start to speciate, develop separate languages, and twitter in words that only they can understand.

People are desperate for the kind of insights philosophers can provide. When I speak to fisheries biologists, or wetland managers, or conservation groups, they are looking for someone who can articulate the worldviews and values that will help them make sound decisions. Scientists can tell us how to save wild salmon, for example. But it's up to others to tell us why we should. The values, the moral imperatives, the framing ideas—all these are missing from the public debate, at least in part because the one group of people who are trained (for years and years) to speak about the justifying ideas, are too busy publishing arcane tracts that no one but the members of a tenure committee will ever read.

Practical wisdom is the business of philosophers. Reasoned judgments are our stock-in-trade. From eight to five, we stand in front of students and talk about moral and spiritual values, and what is right and good and beautiful. If we can't explain the worth of a salmon, who can?

DJ: Why is it so hard for philosophers to write clearly about real-life issues?

KM: I think part of the problem with philosophy has to do with striving for a certain kind of clarity, and a hope for a specific kind of certainty. It took me probably twenty years to realize how steep a price philosophers have paid for this clarity and certainty. The first to go was the philosopher as a person. By writing always about ideas, never about themselves, the authors transformed themselves into disembodied authorities who had no past, no future, no reason for wondering, no reason even for living.

And then what happened is that the range of possible subjects narrowed: the easiest things to write clearly about are the simplest, and nothing in real life is simple. So the philosophers I met in graduate school wrote about pure, slick-surfaced ideas like truth and consistency. But not about home. Not about landscape or work. Not about parents. Not about fish.

DJ: What I would like from a philosophy is something that teaches me how to live and answers these questions: how can I be a better person? How can I live my life more fruitfully, more happily, more relationally?

KM: There are an awful lot of philosophy departments where if you said to a professor, "I want to study philosophy because I want to know how to live," they'd laugh you out of the building. They'd say, "Go to church, or to your mother, or anyplace else, because we're not here about lives, we're here about ideas." If the professor happened to be a logical positivist, he (probably he) would say, "Your question does not have an answer that would have any verifiable consequences in the world, and therefore I..."

DJ: ...must ridicule the question.

KM: "...must ridicule the question." Given the logical positivist's view, if you have an idea—a definition of 'good' or 'beautiful,' for example—that doesn't have verifiable consequences, then the idea becomes meaningless. It follows, of course, that a lot of concepts get declared meaningless simply because they don't fit the definition that anything one cannot understand precisely is not worth understanding, and might not even exist.

DJ: But "How must I live?" seems the only question worth asking.

KM: What's going to give meaning to my life? What makes life worthwhile? Those are traditionally the most significant philosophical questions, and they've been washed off the surface of philosophy by much of what has happened in the twentieth century.

It's a failure of courage, I think. Real-life issues are messy and ambiguous and contradictory and tough and changing—and never clear. But this is a reason for engaging them, not for turning away. The word 'clarity' has two meanings: one ancient and the other modern. The Latin clarus meant clear sounding, ringing out, "clear as a bell'" so in the ancient world "clear" came to mean lustrous, splendid, radiating light. The moon has this kind of clarity when it's full. But that usage is obsolete. Now "clear" is taken to have a negative meaning—without the dimness or blurring that can obscure vision, without the confusion or doubt that can cloud thought. For probably twenty years I thought that the modern kind of clarity was all there was, that what I should be looking for was sharp-edged, single-bladed truth, that anything I couldn't understand precisely wasn't worth thinking about. I'm now beginning to understand that the world is much more interesting than this.

DJ: One of the messy, ambiguous real-life issues you write about is the relation between persons and places, the kind of link that Wallace Stegner had in mind when he wrote, "Tell me where you're from and I'll tell you who you are."

KM: I believe that there is an essential—defining—connection between identity and place.

DJ: What does that mean?

KM: Several things. First, it's trivially true, and profoundly true, that people are made of places. Minerals from eroding mountains strengthen your bones and mine. Willamette River water pushes through my veins, Elk Creek through yours. It's the watery Oregon winter sun that transforms my fat into vitamins. We are calcified by gravity, wrinkled by wind, softened by shopping malls. Gradually, eventually, particle by particle, our bodies are constructed from places.

DJ: But there's more to it than that.

KM: Yes. I believe that not just our bodies, but our minds—our ideas, our emotions, our characters, our personal identities—are shaped, in part, by places. It follows that alienation from the land is an alienation from the self, a kind of sadness. And the opposite is true: there's a goofy kind of joy in finding ourselves in places that have meaning for us.

DJ: How (in what particular way) is it true that our personal identities are constructed from places?

KM: Personal identity: What makes me who I am, as opposed to any other person? In the seventeenth century, John Locke suggested a series of thought experiments that involved transplanting certain parts of the self, to find out what essentially defines us.

You, Derrick, are not your next-door neighbor. But suppose suddenly that she was in your body, and you were in hers. You suddenly have short blonde hair, for example, and broad hips. You would still be you—wouldn't you?—but in a different body. If so, your body is not essential to your personal identity.

Now suppose that suddenly your characters were transposed. You take a lover and lie about it—which is not like you—or you start going to church.

DJ: Which is also not like me.

KM: Are you now a different person? I don't think so. You are the same person, acting in strange and frightening new ways.

But now suppose that, suddenly, your memories are transposed with your neighbor's. When you think of your children, they are your neighbor's children, and you remember the day they were born, and how that felt.

DJ: I don't have children.

KM: You used to remember that you didn't. But now you remember that you have two sons, and they are the people asleep in the house next door, in maple beds you remember inheriting from your mother. Now, I think, you have become someone else. To that extent, it's your memories that make you who you are.

If someone asks me, "Who are you?" it is not enough for me to say, "I am Kathy, or I am Dora's daughter, or I am a professor." The answer is that I am—at least partly—my memories: I am the person who remembers a flock of white pelicans over Thompson Lake, and the apple tree in the backyard of my house. So every time I notice something, every time something strikes me as important enough to store away in my mind, I create another piece of who I am. These pieces of the landscape are the very stuff of my ideas— sense impressions and memories of what I have seen and heard. In this way, I am—literally, at the core of my being—made of the earth.

DJ: So do we have an argument here—something clean and neat? People are made of memories. Memories are made of places. Therefore, people are made of places. Quod erat demonstrandum.

KM: To be honest, it reminds me less of an argument than a novel. The mission of writers is to explore this convoluted landscape where memory and self and landscape come together like molten lava and make an un-holy mess.

DJ: You say that places reside in our memories. But do memories reside in places? Does it work the other way?

KM: Have you ever walked a trail you have walked before, or returned to the front porch of the house you grew up in? Didn't the places speak to you of times long past, recreating memories that you hadn't thought of for years? "Here is where we stopped to check the map and realized we had missed the turn. You had on a knitted cap that was too small and pressed worry wrinkles into your forehead. Here is where we walked the night before you left for Chicago—the place makes me sad all over again." Memories live in places, and you can find them if you go there. Sometimes, if our memory is as unreliable as mine, you can only find them if you go there.

DJ: If our memories and our landscapes are part of who we are, what difference does that make?

KM: It follows that there are two questions we had better be asking ourselves, obsessing over. They are urgent questions. People should stop each other on the street and discuss them in low voices. Parents should call their children long-distance and damn the expense. Question one: If place is this important in our construction of ourselves, and we are never in one place, what will become of us?

DJ: And question two?

KM: Two. If people are defined by their landscapes, what happens to our selves—our integrity, our wholeness—when the landscape is destroyed?

The narrow strip of beach on the outer rim of the wilderness sand dunes in Oregon is part of me and part of my family. The sound of the surf reminds me of the winter when we caught crabs with our bare hands and discovered they were females and let them go. The smell of the air reminds me of my daughter, sitting in the beach grass, leaning against her father's back. When I go back to that beach, I remember this. I am this.

Now what happens to those memories—to me—when that beach is clogged with bunker oil from the New Carissa? What happens to memories when they lose the places they had put down roots? We all know people whose places are gone, the homeless people—the bewildered people.

Environmental destruction is a kind of forgetting, and so it's a kind of self-destruction. If we go around systematically destroying the places that hold meaning for us, the places that hold our memories—then why would we be surprised that we're fragmented, that we don't have a sense of who we are?

DJ: Your work now is about the natural world, but your early work in philosophy, and your first book, was about pardon and forgiveness. Are these issues connected?

KM: Deeply connected. For years, I have been trying to understand how we respond to wrong-doing—justice and forgiveness. There are very powerful parts of us that say that evil should be met with evil. If there is no counterforce—no jail, no lethal injection—the wrong-doing remains as a force in the world. This feeling is the wellspring of retributive justice.

But forgiveness is another possible response when someone does you wrong. I think it's one of the greatest human capacities, the ability to forgive—not to forget, but to renounce resentment, to act as if the wrong had not been done, and so to begin the process of healing. It is our one effective way to triumph over evil. After a war is over, for example, the healing process almost always begins with amnesties and pardons, the formal trappings of forgiveness. Right now, experiments in truth and reconciliation are going on all over the world.

I believe that here, in the United States, we are still involved in a centuries-long war against the land. It has gone on long enough. I believe we need to begin our own process of truth and reconciliation, to release the healing power of the Earth.

DJ: Another way wars end is with show trials of the war criminals.

KM: There are natural consequences to ecological warfare, and so we might think of devastating floods and hurricanes, increased cancer rates, crop failures, as a kind of cosmic justice—tit for tat, no mercy. But the Earth is capable of something very much like forgiveness—the ability to heal itself. When the Earth covers burned-over land with wildflowers, then alder thickets, then pine forests; when a marsh filters water; when plants create oxygen and a river washes silt from gravel beds where salmon spawn—these great natural cycles of renewal, again and again transforming death into life—this is a kind of grace.

DJ: What is grace?

KM: The concept of grace has roots deep in Christian traditions: We are all sinners, the story goes, and God has the right to punish us for our iniquity. But the God of justice is also the God of benevolence, of good will, with the power to forgive, to say, "You have wronged me, but I choose not to inflict the full consequences of your wrong-doing." This is the gift of grace. This is the possibility of redemption.

DJ: How does this relate to the landscape?

KM: When I think of dam-breaching, for example, I think of grace and the possibility of redemption. True, in so many places, we have done irreparable—unforgivable—harm. Extinct species will not be born again. And when corporations cut an ancient forest and poison the bulldozed ground, we will not see that forest again, nor will our children, for fourteen generations. But a river can heal itself, and so it has the power—essentially—to forgive. I can imagine people gathering at the edge of a river as the water draws down and the riverbed re-emerges, water streaming off the shoulders of rocks, a flowing river reborn. I want to be there when sluice gates open and the Columbia River rises from the reservoir behind the John Day Dam.

DJ: The possibility of truth and reconciliation seems dim, unless the war against the landscape is over.

KM: And it's not, of course. Peace-making is hard, slow work. But I think I see the beginnings of a process of reconciliation. Some environmentalists are still struggling to stop the atrocities, to preserve the last scraps of unspoiled land, but the rehabilitation and restoration work has already begun—healing landscapes that have been damaged or destroyed, pulling back the bulldozers, tearing out barbwire fence, opening sluice-gates, releasing young condors, breeching dikes, planting trees—actively trying to undo the damage we have done and make the landscape whole again.

DJ: But what about the truth in the truth-and-reconciliation process? Aren't we still telling each other lies about our relationship to the land?

KM: All the efforts are restoration and healing are piecemeal and, I think, ultimately futile, if we still aren't able to do the true peace work, the truth-telling. In the truth and reconciliation trials in South Africa, if someone who's done terrible things stands up and lies, nothing can be resolved.

DJ: What are some of the lies?

KM: In order of outrageousness: That human beings are separate from—and superior to—the rest of natural creation. That Earth and all its creatures were created to serve human ends. That an act is right if it creates the greatest wealth for the greatest number of people. That a corporation's highest responsibility is to its stockholders. That we can have it all—endlessly mining the land and the sea—and never pay a price. That technology will provide a way to solve every problem, even those created by technology. I can keep going… That it makes sense to barge salmon smelts past the dams to the sea, so that grain can move downriver in barges. That a pine plantation is the same as a forest. That you can poison a river without poisoning your children. And the biggest and most dangerous lie of all: That the Earth is endlessly and infinitely resilient.

DJ: Why is this so dangerous?

KM: We are doing damage now—to the atmosphere, to the seas, to the climate—that may be beyond the power of healing. When the Earth is whole, it is resilient. But once it is damaged, the power of the Earth to heal itself seeps away. In a weakened world, if we turn against the land, pour chemical fertilizers onto worn-out fields, sanitize wastewater with poisons, dam more rivers, burn more oil, bear more children, and never acknowledge that there may be no chance of healing, never admit what we have done and what we have failed to do—then who can forgive us?

DJ: Why is this so hard for us to understand? We see evidence all around us.

KM: Long-standing ways of thinking, even the way we talk, reinforce the fiction. Think of the metaphor of the Earth as a mother, and the slogan, "Love your mother." What does this mean? It might simply acknowledge that humans are created from matter that comes from the Earth. But so are Oldsmobiles, and that doesn't make the Earth the mother of Oldsmobiles.

I think the whole "love your mother" metaphor is just wishful thinking. Mothers can usually be counted on to clean up after their children. They are warm-hearted and forgiving: mothers will follow crying children to their rooms and stroke their hair, even if the child's sorrow is shame at his treatment of his mother. It's nice to think the Earth is a mother who will come after us and clean up the mess and protect us from our mistakes, and then forgive us the monstrous betrayal. But even mothers can be worn out and used up. And then what happens to her children?

There's an ad from an oil company that shows the image of the Earth along with the caption, "Mother Earth is a tough old gal."

DJ: The implication being that the Earth is invulnerable.

KM: A dangerous implication. I wrote a letter to the company saying, "If the Earth really were your mother, she would grab you with one rocky hand and hold you under water until you no longer bubbled." Cosmic justice.

DJ: I actually have some trouble with the linking of truth and reconciliation. I clearly see the importance of telling these stories, getting the truth out there, but simply acknowledging the horrors that you have perpetrated—after your side lost anyway—doesn't make it okay for me. "I spilled a zillion gallons of oil in a wilderness fjord and poisoned everything from the high tide line to the benthic mud." Or, to return to South Africa, "I tortured dozens of people and threw them from airplanes," someone can say, and now we're supposed to let it go? I realize in the case of South Africa, I'm not one of the wronged, so I don't have standing to speak for them, but there's still something missing for me.

KM: Truth doesn't make evil disappear. Truth doesn't make everything okay. But truth makes it possible to go on—to go beyond pain and hatred and begin the process of healing.

DJ: Who can tell the truth? How can it be heard above the 60-second spots, the oil company ads?

KM: I have only one very small answer, one very small piece of what will have to be a huge effort. Many of these lies come directly from western philosophy. So philosophers have a moral responsibility to hold them up to public scrutiny, to examine the harm they have caused, to end the power of the lies to cover up—or define away—crimes against the Earth. And then to tell the truth—Human beings are part of the web of life, not separate and superior. The natural world has value in and of itself, apart from its value to us; it is an end, not a means only. Greed is not a moral justification for anything. If we tell these truths, the reconciliation—the forgiveness—can begin.

DJ: Could you define forgiveness for me? Let's take this step by step. Say I hurt you inadvertently—step on your foot or run you over with my car accidentally. I'm sorry. Where does forgiveness fit in?

KM: Nowhere. You might say, "Forgive me," and I'd say, "I have no right to forgive you, because you haven't committed a wrong against me. I was hurt, but it wasn't a wrong or evil that you did." So there would be no justice in my punishing you for it.

DJ: Now say I run you over on purpose with my car...

KM: And then you beg forgiveness.

DJ: Yes.

KM: I can forgive you or not, it's up to me. You don't deserve forgiveness. You can't demand it as a right. But I may choose to forgive, entirely from good will.

DJ: Even if I later realize what a terrible person I was to run you over with the car, and I no longer do that sort of thing?

KM: The answer depends on what we are punishing people for. For what they do, or for who they are? After you run me over on purpose, are we punishing you because you ran me over on purpose, or are we punishing you because you are the sort of person who deliberately runs people over? If it's the first, then the fact that you're sorry makes no difference whatsoever, because you still caused the harm. But if the whole basis for punishment is that you're the kind of person who deliberately does harm, if you change so you're no longer that person, then you don't deserve punishment. What you would ask for is justice, not mercy.

DJ: Can you give an example of a lie that covers up, or defines away, crimes against the Earth?

KM: So many lies... Well, we can start with utilitarian theories—the claim that an act is right if it results in the greatest good for the greatest number of people. So our obligations to the land are really just obligations to people, to use wild lands in a way that maximizes human benefit. This view has led people to do terrible things for the sake of the "greatest good for the greatest number."

DJ: For example...

KM: The great dams on the Columbia River were celebrated for all the good they did for people—they created jobs, irrigated orchards, created electricity, "turning our darkness to light," according to Woody Guthrie. But the first rule of intelligent exploitation is to take care that in maximizing the benefits, you don't create a greater harm somewhere else. Doing good here, at a cost of greater harm there, is a net loss. And a corollary: remember to count all the costs. While it may sometimes seem that small acts of cruelty or destruction can be justified by a greater good, be aware of the systematically hidden or discounted costs.

It is possible to dynamite Celilo Falls on the Columbia River, where native people gathered for centuries to fish and pray. And then it's possible to dam the river and bury the rubble and the prayers. You can show on a graph how the benefits soar far beyond the measured costs, irrigating orchards and sending cheap electricity to cities on the Pacific coast. But who measured the costs of the dislocation and destruction of native cultures, or the damage to the salmon runs, the slow poisoning of the river? And where is the place on the graph for the brutalization of the human spirit, the hidden costs of cruelty and raised voices, the damage to the integrity of a person who willfully destroys something beautiful?

DJ: So, does your objection to 'enlightened self-interest' come down only to this: don't be dumb about it. Look ahead and count all the costs?

KM: No. What makes me uneasy about theories that measure the worth of rivers against the needs of human beings is that they are built on an arrogant and dubious idea: that human beings are the center of the universe; human beings, imagining that rivers were made especially for them, the way ticks would think, were they to follow the same logic, that hikers were their special gifts from God. The temptation then is to design arrogant policies and undertake arrogant projects, and then we end up doing to rivers what ticks do to us, except ticks have the good grace to drop off when their stomachs are full.

DJ: A river without water, a hiker without blood.

KM: In a hydrology class, where students had been conducting scientific studies of the health of rivers, I was invited to do the one obligatory class on ethics. My colleague calls this "drive-by ethics." I asked the students to tell me the names of their home rivers. I wanted them to say the words, to hear the sounds, to celebrate the gathering of the waters. Down one row and up the next in a big lecture hall, the students said the names of the rivers they loved. Grande Ronde. Umatilla. Klickitat. Malheur. Nestucca. And then suddenly—I don't know what happened—it was as if a cloud had passed over the sun. Students looked up, startled. The saying of the names had become a drum roll for what was lost—the cultures, the free-flowing rivers, the clear water, the salmon—and students listened like children at the feet of the uniformed old man who stands by the war memorial in the park, runs his finger down the engraved words, and reads the names aloud. Snake, dammed and dammed again. Willamette, dammed and poisoned. Klamath, dammed. Santiam, clearcut. Umpqua, dammed. Tahkenitch, dammed. Siletz, clearcut. The Columbia River, dammed, poisoned, dammed again, poisoned, until every river otter in the lower river, every otter, has skin tumors, and any radiologist in this country can tell who has grown up along the river, by the radioisotopes in his bones. The students loved those broken rivers, and maybe love is deeper when it's mixed with grief.

DJ: In your book, *Holdfast*, you have an essay where you find yourself in a marsh at sunset, a week after the suicide of a student. The marsh is a riot of birds and frog-song, and you reflect on the meaning of all this raucous life, the purpose of a marsh. This is what you wrote:

"What is it all for, this magnifying-glass-in-the sun focus on being, this marshland, this wetness, this stewpot, this great splashing and thrusting, this determination among the willows, the flare-up, the colors, the plumage, the effort, the noise, the complexity that leaves no note?

"Nothing, I think, except to continue.

"This is the testimony of the marsh: Life directs all its power to one end, and that is to continue to be. A marsh at nightfall is life loving itself. Nothing more. But nothing less, either, and we should not be fooled into thinking this is a small thing."

What does the marsh tell you about our obligations to the land?

KM: A marsh has instrumental value, there's no denying. Marshes nurture life that nurtures us—body and soul. But a marsh has intrinsic value too.

Even if there were no humans in the universe, it would be better that the marsh exist than not. It has value in and of itself, apart from its usefulness to us.

DJ: So what is the basis of our obligation to rivers and marshes, if it's not maximizing their instrumental value?

KM: Obligations grow out of relationships, the philosopher Nel Noddings pointed out. She's right: we know what it means to care, and we value that. Just as we are connected to our families, and care about them, we are connected to the land, both emotionally and biologically. This is the starting premise: We are all members of a natural community of interdependent parts that includes rivers and wrens and children and stones. The relationships define us, sustain us, create us, fill us with joy. And when we find ourselves alone and apart, our unhappiness becomes a longing close to grief.

If this is so, then to lead a moral life we have to acknowledge the depths and complexity of our ties to the natural communities we are members of, acknowledge our own experience of caring—acknowledge the value we place on caring—and make a commitment to acts that grow out of love. Aldo Leopold says, "Sing our love for the land and our obligation to it," and I am struck by how quickly obligation follows on the heels of love.

What is called for are not just acts of enlightened self-interest, but acts that grow from our connections and acknowledge the worth of what we care for so deeply. A right act isn't the one that makes us happiest. A right act is one that strengthens and reknits the web of relationships, and so it tends, as Aldo Leopold said, "to preserve the integrity, stability, and beauty" of the community.

Figuring out what's right in any given instance isn't going to be easy. You have to learn about your natural communities—how things fit together, what makes communities flourish, what weakens their bonds. You have to study what you might call the ecology of love.

DJ: What is the relationship between the natural world and love?

KM: I'm always surprised when I read nature writing that tells about an individual soul going off alone to commune with nature. It's about isolation, and I don't have much patience with it. To me that's not what it's about at all.

The natural world in my life has always been a way of connecting with people—with my children, my husband, my friends. I think the richness of my experience in the natural world translates immediately into a richer relationship with people.

I've come to think that one of the most romantic and loving things you can say to another person is, "Look." There is the kind of love of two people looking at each other, but I don't think that's as interesting as the love between two people standing side by side and looking out at something else that moves them both.

Think about this in terms of what we've been saying about memory and identity. If we are our memories, then we'd expect that to the extent that we share memories we become one person. The whole notion of the joining of souls that's supposed to happen say in marriage, or in a romance, may be about saying, "Look," and then suddenly having a memory you hold in common.

A few years ago, my husband and I went out howling for wolves, with a dozen strangers. It was a clear, cold night—so cold. Our guide told us to work for discordance, all of us howling on a different pitch, switching keys randomly, to imitate the sound of a wolf pack in full chorus. We always started out that way, but as each group howl drew out at the end, we found we had tuned ourselves into a minor chord—a rich, deep chord, something Bach would recognize. In a clearing, surrounded by pines that cut the shape of wolves sitting on their haunches, the wolves answered our chorus—a full pack-howl coming from behind the wolf-trees. I have never loved my husband more deeply. More than that, I loved all those strangers that night. I didn't know a thing about them but I loved them.

I have come to believe that natural beauty can be the ground of human connection, and the richer your experience of the natural world, the richer your experience of people around you. When we alienate ourselves from the natural world, we alienate ourselves from fundamental parts of ourselves, and become lesser—and impoverish our relationships with other people, too, because we have less to give.

DJ: Your most recent book is about connection.

KM: The book is called *Holdfast*. A holdfast is the structure at the root end of a bull kelp that holds it to the ocean floor, even against all the force of the tides. It's a fist of knobby fingers that stick to the rocks with a glue the plant makes from sunshine and salt water. Biologists don't entirely understand how the holdfast works. Philosophers haven't even begun to try.

I'm fascinated by holdfasts, both for what they are and for the power of the metaphor. What are our holdfasts? As we are pulled back and forth by our chaotic lives, how will we cling to what we value most, to the values that sustain us? As our children leave for college and our parents pass away, what structures of connection will hold us together? How will we find an attachment to the natural world that makes us feel complete and fully alive?

David Abram

Interview Conducted
at his friend's home, Santa Fe, New Mexico
7.7.00

David Abram makes magic in many different ways. He is an accomplished sleight of hand magician, having worked for years at this craft in the United States and Europe. When he returned to college after a year as a street magician in Europe, he began to realize that the use of sleight of hand by healers is an ancient tradition. He became interested in the relationship between magic and healing. So he traveled through Nepal, Sri Lanka, and Indonesia in the hopes of connecting to some of the magicians, or medicine peoples, working within traditional indigenous communities.

Abram was welcomed by them as a fellow practitioner of the craft of magic. Soon he realized that very few traditional medicine people consider healing other humans to be their primary work. They perceive this healing as a by-product of their more primary work, which has to with being intermediaries between the human community and what Abram calls the more-than-human community. As such, a great majority of these healers/magicians live at the fringes of their villages, instead of at the centers, where the clutter and bustle of day-to-day human existence might not only interfere with their ability to hear the animate world, but might be sometimes too painful for these people whose acute sensitivity allows them to be able to form relationships with oak trees, frogs, thunder storms. These magicians consider the animals, plants, trees, rocks, rivers, forests, clouds, to be animate beings who have their own desires and intents.

In Southeast Asia, working with these traditional peoples, Abram was able to fully comprehend that, as he has put it, "The task of the magician is to startle our senses and free us from outmoded ways of thinking."

And this is the second way that Abram makes magic. His writing—and I'm thinking primarily of his extraordinary book *The Spell of the Sensuous*—is aimed toward startling us all into investigating for ourselves the fluid, participatory nature of perception, and the reciprocity that exists between our senses and the sensuous earth. As such Abram is especially concerned with the power that words—the way we use them, the way they inform or constrict our ability to perceive and to think—have to enhance or stifle the spontaneous life of our senses. He wants to change the culture, and he wants to do so by using magic—the magic of sleight of hand, the magic of his words, and the magic that surrounds us at every moment—to startle us back into our bodies.

This brings me to the third way Abram makes magic. His prose is sensuous, lyrical, beautiful—magical. He begins his book, "Humans are tuned for relationships. The eyes, the skin, the tongue, ears, and nostrils—all are gates where our body receives the nourishment of otherness. This landscape of shadowed voices, these feathered bodies and antlers and tumbling streams—these breathing shapes are our family, the beings with whom we are engaged, with whom we struggle and suffer and celebrate. For the largest part of our species' existence, humans have negotiated relationships with every aspect of the sensuous surroundings, exchanging possibilities with every flapping form, with each textured surface, and shivering entity that we happened to focus upon. All could speak, articulating in gesture and whistle and sigh a shifting web of meanings that we felt on our skin or inhaled through our nostrils or focused with our listening ears, and to which we replied—whether with sounds, or through movements, or minute shifts of mood. The color of sky, the rush of waves—every aspect of the earthly sensuous could draw us into a relationship fed with curiosity and spiced with danger. Every sound was a voice, every scrape or blunder was a meeting—with Thunder, with Oak, with Dragonfly. And from all of these relationships our collective sensibilities were nourished."

The problem, as he sees it? "Today we participate almost exclusively with other humans and with our own human-made technologies. It is a precarious situation, given our age-old reciprocity with the many-voiced landscape. We still need that which is other than ourselves and our own creations. The simple premise of this book is that we are human only in contact, and conviviality, with what is not human."

David's educational background is in philosophy. He holds a doctorate in philosophy from the State University of New York at Stony Brook. He has been the recipient of fellowships from the Watson and the Rockefeller Foundations. *The Spell of the Sensuous* won the prestigious Lannan Literary Award for non-fiction. He was named by the *Utne Reader* as one of a hundred leading visionaries currently changing the world.

We met on a hot July afternoon in Santa Fe, New Mexico, and talked through the afternoon. As we talked David sometimes rolled a coin across his fingers. Suddenly the coin would disappear, to reappear elsewhere a little while later. Birds flitted among the branches of overhanging trees, and as I later transcribed the tape, I was reminded of their beauty by their constant songs in the background.

DJ: I'd like to start with two questions that might actually be one. They are: Is the natural world alive? and, What is magic?

DA: Is there anything that is not alive? Certainly we are alive, and if we assume that the natural world is in some sense not alive, it can only be because we imagine we're not fully in it, and of it. Actually, it's difficult for me to conclude that any phenomenon I perceive is utterly inert and lifeless; or even to imagine anything that is not in some sense alive, that does not have its own spontaneity, its own openness, its own creativity, its own interior animation, its own pulse—although in the case of the ground, or this rock right here, its pulse may move a lot slower than yours or mine.

Now your other question: what's magic? In the deepest sense, magic is an experience. It's the experience of finding oneself alive inside a world that is itself alive. It is the experience of contact and communication between oneself and something that is profoundly different from oneself: a swallow, a frog, a spider weaving its web...

DJ: Another human being.

DA: That too. Sure. Magic is that astonishing experience of contact and conviviality between myself and another shape of existence, whether that be a person or a gust of wind. It's that sense of wonderment that arises from the encounter with that which I cannot fathom, with something that I cannot ever fully exhaust with my thoughts or understanding. Many of my most intense experiences of magic have been encounters in the wild with other species, other shapes of earthly intelligence. From the meeting and exchange that one might call interspecies communication.

DJ: When most people think of magic, they think either of sleight-of-hand or sorcerers casting spells. Is there a relationship between these definitions and yours?

DA: Hmmm... I wouldn't call what I've said a definition. If you try to define something as unruly and wild as "magic," you're asking for trouble. But these other, more restricted notions of magic are still dependent upon the sense of a world all animate and alive: a magician, really, is one who is able to participate richly in that world; who can communicate with the elements, or call a wild hawk down out of the sky—one who can understand something of the language of the other animals, or who can communicate with certain plants and so is able to draw upon the particular powers of certain herbs in order to heal or alleviate illness.

Sleight-of-hand magic is somewhat more distantly related but still utterly dependent upon the animistic experience of a world all alive and aware. In our modern, technological civilization, the sense that the natural world is alive is considered a delusion or superstition. We conceive of nature—and indeed of the material world in general—as a set of basically inert or mechanical objects. Such a conception profoundly influences the way we see the world around us—or rather the way we don't see the world. It keeps us from making contact with the inexhaustible strangeness and wild otherness of the things around us. For instance, when we speak of the behavior of other animals as just "programmed" in their genes, it deadens our ears to the all the birdsong going on around us; because those birds, we assume, are not really saying anything; its just automatic sounds. Our ears begin to close down—we become deaf to all the living voices around us. And our eyes, too, begin to glaze over. If we speak of the world as a mechanically determined set of processes, then there's no real openness or mystery to engage our senses, and so our senses begin to shut down, and we come to live more and more in our heads.

But the sleight-of-hand magician is one who can startle the senses out of the slumber induced by such obsolete ways of speaking. By making a coin vanish from one hand and appear under your foot, making a stone float between his hands or a silk scarf change its colors, the magician wakes up that old, animistic awareness of objects as living, animate entities with their own styles and secrets; he coaxes our senses to engage the strangeness of things once again. This was my own profession, or craft, for many years. As a sleight-of-hand magician working in the late twentieth century, I felt my task was to undermine, to disrupt, to explode the determinate and habitual ways of perceiving that we fall into in a culture that speaks of and defines nature to be a set of inert and inanimate objects. A skilled sleight-of-hand magician is involved in shaking that accepted view of reality until it begins to disjoin and fall apart; freeing up our sensing bodies to begin to see and to hear and taste the world creatively once again. In order to do this, I make use of various "sleights," these little manipulations of my fingers that I use to capture your senses and to loosen them out of their expectations. I have to roll this coin around my fingers enough times so that at some point it starts to come alive. Then it can vanish, and reappear over here.

People expect so much to see things in certain habitual ways that they've stopped actually seeing them at all. Because they always know exactly what they're going to see, they no longer really see the world; they're not participating with their eyes in the life of that tree, or in the sky overhead. But a sleight of hand magician disrupts our expected sense and experience of the visible so that we actually start looking again, and gazing and peering at things, and participating in them.

DJ: So magic has a lot to do with perception.

DA: Absolutely! The magician—whether an indigenous sorcerer or a modern sleight-of-hand conjuror—is someone who is adept at altering the perceptual field, adept at shifting others' senses, or at altering his or her own senses in order to make contact with another shape of awareness, another entity that perceives the world very differently than we do—with a coyote, perhaps, or a frog. Or a whole forest, for that matter.

We've been taught to think of perception as a kind of one-way process, whereby information from the world out there is picked up by our senses and transferred to our nervous system in here. But when we really attend, mindfully, to the experience of perception, we discover that it's a reciprocal, interactive process—a dynamic interaction, or participation, between oneself and what one perceives. To our own sensing, animal bodies, the things are not passive. We walk down the street, and a particular building, or leaf, or stone, actively catches my attention.

DJ: It grabs your awareness.

DA: It calls my eyes, or captures my focus. And thus I'm drawn into a relationship with this other body, this other being. And the more I enter into this relationship, the more I grant it my attention, perhaps moving toward that stone, picking it up and hefting it in my hands, feeling its textures with my fingers, the more articulately that rock speaks to my body, and begins to teach me. It moves me.

DJ: What would you say to try to convince a skeptic, someone who claims that all this stuff about nature as alive, or stones as animate beings, is all projection?

DA: Hmmm... Perhaps I'd take him or her walking along a particular stream that I love, to where at one spot you're suddenly confronted by an immense sandstone cliff rising from the opposite bank. It towers above you, and never fails to move someone—especially someone who's not seen it before. And I'd watch to see the way that rock moves him—the way it makes him step back and utter a little gasp. I'd ask him if he really thinks the rock is inanimate. If he says yes, I'd say "but that rock clearly moves you. How, then, can you say it does not move?"

Maybe he'd reply that that movement is not really a physical action—that its a purely mental experience, a projection. But then I'd point out how his own body had indeed stepped back when he first saw the rock cliff—that it was indeed a physical interaction between his body and the vast body of that red rock, between two different kinds of dynamism, two different ways of being earth.

DJ: So by denying that the rock face is animate, he's denying his own direct experience...

DA: Exactly.

Much of my work, I suppose, is about noticing that we are really inside this world, palpably immersed in something much bigger than we are, something much vaster than we can fathom. In terms of bodily reality, of course, its obvious. We're quite physically immersed in the air and winds, in the thick of a world that's outrageously vast. But somehow today we seem very adept at convincing ourselves, mentally, that we're really not inside of this outrageous mystery, and we're not embedded and immersed in something inexplicable. Our intellects seem to hover outside the world, looking at it all from outside and trying always to figure it out, as though we were spectators of the world rather than participants in it. Because of that I think most people have come to ignore their sensory experience and to construe the earthly world the way their intellects tell them to: as though they were somehow outside of and apart from it. And as a result they feel very little affinity, or kinship, with the surrounding earth.

My work is motivated in great measure by my sense of loss, by the spreading destruction and desecration of so much earthly beauty. By the accelerating loss of other species—the extinction of so many other styles of sensitivity and sentience, by the destruction of wetlands and forests, the damming and draining of so many rivers to serve our own, purely human interests. I'm trying to understand how it's possible that a culture of intelligent critters like ourselves can so recklessly and so casually destroy so much that is mysterious and alive, and in the course of it destroy so much of ourselves and our own capacity for wonder.

And it seems to me that it is not out of any real meanness that we are destroying so much of our world; but rather it's simply that we no longer notice these other beings, no longer really notice or feel that we are a part of the same world that the ravens and the rivers inhabit. We don't sense that we're inside the same story in which the squirrels and the salmon are characters. Somehow our ways of speaking, and our ways of living, perpetuate this odd notion that we stand outside of the world, apart from the world, looking at it, pondering it as if from some distant vantage point. And our science steadily tries to figure out the world, to come up with a precise blueprint of how it all works—as if the world were a vast machine we could somehow diagram and control if we can just get the right perspective.

Logically, however, this is all a bit silly. We're obviously immersed in this world, utterly dependent upon it, our nervous systems coevolved in delicate interaction with all these other beings and shapes and textures. Rather than figuring out the workings of this machine from outside, in hopes of trying to engineer it to suit our purposes, it would make much more sense for our sciences to study the world from our experienced place within this world— using our experiments to discern how we might establish a more sustaining relationship with a particular species, or with a particular wetland or forest, rather than trying to figure just out that how that species or that wetland works in itself, as though we were somehow not participant in its processes. Those are the sort of questions our sciences should be asking: how can both we and these frogs flourish in right relationship to one another; how can we humans live in right relation to this river valley so that both we and the river and the salmon all flourish—rather than: what kind of a machine is a salmon in itself, or what are the mechanisms that make this forest tick? By asking these latter questions we take ourselves out of relation to the forest, out of relation to the salmon, in order to comprehend their workings. I suppose it would be okay if we then brought ourselves back into a living relation with them. But we don't—instead we begin to focus on how to manipulate the forest, how to engineer the genome of the salmon for our own ostensible benefit. So much research, today, seems motivated less by a sense of wonder than by a great will-to-control. It's a mark of immaturity, I think, a sign that our science is still in its adolescence. A more mature science would be motivated by a wish for richer relationship, for deeper reciprocity with the world that we study.

But perhaps today we do see some stirrings of such a mature science—in the emergence and development of conservation biology, for instance, or in the empathy cultivated by certain field biologists for the animals and plants that they study—or even in the growing recognition of indeterminacy, and "chaos," as a principle that undermines all our attempts to understand the world from outside.

In our culture we speak about nature a great deal. Mature cultures speak to nature. They feel the rest of nature speak to them. They feel the ground where they stand as it speaks through them. They feel themselves inside and a part of the unfolding story in which storm clouds and spiders are just as much players as they are. So that's what I wonder: how to coax people back inside the world, how to startle their senses awake so they suddenly notice that they're immersed in the world, not spectators but participants.

DJ: A few minutes ago, you were suggesting that perception, itself, is participatory.

DA: When we speak of the world as a set of objects, or of mechanisms waiting to be figured out by us, we are implicitly saying that the world has nothing that is, in principle, hidden from us, that given enough time and research we could plumb the depths of the whole shebang, and know how it all works. It's the God trick—the idea that we can understand the world from outside, from a God's perspective. But when we pay attention to our actual experience of things and of the world, we realize that we never encounter the totality of anything all at once. There is always some aspect of what we encounter that is hidden from us: the other side of that tree, or its roots under the ground. It's these hidden aspects, these mysteries or uncertainties, that invite us to look further, that draw us into relation, into participation with whatever we meet. Perception is a kind of primordial participation with the world, a dynamic interaction between my body and the world. Simply to be gazing the blue sky, or watching those storm clouds approach, is already to be in relationship, to be participating in an active exchange between my body and those roiling clouds. But if I speak of the clouds or the weather as a purely mechanical, quantifiable set of processes, then I'm speaking of them as things that have no life of their own, no otherness, nothing really hidden from our awareness, and so I'm stifling the possibility of an ongoing relation with those storm clouds, which is to say, I stop seeing them. I no longer really notice the sky with all its shifting patterns. To the extent that we speak of the world as a set of objects, we stop seeing with our eyes, and hearing with our ears. We climb into our heads and live in a world of abstractions, because we cut off the spontaneous reciprocity between our bodily senses and the sensuous flesh of a living world.

If we want to actually start noticing where we are, and finding ourselves in a better relation with the rest of the earth around us, the simplest and most elegant way I know of is to simply to stop insulting everything around us by speaking of them as passive objects, and instead begin to allow things their own spontaneity, their own life. As soon as you start speaking in such a way, you start noticing things a hell of a lot more. You suddenly find yourself in a dynamic relationship with all the things around you, including the air you breathe, the chair you're sitting on, the house in which you live. You find yourself negotiating relationships all the time. And you realize that ethics is not something to be practiced only with other humans—that all of our actions have ethical consequences.

DJ: You said a chair. When you talk about things being alive, you're not just talking about rocks, salmon, clouds, wind...

DA: I'm also talking about telephone poles, about houses...

DJ: So you perceive this tape recorder as something to be entered into relationship with—or rather as something that we're already in relationship with, if we would just notice and acknowledge it?

DA: Sure. To speak of anything as inanimate is kind of disrespectful. It's insulting to the thing. Why do it? It cuts me off from listening to what that thing might want in the world, to what that object, that presence, might be asking of me. I don't see any usefulness in making a conceptual division between that which is animate on one hand, and that which is inanimate on the other. And I know of no healthy culture that makes such a division, between animate and inanimate matter. Often when discussing these notions, people will say, "Okay, well, sure, humans are alive; even aspects of the human community I sometimes tend to think of as not being fully alive, well, they're alive, too. Other animals, okay, I can get that. Critters, they have their own lives, sure. And even plants, I get that they're alive. But stones? Rocks? Matter? The matter of which this table or that chair is made? You're going to tell me that's alive? I can't go there—forget it!—because that's just base matter."

People always want to draw the line somewhere. But you see, it's drawing the line at all that's the problem: the idea that at bottom matter is ultimately inert, or inanimate. The word matter, if you listen with your animal ears, is basically the word "mater," or mother. It comes from the same Indo-European root as does the word "matrix," which is Latin for "womb."

We all carry within us an ancient, ancestral awareness that matter as the womb of all things, that matter is alive through and through. But to speak of matter as inanimate is to think of mother as inanimate, that somehow the female, earthly side of things, is inert, is just an object. If we want to really throw a monkeywrench into the workings of the patriarchy, then we should stop speaking as though matter is in any way, at any depth, inanimate or inert.

Every indigenous, oral culture that we know of—every culture that has managed to sustain itself over the course of many centuries without destroying the land that supports it—simply refuses to draw such a distinction between animate and inanimate matter.

If we speak of matter as essentially inanimate, or inert, we establish the need for a graded hierarchy of beings: stones have no agency or experience whatsoever; bacteria have a minimal degree of life; plants have a bit more life, with a rudimentary degree of sensitivity; "lower" animals are more sentient, yet still stuck in their instincts; "higher" animals are more aware; while humans alone are really awake and intelligent. In this manner we continually isolate human awareness above, and apart from, the sensuous world. If, however, we assume that matter is animate from the get-go, then hierarchies vanish, and we are left with a diversely differentiated field of animate beings, each of which has its gifts relative to the others. And we find ourselves not above, but in the very midst of this web, our own sentience part and parcel of the sensuous landscape.

Our own artifacts—our homes, office buildings, automobiles, computers—are made of living materials: why should they not be alive themselves? But sometimes it's hard—at least for me—to feel the spontaneous life in those things have that have been manufactured by us humans. In certain artifacts, particularly the mass-produced ones, it's so hard to make contact with the unique life of that presence. But often one can find that life pulsing, most readily, in the materials of which that object is made. In the wood of the telephone pole, which was once standing in a forest, in the clay bricks of the apartment building, even in the smooth metal alloy of the car door that you lean against—there, in those metals originally mined from the bones of the breathing earth, one can still feel the presence of patterns that are earth-born, and that still carry something of that wider life. But if I look at the car just as a Ford Taurus, what I see is not something that is born, but something that is made. And there is surely an important distinction between the born and the made. But even with that distinction, the made things are still made from matter, from the flesh of a living cosmos.

DJ: Back to my earlier question: how would you convince a skeptic that a river, or a mountain, is alive?

DA: I would simply invite the skeptic to try speaking this way, and see what it does to his senses, see if it makes his eyes and his ears come awake, so that he starts experiencing the sensuous world around him much more deeply. See if it makes his skin wake up, so he notices the caress of the wind on his arms and face, and begins feeling the wildness and of being alive much more intensely.

Actually, Derrick, I'm not interested in convincing anyone that this is the truth in some objective, literal sense. Because it seems to me that the objective, literal view of the world is part of the problem. I'm not trying to get people to just replace one view of what is literally the case with another view of what is absolutely literally true. No.

I know, however, that we cannot change the way we live, the way we interact with the world, without changing the way we speak. We currently speak about the world in a very goofy way that holds us apart from it, and makes us feel like we're outside, and hence able to control it, master it, manipulate it. There are other ways of speaking that hold us in a very different relation to the world. I don't think that any of these ways of speaking are "true" in some utterly objective sense. I think they're all just different strategies for speaking, different ways of wielding our words. And one strategy, it seems to me, leads us into a much finer, fuller, more reciprocal way of living with the world around us. Hence in that sense I think it is much more true. But here I'm thinking of truth no longer as a measure of the match, or fit, between my representations and the way the world actually is. I'm suggesting that truth is something entirely different, that language is not at all about representations—that language doesn't represent the world from outside, but rather that our language is itself a part of the world, that it bubbles forth in the midst of the world. Hence it can't represent things; it is a way of relating to things… Truth, then, is not a match between my representations and the way things are. Truth is a right relationship between me and the world around me. Truth is an index, if you will, of the quality of relationship that a particular culture has with the land that it inhabits. If the land is ailing, or is dying, as a result of the lousy way that that culture interacts with the rivers and the soils, then I'd say that culture knows very little about truth—regardless of how many supposed facts it has amassed regarding the measurable aspects of its world. As I mentioned earlier, this is a very different notion of truth from the one that holds sway right now within conventional science, which is still trying to figure out the "truth" of "how nature works." It seems to me that a more mature understanding of truth would ask how we can live in right relation with this wetland, so that neither we nor the wetland are ailing. If we're going to study humpback whales, how can we as a human community and a humpback whale community flourish as parts of the same world? I'm not interested in pursuing the questions of: what is a humpback whale? How does it work? What are its mechanisms? To even ask those questions presumes that I am something other than an animal myself—that I am some kind of bodiless mind, a pure spectator of nature, rather than a participant in it.

So there's this problem with much of what we've been talking about. Within our contemporary technologized civilization, it is all too easy to say "that rock is alive, that tree is aware and awake." It's too facile, because it's so simple for people to just translate this into their objectified, literal view of the world, and to believe: oh, so it is literally alive and aware and awake. It feels to me too much like a perpetuation our current way of speaking, which uses language to dominate the world, to say what really is, as opposed to using language to make contact with the world, to invoke, to touch things, and to feel them touching us, to respond to things. At this strange cultural moment in the West, our way of wielding words is even more of a problem than the content of those words. Of course, when we speak of the world around us merely as a conglomeration of objects, that is a problem. But even more of a problem is that when we speak, we speak as though nothing else is listening. We speak as though none of these other beings can hear what's being said, or can be influenced by our speaking.

DJ: As though nothing else is listening...

DA: Yes. Not in the sense that the birds or the trees could understand the dictionary definitions of our words. I don't think that the creatures around here—the coyotes and the ravens and the magpies—know the denotative meanings of the words I say, but I suspect they can hear the tonality in our speaking. They feel the rhythm in our words. They can hear the music and the melody in our conversation. And in that sense some of the meaning comes across. Yet we speak as though nothing else hears, as though we needn't take care how we speak of these other beings. We like to assume that language is a purely human property, our exclusive possession, and that everything else is basically mute.

But what I'm trying to suggest is that those of us who work for a tikkun, we who work to heal or mend the rift between humankind and the more-than-human earth, oughta pay more attention to how we speak, we oughta be way more mindful about how we wield our words. If you already know that you're entirely inside this wild world, if you've already entered, now and then, into a deeply felt reciprocity with another species, or have tasted a profound kinship and solidarity with the living land around you, still: how do you find the right way to speak from within that? It is not easy, today, to find a way of speaking that does not violate that experience, that does not tear you out of that world. It's real hard to flow your phrases in a manner that invokes and allows that living world to become fully present not just for yourself but for those around you. Our civilization is masterful at twisting even our richest words to make them into slogans for a commodity-based reality. Our language and our habits of speech have coevolved with a violent relation to the world for so many generations, for so many centuries, and one does not step out of them very easily.

Given the power of this crazed culture to co-opt even the best of our terms, I think that even more important than the content of what we say is the style of our saying, the form of our speaking, the rhythm of our rap. Somehow the music and the texture of our speaking has to carry the meaning, has be appropriate to the meaning at every point. Our deepest intent makes itself felt in the cadence, in the rhythm and the melody of our discourse. If we are not, in fact, disembodied minds hovering outside the world, but are sensitive and sentient animals, bodily beings palpably immersed in the breathing body of the world, then language is first and foremost an expressive thing, the patterned sounds by which our body calls to other bodies—whether to the moon, or to the geese honking overhead, or to another person. Its really a kind of singing. Even the most high-falutin and abstract discourse is still a kind of song, a way of singing the world. It may be a really lousy song—a song that's awfully insulting to many of the beings that hear it, one which grates on the ears of owls and makes the coyotes wince—but its still a song. And those of us who are working to transform things, we're trying to change the tune, to shift a few of the patterns within the language.

If we really wish to open our senses back up to the wonder and subtlety of the earth around us, we all have to be poets. I don't mean we should write poems, for poetry anthologies—no: rather, that our everyday speaking has to be poetic, has to touch people bodily as well as mentally. We have to notice the music in our speaking, and take care that the music has a bit of beauty to it, so that we're not just talking as disembodied minds to other abstract minds but as sensuous and sentient creatures addressing other sensuous bodies, so that our bodies are stirred, and are brought into the conversation, and so that the other animals are not shut out either. We feel their presence nearby, and so we take care not to violate our solidarity with the other animals, and with the animate earth.

DJ: When I write, I don't want anyone to say, "What a great idea." I want them to burst out sobbing, or to become agitated: to have a bodily response. Ultimately of course I want them to bring down civilization.

DA: Uh-huh. When I write, I sometimes feel I'm in service to the life of the language itself. Maybe I write to rejuvenate that life, to open it back on to the wider life of the land, so it can draw sustenance there. I'm working to return meaning to the more-than-human terrain, which is where all our words are rooted in the first place. I guess I really don't think language is a particularly human thing at all—seems to me it's a power of the earth, in which we happen to participate.

So I guess for me, then, the question is not really: "Is the world alive?" but rather "How is it alive? How does that life hit us? How can we give voice to that life, or let it sing through us?"

DJ: If all traditional, indigenous cultures speak of the world as animate and alive, and if, as you've suggested, our own most immediate and spontaneous experience of the world is inherently animistic, disclosing a nature that is all alive, awake, and aware—then how did we ever lose this experience? How did civilized humankind lose this participatory sense of kinship and reciprocity with a living world? How did we tear ourselves out of the world?

DA: Hmmm... Lots of factors. Settlement. The development of large-scale agriculture. New technologies. But I believe it had a great deal to do with one of the oldest and most powerful of our technologies: writing. And, in particular, the alphabet.

But in order to understand why, you have to recognize that the animistic experience is not just a sense that everything is alive, but also that everything speaks, that everything, at least potentially, is expressive. The evidence suggests this is ground zero for the human organism, an experience common to all our ancestors. For most of us today, it seems an extraordinary and unusual experience, but in fact it could not be more ordinary and more normal. The baseline human way of encountering the world and the things around us is to sense that they are also encountering us, and that they are experiencing each other, and to sense as well that the things are speaking to one another, and to us at times—not in words, but in the rustle of the leaves...

DJ: ...which are quite possibly tree words. It hit me about a year ago that there is no difference between us speaking and trees speaking. We both use the wind, or maybe the wind uses us. The wind going over the vocal cords and the wind going over the leaves.

DA: Sure. Language is just the wind blowing through us.

DJ: I took us down a side alley. You were saying…

DA: That everything speaks. The howl of a wolf, the rhythms of cricketsong, but also the splashing speech of waves on the beach. And of course, as you suggest, the wind in the willows. To indigenous people, there are many different kinds of speech. Many manifold ways of pouring meaning into the world. But if that is our ordinary normal human way of experiencing the world, how could we ever have lost it? How could we ever have broken out of that living animate expressive field into this basically mute world that we seem to experience today, where the sun and moon no longer draw salutations from us, but just arc blindly across the sky in mechanical trajectories, and we no longer think that we have to get up just before dawn in order to pray the sun up out of the ground? How did that happen?

I think one of the factors that has been too easily overlooked until now is the amazing influence of writing. All of the genuinely animistic cultures that we know of—whether we talk of the Koyukon people of Alaska or the Hopi of the southwest desert, Lakota of the plains or the Huaorani of the Amazon Basin, whether we think of the Ogoni of Nigeria, or the Sami of Scandinavia, or the Pintupi and Pitjantjarra of the Australia—all of these cultures, these peoples who know that everything is at least potentially alive and indeed that everything speaks—these are all oral cultures, cultures that have developed and flourished in the absence of any formalized writing system (in the absence, that is, of any formal set of written signs that was coupled to their spoken language).

Animistic cultures are oral cultures, cultures without any formal systems of writing. And so we should wonder: what is it that writing does to our animistic experience of the world?

And here's what I would say: Writing is itself a form of animism, a kind of magic. The fact is that writing makes use of the same animistic proclivity that led our oral ancestors to experience the leaves as alive, the branches as gesturing to us. To begin to read is to enter into an intense sensorial participation with the letters on the page. I focus my eyes so intently on those letters that the letters themselves begin to speak to me. Suddenly, I see what "it says." I open a book and gaze down at a page, and straightaway it speaks to me. This is animism! It's another form of that sensorial participation that led our indigenous ancestors to listen to the speech of trees and rivers.

So if the question we ask is: "How did we ever lose our animistic experience of things?" the answer is that we never really lost it! We can't lose it: we are animistic by nature, since indeed we are animals ourselves. If we no longer seem to engage animistically, in the life of the wind, and the forest, and the lizards slithering over the rocks, if we're no longer participating with the life of the rocks themselves, it's because we've transferred our own animistic engagement to something else. We can't get rid of the magic; we're made of it! If we're no longer experiencing the sensuous world around us a field of animate, expressive presences, it must be that something else has taken on that magic for us, that fascination.

The primary shift, I'd suggest, was when we began participating so intensely with our own written signs that the signs themselves began to speak to us. That's really what reading is. We come down in the morning, we open the newspaper, and we focus our eyes on these little bits of ink on the page, and we hear voices! We feel ourselves addressed, spoken to! We see visions, of events unfolding in other places! This is not very different from an old Hopi elder who walks outside the pueblo, and finds his attention drawn to a large rock at the edge of the mesa: he focuses his eyes on a shadowed part of that rock and suddenly hears himself addressed by the rock! Or a Kayapo woman who steps into the rainforest, notices a spider weaving its web, and when focusing her eyes on that web suddenly hears the spider speaking to her. "Superstition," we call it. But we do the same thing with our own scratches and scripts! To focus our eyes on the inert letters on the page, and abruptly to hear a flood of speech, of words and ideas that are not your own, is an intensely concentrated form of animism, no less outrageous than a storytelling stone, or a talking spider... The difference is that now it is only our own scratches, our own marks and signs, that now speak to us. We have entered into a deeply animistic participation with our own signs, a concentrated interaction that has short-circuited the more spontaneous participation between our senses and the sensuous surroundings. Written signs have usurped the expressive power that once resided in the whole of the sensuous landscape: what we do now with the scratches on the page, our oral ancestors did with aspen leaves and spider webs, the tracks of deer and elk, with the cycling moon and the gathering clouds.

Our own writing, our own signs have tremendous power over us. It's certainly not by coincidence that the word "spell" has this double meaning: to arrange the letters of a word in the correct order, or to cast a magic spell—'cause to learn to read and write with this new technology was indeed to learn a new magic, to enter into a profound new world, to cast a kind of spell upon our own senses. I think we've all been in the grip of that spell—the spell, we might say, of spelling—and of all the other technologies that have been spawned by the alphabet, made possible by this new distance from the rest of the living landscape that opens when we practice this magic with our own creations, with our own signs. Our own written signs now speak so powerfully that they have effectively eclipsed all of the other forms of participation in which we used to engage. And of course it is no longer just our written signs, but our TV screens and our computers and our cars, and indeed all of our fancy technologies. The alphabet is really the mother of all our Western technologies. We first needed to enter into the spell of the alphabet before we could fall into this fever of technological invention.

I don't mean to be getting down on technology, only to say that many of these very complex technologies (not tools like the hammer and the wheel and the shovel, but these technologies—like the television and the computer—that you can't put down when your finished with them, since once you engage them they restructure the whole of your awareness) these could only have emerged from the alphabetic mindset. And shucks, I don't mean to be demeaning the alphabet here—I'm a writer, after all—I'm not saying that the alphabet is something bad, not at all. What I'm trying to say is that the alphabet is magic—that it is a very powerful magic, and that like all magics it must be used with real care, and that when we just take it for granted, when we don't notice its potency, then we tend to fall under its spell.

So while our indigenous ancestors dialogue richly with the surrounding field of nature, consulting with the other animals and the earthly elements as they go about their lives, the emergence of writing—and particularly alphabetic writing—made it possible for us to begin to dialogue solely with our own signs in isolation from the rest of nature. By shortcircuiting the ancestral reciprocity between our sensing bodies and the sensuous flesh of the world, the new participation with our own written signs enabled human language to close in on itself, enabled language to begin to seem like our own possession, and not something born of our encounter with other speaking critters—born of singing with birds, born of hunters uttering the cries of certain animals in order to draw them close, and of responding to the speech of thunder and the babbling streams.

We no longer notice that language is something taught to us by the sounds and gestures of the other animals, and by the roar of the wind as it pours through the trees. Suddenly language seems a purely human power—since it's now something we practice in relation to our own signs, a strictly human interaction with our own scratches and scripts, and in which nothing but the human needs to play any role. And so the rest of the landscape gradually loses its voice; it begins to fall mute. And to seem of much less consequence.

We no longer need to interact with the animate, expressive landscape in order to think clearly. I now look out at nature from within my privileged interior sphere of mental subjectivity and creativity, but this subjectivity and creativity is not shared by the coyotes or the swallows or the salmon. They now seem to inhabit another world—an objective, purely exterior world.

They just do their own thing automatically. All the creativity, all the imagi-nation—for so many of us today these are purely human traits. The mind, we think, is a purely human thing, and it resides inside our individual skulls. You have your mind, and I have my mind; we have this sense that it is some-thing that is ours. We own it.

DJ: Why can't we engage our own writing and still engage with an animate natural world as well?

DA: It's a good question. The written word doesn't necessitate that we cease participating with everything else: it just makes it possible. It doesn't neces-sitate that the land become superfluous to us, or that we no longer pay at-tention to the more-than-human world. But we no longer need to interact with the land in order to recall all the stories that are held in those valleys, we no longer need to encounter coyotes and dialogue with ravens in order to remember all the knowledge originally carried in the old Coyote tales and Raven tales, because now all that knowledge has been written down, preserved on the page. Once the language is carried in books, it no longer needs to be carried by the land, and we no longer need to consult the intel-ligent earth in order to think clearly ourselves. For the first time we no lon-ger need to speak to the mountains and the wind, or to honor the land's life with prayers and propititiations, because all our ancestrally gathered insights are preserved on the page. So, the written word was not a sufficient cause of our forgetting, as we philosophers say, but it was a necessary ingredient in our forgetfulness.

DJ: This reminds me of something John A. Livingston wrote in *The Fallacy of Wildlife Conservation*. He says that once we reduce our input to everything being mediated by humans, we're essentially in an echo chamber, and we begin to hallucinate. We're sensorily deprived, because we're not getting the variety of sensory stimulation we need. His point is that much of our ideology, much of our discourse, is insane, delusional, hallucinations based on the fact that we've put ourselves in solitary confinement.

DA: I think I share a similar intuition, which I might put a little differently. Our senses have coevolved with the whole of the sensuous world, with all these other sentient shapes and forms, all these other styles of life. Our nervous system emerged in reciprocity with all that rich otherness, in relationship and reciprocity with hawks and waves and stormclouds and waterfalls, with an animate, living land that spoke to us in a multiplicity of voices. I mean, human intelligence evolved during the countless millennia when we lived as gatherers and hunters, and hence in a thoroughly animistic context, wherein every phenomenon that we encountered could draw us into relationship.

Yet suddenly we find ourselves cut off from that full range of relationships, born into a world in which none of those other beings are acknowledged as really sentient or aware. We abruptly find ourselves in a world that has been defined as a set of inert or determinate objects, rather than as a community of animate powers with whom one could enter into relationship. A dynamic or living relationship is simply not possible with an object. The only things you can enter into relationship with, the only other sentient beings around, are other humans. Yet the human nervous system still needs the nourishment that it once got from being in reciprocity with all these other beings and entities. And so we turn toward each other, toward our human lovers and friends, in hopes of meeting that need. We turn toward our human lovers demanding a depth and range of otherness that they cannot possibly provide. Another human cannot possibly provide all of the outrageously diverse and vital nourishment that we once got from being in relationship with dragonflies and swallowtails and stones and lichen and wolves. It's just not possible. We used to carry on personal relationships with the sun and the moon and the stars! To try and get all that, now, from another person—from another nervous system shaped so much like our own—continually blows apart our marriages, it explodes so many of our human relationships, because they can't withstand that pressure.

DJ: That reminds me of something I wrote in my book *A Language Older Than Words*: "One of the great losses we endure in this prison of our own making is the collapse of intimacy with others, the rending of community, like tearing and retearing a piece of paper until there only remains the tiniest scrap. To place our needs for intimacy and ecstasy—needs like food, water, acceptance—onto only one species, onto only one person, onto only the area of joined genitalia for only the time of intercourse, is to ask quite a lot of our sex."

DA: Indeed. Our intimate relationships become increasingly brittle. We finally turn toward our lover and say "I really care about you, Darlin', but I'm somehow not quite feeling... met. I'm just not feeling met by you in all the ways I feel that I should be." Of course not! Another person cannot possibly meet us in all those manifold ways that we were once engaged by the breathing world! Even a large bunch of human relationships cannot make up for the loss of all that more-than-human otherness, and it is this that makes all our human communities intensely brittle and violence-prone. I don't think we have a hoot of a chance of healing our societal ills and the manifold injustices we inflict on various parts of the human community, without renewing the wild Eros between ourselves and the sensuous surroundings—without "falling in love outward" (in Robinson Jeffers' wise words) with the living land that enfolds us.

As long as we neglect the rest of nature, as long as we continue to construe the land as little more than a passive background, or backdrop, against which our human projects unfold, we'll continue to close ourselves off from the very sustenance and guidance that our human communities most need in order to thrive and flourish. Truly. As long as we hold ourselves out of relationship with the living land that our community inhabits, we'll be unable to tap the necessary guidance that we need from those forests, from those winds and weather patterns, and from the soil and the supporting ground, from all these other beings, those mountains and rivers, many of whom live at scales much vaster than our own, and so can offer us some real perspective, and gift us all with a sense of humility. We simply need their wild guidance. Every human community is nested within a more-than-human community of beings. And until we notice this, we're going to keep slamming each other in frustration, busting each other up with bullets and with bombs, violating the integrity of other folks within our cities, undermining our own relationships.

Do you really want a healthy and lasting relationship with your sweetheart? Then instill it with a wider affection for the local earth—with an active affection for the local critters, and plants, and elements—and that will hold your relationship and nourish it and feed it and keep you and your lover able to be fluid with each other, since there are so many other beings who witness and contribute to your partnership.

DJ: You've talked eloquently already about not needing to enter into new relationships, but simply noticing and acknowledging the relationships that already exist…

DA: Well we're obviously embedded and entangled in a complex web of relationships, both with our own kind and with many entities very very different from us. How then is it that we don't notice them, don't honor them, don't respect these relationships with all these others who encounter and feed us? It can only be because somehow we're oblivious to that direct, unmediated layer of intimate relationship and carnal exchange that is always going on—because we're oblivious to the bodily level of our existence. It is my body that steadily drinks of the air breathed out by these green and growing plants, and my body that breathes out the carbon dioxide these plants steadily draw upon in order to photosynthesize and flourish. It is my body, my muscled flesh that rests in intimate relationship with the tree-trunk I'm now sitting on. My toes are well acquainted with the life and texture of the soil, from walking barefoot in the garden or wandering through all these arroyos. But we don't live our body's lives anymore. We live a life of abstractions, we live a life of the mental cogitations massively influenced and informed by all of the human-made signs that surround us. We're incessantly reflecting off of our own reflections. We have been taught not to trust our senses, and our direct sensory experience. The senses, which are our most instinctive animal access to the world, our eyes, our ears, our tongue, our nose, all these magic organs that open us directly onto the more-than-human field: we've been taught not to trust any of these powers. We're told that the senses lie, we're taught in school that the senses are deceptive.

What do our senses tell us? I step out at dawn, walk out across the arroyo, and I see with my own eyes the sun rising out of the nearby Sangré de Cristo Mountains, and in the evening I see it sinking down into the distant Jemez Mountains. And then I watch the moon being hatched from the Sangrés, arcing across the sky, and then slip down into the ground far to the west. But at school I'm told, "No, no, no, no, no! The sun is not really moving at all! It's the earth that's moving. Don't trust your senses. The sun is not rising up and setting down. The truth of the matter is that it is the earth that is turning."

Fair enough. But do we really need to disparage our sensory experience in this manner? Surely there is also a truth to our more spontaneous experience of the rising and setting of the sun. I mean, everyone still says that "the sun rises" and "the sun sets," whether they are scientists or janitors, and it's kinda bizarre to simply invalidate this collective experience, as though our bodies have no wisdom of their own. So many indigenous cultures speak of how the sun, after sinking down into the western earth every evening, journeys all night through the ground underfoot on its way toward the east, and how in the course of this journey the sun feeds the deep earth with its fiery life, seeding the depths with the multiple plants that continually sprout from the earth's surface. It's a tale that honors our direct experience. There is a deep truth to the body's spontaneous experience of things, a truth that underlies, and secretly supports, all the more abstract and rational insights that we erect upon it. It's a truth that we ought not to toss aside when we teach the modern, "more sophisticated" cosmology. Rather, we should show how the new view grows out of this older, more primordial experience that has never been lost—that these are like different layers of our encounter with the world, different levels of interpretation. Just as a text has different layers of interpretation, so does the world. And each entails a different kind of awareness.

Nevertheless, ever since Copernicus and Galileo and their grand intuition, we have all learned to distrust our senses. We generally pay far more attention to what we are told by the experts than to what we can learn with our unaided senses. We have split our reasoning minds off from our sensing bodies. Descartes laid out the blueprint for how to do so. The thinking mind is one kind of substance, he said, and the body is another kind of substance: pure matter. And in order to buy into the Copernican worldview, it would seem we had to accept this split, had to hold our thinking selves apart from the sensuous and sensing life of the body. But what great damage that's done—we've forgotten our solidarity with the breathing earth.

After all, we now know that the sun, too, is in motion, and that even the "fixed" stars are rapidly rushing apart from one another—all of the celestial bodies are in motion relative to one another. Hence it seems an arbitrary choice where one chooses to stabilize one's perspective. But since we find ourselves here, on this earth, it perhaps makes just as much sense to consider the breathing earth as the stable center of our world (to recognize the ground underfoot as the very ground of our reality) then to consider the Sun as the unmoving center.

DJ: This reminds me of the Groucho Marx line when he was caught in an obvious lie: "What are you going to believe, me or your own eyes?"

DA: I'm interested in helping folks to think with their senses, once again, to trust their direct experience of the world, to stop buying into this bizarre notion that their senses are deceptive. Of course the senses reveal a world that is ambiguous and open ended, and by looking more closely, or by listening more carefully, we will always discover new things. But if you don't trust the intelligence of your senses, then what is it that you are going to trust? You will have to place all your trust in the experts to tell you what is really going on, because the truth then is always hidden behind the scenes. It is rather like the situation of a church, or a temple, that tells you, "Well, the real truth is not here but is in that heavenly dimension hidden beyond the stars, and only our high priests have access to that unseen realm."

Such is the situation that we're in, today, when we neglect our direct sensory experience of things. I mean, of course it's so difficult to mobilize people on behalf of the vanishing species, or the dwindling rivers, or the ailing life of the land around them! Of course the surrounding earth is only a peripheral concern for most folks! Because the real truth, we have heard, is somewhere else; it is not in this world that our senses experience. Our physicists say that the real truth of things is hidden in the subatomic world. The molecular biologists now say that it is in the ultra-microscopic dimension of DNA base-pairs and gene sequences that the real truth of nature—and of our own life and behavior—resides. The neurobiologists say the real truth of our behavior is to be found in the neuronal structure hidden within the brain.

These are all worlds to which we feel we're beholden, but to which we don't have direct access: one needs very fancy instrumentation, very high-powered microscopes and cyclotrons and such to get at them. And so we take our truth from the experts with the instruments, and we forfeit our own power, our own access to the real. Or perhaps we've heard that the deepest source and truth of things is to be found in the breaking of the initial symmetries in the Big Bang—another dimension which most persons have no way of glimpsing: you need massive orbiting telescopes to gain even a provisional entry to that realm so far beyond the scale of our direct experience. The truth is always hidden somewhere else for a culture that has forsaken the evidence of its own senses.

I mean, hey: all these investigations into other dimensions are very elegant and sometimes even useful, but in our lust for Truth with a capital T we forfeit our responsibility to the scale at which we live, this ambiguous and uncertain world that moves all around us. We hide ourselves from the most outrageous and mysterious truth of all, which is our ongoing immersion in this wild web of relationships—with other persons and other beings—all of whom request our awareness and our humble respect. After three full centuries of science in the West, it should be obvious to all that we humans are one little aspect of one little part of one little facet of the cosmos, and so I can't understand how anyone could think that we could ever figure it out in its totality. The most we can really attain, with humility and humor, is a richer relationship, a deeper reciprocity with the persons, beings, and elements that surround us.

For all our dreams of a final certainty, the only thing we can ultimately be certain of is the world disclosed to us by our direct sensory experience. The sensuous world is always local. It is not, for me, what's going on in China right now. It is this place that I happen to inhabit. This Rio Grande watershed, with these particular critters who like to hang out around these plants who happen to root themselves in these soils. These junipers and ponderosas and pinon pines. And that raven squawking from the telephone wire, and the lizards and horny toads that haunt this terrain, and the coyotes howling out there in the arroyos, and the particular color of these skies, and the reddish tone in these rocks. This is my local universe. This is the primary cosmos for me. The sensuous world is always local, and it is never a merely human world. There is no aspect of the sensuous world that is exclusively human—since even on the eighteenth floor of a city building, I'd still be inhaling air that's been breathed out by the green and growing plants that surround the city; and I'd still be under the influence of gravity, the mysterious draw of my body toward the earth.

DJ: Are we wise enough to remember this?

DA: We don't have to be wise enough. It's more a matter of realizing that the wisdom, or intelligence, was never ours to begin with, because the mind is not ours, it's the earth's. Sure, there is something interior about the mind, but it is not because it's inside us, but rather because we are inside it. Mind is not a human property, it's a quality of the earth. As soon as we begin to loosen up, to allow the life of the things around us, and as soon as we begin to speak accordingly, we'll begin to notice that the awareness that we thought was ours does not in fact belong to us. We're breathing it in and out. Along with all the other animals, the plants, and the drifting clouds, we are immersed in the mind of this living world.

So I don't need to become wise. I need to open up to, and begin to learn from—and begin again to be fed by—these other beings. And I need to notice that each place has its own particular style of awareness. The intelligence of this place, the mind of this land, here in this valley, is quite different from the mind of the Puget Sound, which is quite different from the mind of the eastern forests.

If we just start listening somewhat, something will snap us up, and suddenly we'll be just practicing: we'll be in it. Just discovering once again that we are inside of the world will, I think, be vital, sufficient, strong enough to enable us to work with whatever we must face.

DJ: Many of my environmentalist friends say that as things become increasingly chaotic, they want to make sure that some doors stay open. If Grizzly bears are still alive in fifty years, that door is still open. What I hear you saying is that one of the doors you would like to make sure stays open is the door to the body…

DA: It's not one of the doors. It's the door. If we remain open to our own breathing bodies, and to the imaginative life of our bodily senses, then these open us up to everything else. If that door is closed—as it has been for us mentally because we've closed it off linguistically—then we have no way to orient ourselves in the world. No wonder we are destroying so many eco-systems and so many other species. No wonder we're destroying our communities. Because we're completely out of relation with the one source of grounding and guidance that can make it all make sense. Ethics is not learnable off the page. You can't learn it in a book. You can't learn ethics off a computer screen. Ethics is what we learn, first, as a willful and sensitive body bumping into other sensitive bodies, discovering that you have to make space for them.

So many people have a sense of the world as unreal, as a dream, as something ephemeral. We're all suffering from a confusion of worlds, because we have given far more weight to abstractions—whether the abstract truths propounded by our scientific colleagues or the disembodied certainties propounded by so many new-age spiritual teachings—than we do to the much more ambiguous, difficult, and outrageously wondrous world that we experience face-to-face, here and now, in the flesh. The animate earth around us—this land swept by the wind and pounded by rain—is far more lovely than any heaven we can dream up. But to awaken to this awesome beauty we must give up our spectator perspective, and the illusion of control that it gives us, in order to gaze out at the world from within its own depths. This is, alas, a terrifying move for most overcivilized folks today—because to renounce control is to notice that we are vulnerable: to suffering, to loss, to disease, to death. But also that we are vulnerable to the purest joy. The wild world to which our senses give us access is an inexhaustibly beautiful realm, but it is hardly safe—it is filled with shifting shadows, and is plenty dangerous. I guess that's why everyone seems so terrified to drop the pretense of the view from outside, the God-trick, the odd belief that we can master and manage the earth.

We can't master it—never have, never will. What we can do is participate in the life of this breathing world far more deeply and creatively than we have these last few thousand years.

Vine Deloria

Interview Conducted
By Telephone
7.22.99

Vine Deloria was one of the most important living Native American writers. For more than a quarter century he produced an extraordinarily readable critique of Western culture. Central to Deloria's work was the understanding that, by subduing nature we have become slaves to technology and its underlying belief system. We've given up not only our freedom, but also our relationship with the natural world.

Deloria was born in 1933 on the Pine Ridge Sioux Reservation in South Dakota. His family has straddled white and Indian cultures for many generations. One of his ancestors, the son of a fur trader and a Yankton Sioux headman's daughter, had a vision that his descendants would serve as mediators with the dominant society.

Deloria's father, a South Dakota Episcopal priest, took his young son to the site of the 1890 Wounded Knee massacre and pointed out to him the survivors who still lived on the reservation. Deloria left home at sixteen to go to a college-preparatory school in Connecticut. After graduation, he turned down an acceptance to the University of Colorado and bought a used car with his tuition money. He went on to study geology for two years at the Colorado School of Mines (my own alma mater) before enlisting in the Marine Corps reserve. In 1956 he enrolled in Iowa State University, where he met his future wife, Barbara Jeanne Nystrom.

They moved to Illinois so that Vine could attend a Lutheran seminary in preparation for becoming a minister, like his father. For four years, he studied philosophy and theology by day and earned money as a welder at night. Although he completed his education, he grew increasingly disappointed with "the glaring lack of solutions" the seminary provided.

In 1964, Deloria went to work as the executive director of the National Congress of American Indians, and there he began to see the importance of building a national power base for Indians through grassroots organizing. He soon came to appreciate the need for trained Indian lawyers who could defend tribal sovereignty and treaty rights within the legal system, and in 1967 he enrolled in law school at the University of Colorado.

Deloria maintained his ties to Christianity. He was even elected to the Executive Council of the Episcopal Church. However, he posed a challenge to the religion: "If, as they claim, Christianity is for all people, why not let Indian people worship God after their own conception of Him?" Deloria stopped identifying himself as a Christian, but, when pressed, offered that he was a "Seven Day Absentist."

After receiving his law degree in 1970, Deloria wrote many books and lectured at colleges all over the country. In both his writing and his speaking, he never shied away from direct assaults on injustice. It was as though he didn't have time or patience for the polite indirectness that characterizes so much political dialogue today. His book titles alone testify to this directness: *Red Earth, White Lies* (Fulcrum Books) won the 1996 Nonfiction Book of the Year Award from the Colorado Center for the Book; *Custer Died for Your Sins* (University of Oklahoma Press) brought accounts of the trail of broken treaties up to date; and *God Is Red* (Fulcrum Books) remains one of the best books written on Native American spirituality.

Deloria died in 2006.

DJ: What would you say is the fundamental difference between Western and indigenous ways of life?

VD: I think the primary thing is that Indians experience and relate to a living universe, whereas Western philosophy, especially science, reduces things to objects, whether they're alive or not.

The implications are immense. If you see the world around you as made up of objects for you to manipulate and exploit, it is inevitable that you will destroy the world by attempting to control it. Perceiving the world as lifeless also robs you of the richness, beauty, and wisdom of participating in the larger pattern of life.

In order to maintain the fiction that the world is dead and that those who believe it is alive are succumbing to primitive superstition, scientists, and more broadly scientific explanation, have to reject any nuance of interpretation of activities in the natural world that imply natural sentience, or an ability to communicate back and forth between humans and nonhumans, or, leaving humans out of the picture, between nonhumans.

Science insists, at a great price in understanding, that the observer be as detached as possible from the event he or she is observing. I would contrast that with traditional indigenous peoples, who know that humans must participate in events. They must attempt to determine the spiritual activity that supports or undergirds these physical activities, rather than determining how they can use those events for their material advantage.

Ironically, and it's ironic because science prides itself on being a search for knowledge, this way of relating to the world allows Indians to gain information from birds, animals, rivers, and mountains which is inaccessible to modern scientists. Even more ironically, it allows Indians a degree of insight that Westerners will never achieve through science. Take meteorology. We know that seeding clouds with certain chemicals can bring rain. This method of dealing with natural forces is wholly mechanical and is in essence forcing nature to do our bidding. Yet Indians achieved the same goal of affecting the weather by conducting ceremonies to ask the spirits for rain. Science cannot affect winds, clouds, and storms except in very specific and limited ways, but Indians could affect all of these in a diametrically opposed manner, similar to the difference between attempting to get a slave to do something, and asking a friend for help.

Acting in concert with friendly thunder and storm spirits was commonplace among many Indian tribes. The knowledge that all things are related was often gained and imparted through religious rituals, but it was also a methodology that informed daily lives. Attuned to their environment, Indians could also find food, locate trails, protect themselves from inclement weather, and anticipate events using their understanding of how all these different entities relate to each other.

DJ: I've read that after the Sand Creek Massacre, two Arapahoe women and their children were huddling in a cave, and a wolf came up to them. It slept with them to keep them warm, and guided them by day, keeping them safe from the cavalry. When they were hungry it led them to buffalo kills. Finally it took them to another Arapahoe camp, and after receiving a meal in thanks, disappeared.

VD: This knowledge isn't unique to American Indians. It is available to anyone who lives primarily in the natural world, is reasonably intelligent, and who gives other life forms respect for their intelligence and power of thought.

On the other hand, those who have a scientific perception of the world as lifeless and who objectify others are committing to a totally materialistic universe.

The central idea of science as it has been developed and applied is to get machines or nature to do the work human beings don't want to do. And in a capitalist system, whoever supplies money for scientific research becomes the owner of the technology. This means that as it's applied, science is really never for the good of humankind, but instead for the financial elite or the military, and that each field of science is dominated by biased authorities who have found institutional favor.

But it goes deeper than this. It is not only other living beings who are being objectified and dominated; experiences, beliefs, and knowledge harden and become lifeless, too. People who are educated should be bringing wisdom to their communities and making it available to others so that the lives they are leading make sense. Instead, problem solving, philosophy, and religion have become mystified and meaningless. People purchase food grown by others, settle their conflicts in courts and legislatures and not by informal mutually-agreed-upon solutions, and wage extended and terrible wars over abstract principles instead of enacting small battles over the right to occupy land for hunting and fishing. Beliefs about the world are processed into philosophical systems that articulate rational principles rather than emphasizing anecdotal experiences, and religion is reduced to creeds, dogmas, and doctrines.

The people who maintain the structures of science, religion, and politics have one thing in common that they don't share with the rest of society. They are responsible for creating a technical language, incomprehensible to the rest of us, whereby we cede to them our right and responsibility to think. They in turn formulate a beautiful set of lies that lull us to sleep and allow us to forget about our troubles, eventually depriving us of all rights, including, increasingly, the right to live in a livable world.

People often look to scientists for reliable explanations about the world instead of trusting their own experience and senses. These scientists, after passing through universities and colleges, defer to dogma and doctrine to determine what truths will be admitted into the Scientific canon. This has gotten to the point where almost anything anyone with a Ph.D. says is accepted as truth, and almost any press release that reads, "Science says this" or "Science says that" is taken as gospel, rather than as someone's opinion.

One example of this is the notion that Indians came to the Americas across the Bering Strait. We've seen reports coming out of the Monte Verde digs that say, "We verified human occupation at 12,500 years in Chile." Immediately the newspapers say this proves there were waves of people traveling to and fro across the Bering Strait. But it doesn't prove anything. Assuming that radiocarbon dating is anywhere near accurate, and assuming the researchers didn't throw out as "noise" any dates they didn't agree with, all this shows is that a group of people lived there 12,500 years ago.

DJ: You view the theory that human beings came to be in North and South America by crossing the Bering Strait as an article of faith, rather than as proven fact.

VD: Well, I've yet to see any even remotely convincing evidence of it. It's a longstanding doctrinal belief that anthropology imposed on itself, and that really started with the old Spanish Clerics who were trying to identify Indians as either survivors of Noah's flood or part of the lost tribes of Israel.

DJ: I'm not sure how the issue of deep origins is important.

VD: It's vitally important, for a couple of reasons. The first is that if the clerics could convince themselves Indians were descendants of Ham, or some tribes of Israel who had lost their way, they could further rationalize their enslavement of Indians based on the Indians' ancient sinfulness, or their falling away from the one true path of Judeo-Christian righteousness. And it reveals something deeper, that lasts until today, which is a steadfast refusal to see the world any way other than through Eurocentric eyes. Indians cannot simply be Indians. They have to come from somewhere else.

That leads to the second reason this question of origins is so important. Five centuries of violence perpetrated on Indians and on their land by Westerners lies uneasily on the conscience, which leads, if justification isn't available, to considerable residual guilt. Consequently a couple of beliefs have arisen to explain away this history. People want to believe that the Western Hemisphere, and particularly North America, was vacant, unexploited, fertile land waiting to be put under cultivation according to God's holy dictates. The hemisphere thus belonged to whoever was able to rescue it from its wilderness state. Of course we see the same thing today in the Amazon and elsewhere.

Coupled with this belief is the idea that American Indians were not original inhabitants but relative latecomers who had barely unpacked when Columbus came knocking on the door. If Indians arrived only shortly before, they had no real claim to the land, and could be swept away with impunity. Even today I hear some non-Indians say, "Well, aren't we all immigrants from somewhere?" The short answer is, No. And by making us immigrants to North America they are able to deny the fact that this is our continent.

Another way I've seen the Bering Strait theory used to assuage Western guilt is by allowing Westerners to pretend Indians are just as destructive as Westerners. I'm sure you've heard of the "Pleistocene overkill" hypothesis, which basically states, with no real evidence, that as soon as Indians got over here they started killing everything in sight. The theory was first proposed some fifty years ago by Carl Sauer. It was shot down almost immediately by Loren C. Eiseley, who raised numerous concerns that have never been satisfactorily resolved, such as the fact that not only megafauna disappeared at the time, but also birds, mollusks, and frogs, which of course could simply not have been hunted to extinction, and the fact that there is no evidence, comparing modern examples of tribal hunting groups with possible ancient techniques, for any group to exterminate or even significantly affect an animal population unless the hunters and prey are restricted to a very small area.

The theory remained dead in the water until it was revived in the 1960s by a book called *Pleistocene Extinctions*. Since that time, as the destruction of the natural world has become ever more difficult to ignore, and as Europeans have needed ever stronger salves for their consciences, the theory has risen up again full force. Although there is still no real evidence to support it, its ideological function—if the Indians were destructive, too, then it must be part of human nature, and not just the result of a destructive way of living and a destructive way of perceiving the world—is important enough to justify its admission into the scientific canon.

I discuss this extensively in my book *Red Earth, White Lies*. That book has been out for years now, and there's not yet been a single scientist or scholar or anthropologist who has provided me or a lot of other people with any real evidence that Indians crossed the Bering Strait, or that they caused a massive wave of extinctions on their "arrival."

DJ: A couple of years ago I read a book that really infuriated me. It was called *Demonic Males*, and it purported to show that rape was "normal" for humans. The authors discussed human cultures (indigenous and non-indigenous) in which rape has existed, ignoring the many cultures in which rape was—beyond nonexistent—inconceivable until the members of these cultures were taught by example what it means to be civilized. They went on to say that there has never been a human culture in which women have not been abused, and there's never been a peaceful human culture. To claim this they had to ignore, even within their own fields, mountains of unimpeachable evidence. This book was very popular, and I was astounded that they were able to ignore all this obvious evidence in such a bald-faced way.

VD: You see that all over. There's a current theory that Indians are responsible for the destruction of the buffalo. They say Indian winter encampments deprived the buffalo of food, and so the population plummeted.

DJ: How could they say this?

VD: Simple. By ignoring all evidence that doesn't support their thesis. This happens all the time. In this case they simply ignore every newspaper in the 1870s reporting every time a trainload of buffalo hides went out. In the Dodge City area alone hunters killed three million buffalo in three years. Yet these guys are becoming famous by saying it was the Indians who did it.

DJ: How did the Indians become inhabitants of this continent? What do the Indians say?

VD: That's a question not asked often enough, and points out another problem with the Western scientific tradition. Somehow it is presumed that science, and thus Europeans, know better how Indians got here, or how they lived prior to Columbus, than the Indians themselves. That attitude is at best patronizing. Instead of doing all these studies, why don't they just ask the Indians? And when they do ask, why don't they take the answers seriously?

As to what Indians say about their origins, tribal traditions vary considerably. Many tribes begin their story at a certain location and describe their migrations. When you ask where they came from, they say, "We don't know, it was a long time ago." Others say they came from another continent by boat. Of course archaeologists generally refuse to believe them because they think ancient peoples didn't know about boats, which is absurd.

A number of tribes say they were created here and their stories generally describe the process of creation not unlike other non-Indian stories. I like the Pacific Northwest ideas that there was a world in which the physical was not dominant, and you could change your shape and experience what it was like to be an animal, plant, or bird. Then that world changed and some people were caught in different shapes and became animals and so on. This may sound like Neo-Platonism, but it has much to recommend it.

A few tribes say they came into this world from another world that had portals, which were physical points that were tangent to our world. The best example I have been given is that you would walk into a cave or tunnel, walk until it was completely dark. After a while you would find a tiny light ahead of you. As you kept moving toward it, it would grow bigger, gradually revealing itself as an entrance. Upon leaving the cave you would find you were in a completely new world.

Much of the knowledge is esoteric, revealed in ceremonial settings and dependent on views of time, space, matter, and cosmic purpose that are heretical from the Western perspective. Because of this they are generally dismissed out of hand as superstitious campfire stories that have no connection to physical reality.

DJ: You've cited Feyerabend as saying that "whatever fails to fit into the established category system or is said to be incompatible with this system is either viewed as something quite horrifying, or, more frequently, simply declared to be non-existent."

VD: That's standard scientific procedure. You use carbon dating, and you throw out the dates you don't agree with. Then you turn to the dates that "make sense," and you say, "See, this is proven." It's nonsense.

We have to ask ourselves precisely what it is that scientists do. They gather data from what appear to be similar entities and circumstances, and after much meditation, announce the discovery of "laws" that, with some notable exceptions we rarely hear about, describe the universe. Sometimes the anomalies are acknowledged, and become the basis for fruitful discussion. But more often they're simply swept under the rug. That the increasingly sophisticated scientific measuring instruments continue to negate the previously-agreed-upon canon does not seem to bother the great majority of scientists, and for that matter the rest of us, who should care far more than we do. Nor does it bother most of us that science imposes highly restricted patterns upon the natural world, thereby limiting its potential for response. Scientists—and once again more broadly all of us—are not asking complete questions of nature, and in many cases are asking irrelevant ones.

DJ: Is science redeemable, or does it need to be chucked wholesale?

VD: In the long run, much of Western science has to go, all of Western religion should go, and if we're in any way successful in ridding ourselves of these burdens, we'll find we can fundamentally change government so it will function more sensibly, and enable us to solve our problems. But in the short term I think science needs two things. One is that various fields alleging to be scientific should devote considerable time to a restatement of principles, and examine what they really can prove, and what is speculation. And they should make that clear. Second is that standards of evidence need to be erected. There's got to be some discipline. And some courage. I had a lot of anthropologists call me up and apologize for that *Newsweek* cover on the peopling of America. They told me, "I'm furious. That's a big pack of lies." I responded, "I didn't write the article. Why don't you write to *Newsweek*?" And then they'd say, "I just wanted to let you know I'm in sympathy with you." Well, that doesn't do anybody any good.

DJ: Why do you think they wouldn't write to *Newsweek*?

VD: They're worried about their status. I know people who have brilliant articles written along the lines of what I did in *Red Earth*, and they won't publish them, because they're afraid the profession would laugh at them. Well, that doesn't mean you don't speak out when you have something important to say.

DJ: A friend of mine once said she thought science was an even better means of social control than Christianity, because if you don't believe in Christianity you're simply doomed to hell after you die, but if you don't believe in science you must be stupid.

VD: Well, I think science replaced Christianity as the acceptable religion of our society. You see that whenever someone goes to court to try to establish or protect religious rights. If science and religion come into conflict, religion always loses. That's true from Christian fundamentalists through Indians through Orthodox Jews: anybody who has a religious view that would not be acceptable to a small clique in science, that's the end of it.

DJ: Let's return to another way of being, and of perceiving the world.

VD: I would say an alternative to forcing nature to tell us its secrets is that of observing nature and adjusting to its larger rhythms. This is the alternative practiced by so many other cultural traditions. The practice scares a lot of people within the dominant tradition because much of the information comes from "suspect" sources that are be tinged with emotion and mysticism.

I'll give an example from American Indian knowledge. Many centuries ago the Senecas had a revelation. Three sisters appeared and informed them they wished to establish a relationship with the people, with the "two-leggeds." In return for the performance of certain ceremonies that helped the sisters to thrive, they would become plants and feed the people. The three sisters became beans, corn, and squash. The lands of the Seneca were never exhausted because these plants, in addition to sharing a spiritual relationship as sisters, were also a sophisticated natural nitrogen cycle that kept the land fertile and productive.

DJ: That leads to a question I've always pondered. You always hear about these South American tribes who process some poisonous plant by boiling it three times and skimming off the froth. After they complete an extremely complex process, they end up with medicine. Historically I've always heard that these processes were gained through trial and error, which seemed to me ludicrous because sometimes the original plant is deadly poison. But you've written that "getting information from birds and animals regarding plants is an absurdly self-evident proposition for American Indians."

VD: Oh yeah. There are lots of Indian stories where a plant will appear in a dream and speak to them, or someone is walking through the forest and suddenly a plant will say, "I'm edible, but you've got to do these various things to use me correctly."

When I was much younger I was very interested in getting Indian plant knowledge to scientists for them to take a look at it. But they wanted to take the plant and break it down to see what its constituents were. I said, "No, no, that's not the way the medicine men use it. They use it whole, and then they get the natural product out of it. Make a tea, or a poultice, but don't start chemically disassembling it, because it's the unity of the plant that cures, not any one ingredient."

DJ: That seems to get at the heart of the fundamental difference between Western and indigenous cultures, having to do with seeing the plant as a whole as it literally speaks to you, versus "putting nature on the rack and extracting her secrets from her," as Francis Bacon said.

VD: That's true, but what many scientists will not admit is that most of the greatest scientists dabbled considerably in spiritual matters and were aware that mysticism and intuitive unusual experiences provided most of the information and knowledge they had. This includes even Descartes, who was a major materialist famous for articulating the mind/body, human/nature split; he said that an angel came and explained things to him. There are so many of them: Heisenberg, Einstein, Bohr, the guy who discovered the benzene ring. There is stuff written all over about how they had these sudden insights. What's the difference between one of those guys having a sudden insight and the Indian doing a ceremony in which the spirit of the plant says, "Do this"?

DJ: I would say one difference lies in cultural context, leading to differences in how the information will be perceived, and then used.

VD: That's true. To go back to the story of the three sisters, the white man later came and planted only corn and wheat, and soon exhausted the soil. So after conducting many experiments, scientists "discovered" the nitrogen cycle and produced tons of chemical fertilizers to replace the natural nitrogen. But now we learn that these chemicals have unpleasant side effects that may be even worse on us than they are on the soil.

My point of this whole three sisters story is that for every scientific "discovery," there exists one or more alternative ways of understanding natural processes. But we can't know what these alternatives are until we begin to observe nature and listen to its rhythms, absolutely rejecting the idea of forcing nature to tell us about itself.

DJ: I've long heard of ceremonies where Indians sing to the corn. How does that help? What does the person who sings give to the plant?

VD: We're giving energy and respect to the plant. It's kind of like when you're trying to teach your kid how to play basketball, and even though he can't hit the hoop, as he shoots higher you say, "Hey, that was really a good one." And so what you're telling the plant, is, "Gee, we not only respect and appreciate you, but we make a fuss over the fact that you are growing better than you would have." It's straight transfer of energy.

DJ: Everybody likes to get strokes.

VD: That's right.

It's hard for me to understand why Western peoples believe they are so clever. Any damn fool can treat a living thing as if it were a machine and force it to perform certain functions. All that's required is sufficient application of force. But the result of force is slavery, both for the victim and the wielder.

DJ: You cite the Osage chief Big Soldier, "I see and admire your manner of living… In short you can do almost what you choose. You whites possess the power of subduing almost every animal to your use. You are surrounded by slaves. Every thing about you is in chains and you are slaves yourselves. I fear that if I should exchange my pursuits for yours, I too should become a slave."

VD: That's the best thing any Indian ever said, and I think it applies straight across the board. I teach at the University of Colorado, and so many of the students are convinced that they are free because they act just like each other. They all do the same things. They think alike. They're almost like a herd, or like they've all been cloned. They're enslaved to a certain way of life. Once you've traded away spiritual insight for material comfort, it is extremely difficult to ever get back to any sense of authenticity. You see these poor kids going out hiking in the mountains, trying to commune with nature, but you can't commune with nature just taking a walk. You have to actually live it. And these young people have no way of critiquing the society that is enslaving them, because the only experiences they're really going to have are the occasional weekend hikes. They may see beautiful vistas, and they may get a sense of this other aesthetic, but they're not going to get to the metaphysical sense of who they really are.

In this sense, Appalachian whites, rural blacks, and Scandinavian farmers are all so much closer to the natural world because they live in it twenty-four hours a day. These groups may not see themselves as a single group, yet they are all connected by their oppression by industrialization, by the destruction of the land bases on which their lives depend, and by their connection to the natural world that teaches them who they are. What's important is not just an abstract connection to an abstract earth, but instead the relationship you have with a particular tree or a particular mountain.

DJ: How does being in one place for a long time teach you who you are?

VD: As you live in one place, it becomes so familiar to you that you begin to tear down the defenses you've erected in order to survive in industrial civilization, and you begin to fall into the rhythm of the land. So the first thing is that you begin to have a different sense of the natural. You spontaneously don't have to think of abstract things. You think more in terms of how the land itself looks, and what it's telling you. I would think many people in Appalachia have this sense already developed. There've been families there now for what, five, six generations? I would think the ones who live back in the hills have really begun to adjust themselves to the land. Note, and this is very important, that I'm talking about them adjusting to the land, and not the other way around: forcing the land to adjust to them. So if you look at them, and if you talk to them, they don't have all the abstract concerns that all the so-called civilized people have.

DJ: What sort of abstract concerns are you talking about?

VD: This sense of always wondering who you are. Always trying to prove yourself, to prove to yourself that you are good enough, strong enough, rich enough, good looking enough. Whatever. I can see how that could be a good survival technique in New York City, but if you're not always having your identity called into question, you don't need to worry about those things. You can simply become your own self, can become what in the old days would have been called a character. Sometimes I still read in an obituary that this old man or this old woman did all these incredible things, and I have to ask myself how they did so much of substance.

DJ: What's the difference between a "character," as you are using the word, and an entrepreneur, say?

VD: I would say that the actions of the entrepreneur are always in terms of the economic machine, to gain some kind of security, even if the person is not greedy like Bill Gates. Or even if we extend this a little bit, I would see a world of difference between a character whose actions emerge spontaneously out of who they are because they've lived in a certain place for a long time, and someone whose actions—striving to own a new boutique, to become a scuba diver, an attorney, or a dress designer—emerge from a desperate search to define who they are.

If you live in one place you have ongoing experiential context, which is the land. If you don't, your experiences are limited to little soundbites. And if you really want to feel alive, you've got to grab sound bite after sound bite. Thus you've got the MTVs, the discos, the Bolder Boulder race where everybody runs for seven miles, and then you've got to maintain that experiential high for yourself. It's a treadmill.

What I'm really getting at is that because of the industrial machine, no one really has an identity. So you have to keep giving them numbers, and you have to keep making plans for them. If you live out in the rural areas, you quickly learn that people and animals and the land itself are all judged on character, how they respond to each other, to the land, the seasons, and this then becomes kind of a holistic response to things. If you look at the bestseller list, you see all these books trying to tell you how to be yourself. Well, when the land gives you a foundation you don't have to fight that question.

DJ: Where do modern Indians fit into this? What about Indians whose stories came from the swamps of south Georgia, and now their reservation is in Oklahoma? Or what if the individual is now living on the south side of LA?

VD: That's a problem we're having in this generational changeover. People my age grew up on reservations, or towns near reservations. Now you've got a substantial number of young Indians in college who grew up in San Leandro and Bel Aire and Englewood, Colorado. These kids are genetically Indian, but culturally they're suburban. And when so many of these young kids come back, they are grabbing the images of things, rather than the substance of them.

DJ: Can you say more about that?

VD: These young Indians often can't distinguish between the real Indians of their tribe and their past, and all the information put out about Indians. *Black Elk Speaks* has become a kind of a bible for a whole generation of Indians, but it's really only about one Sioux medicine man.

We need to try to get them to look at their own cultural traditions, to ask the questions, How did my people do this? How was it organized? Who were the people who made the decisions? For example, the Muscogees had incredibly sophisticated cultural, religious, and educational systems, all integrated into one overarching system that produced brilliant people. Yet it's very hard to get young Muscogees to look back at it, and get totally immersed in it. You've got to go youngster by youngster, and point them back. About five or six years ago, I had some funds, and so pulled together traditional people of different tribes for two conferences on star knowledge, one on animal knowledge, and one on plant knowledge. The whole thing was really traumatic, because we had an audience of Indians, most of whom had very seldom heard real Indian storytellers tell about traditions. These people got up and spoke for forty minutes, and the audience would be in tears. They'd come to me and say, "I never experienced anything in my life like this." I'd respond, "Well, of course, that's what our ancestors did. They didn't spend twenty-four hours a day trying to hunt buffalo. They'd kill a buffalo, have a feast, and then people would take a few days off, sit around the campfire and tell all these stories." That experience of constantly being in a community that renewed itself historically and geographically built incredibly strong characters and happy people.

If you can't have that all the time, if you don't have it, you better try and get it back. You ought to look around and ask, "What was it really, and how can we revive it?"

DJ: How can we revive it?

VD: Well, I would start by pulling together what's written down, and getting to know that reasonably thoroughly, and then going out and talking to some of the elders, and asking them, "This is what the books say, now what do you say about how this was done?" When I've done that I've gotten an incredible amount of information, because what's written down is pretty familiar to most traditional people. It includes stories they've told over and over again.

But when scholars just happen to find some Indian who wants to talk about the traditions, they write it up and absolutize it, saying, "This is what Sioux Indians must believe," or "This is what Shoshones must believe." Then you talk to medicine men and they'll say, "Oh, yeah, in that written version they didn't include this and this and this and this."

Many of these elders probably reached adulthood in the 1930s. This means their grandfathers were the guys who fought Custer and Miles, and who in the 1930s were sitting on their reservations getting ready to die. Those people had been brought up in freedom. They had not had reservation experiences in their early years. We're now losing the last people who ever spoke to the last people who were free. This means we're at a very hazardous time.

When my generation goes, people are not even going to remember rural communities with no paved roads. You lose that context of place over and over again. You go through small towns near reservations, and there are no benches for anyone to sit on and talk. How do people get together now? At a tribal council where somebody asks your opinion on a policy decision? At a pow-wow where it seems everybody's trying to win the dance competition? Where is the coming together, the old visiting, the old kinship responsibility? Those are all fading away.

DJ: It seems to me that an inevitable consequence of losing that continuity is a devaluing of the elderly, because they are the carriers of memory. I grew up in Boulder, Colorado, and left when I was 24. A few years after I moved, a friend told me he'd been by my childhood home, and someone had cut down the trees I planted when I was a kid. It occurred to me that in a healthy functioning community, one of the responsibilities of the elderly is to be able to say, "This is where this happened… And the year you were born, there was a big snowstorm." When you move around, communities lose that function.

VD: Yes. And there is all this concern for families, but how many people know where their grandparents are buried? There are no family cemeteries any more. There is no returning to a place where you feel at home.

DJ: I want to ask a question I don't often see asked, yet seems crucial to explore. Why do you think it is that the dominant culture commits genocide against essentially every traditional culture it can?

VD: I don't think they want it known that there are other ways of living, because the whole success of the industrial state is based on having all the citizens be part of the economic machine. If you have people wandering around singing or making music or writing poetry, or living out in a rural area pretty much self-sufficient, it's a tremendous temptation for those others back in the machine to try to seek better lives for themselves. That's the first reason. The second reason is that if you look at the lack of stress in those people, and you look at the stress created by the industrial machine, you realize that the whole culture has gone crazy. We don't control machines. They control us. So the machine has got to crush any dissidence, any disagreements. This goes clear back to Christianity. The stated Christian ethic is to love your neighbor as yourself, but we have to look at how is in practice. Certainly millions of Indians were given the choice of Christianity—and enslavement—or death. We see the same thing today, though now it's generally couched in economic terms.

DJ: Tell me about Indian religions.

VD: Most Indian traditions never had a religion in the sense of dogmas and creeds, nor did they have the sort of ongoing deity that Christians speak of, by which I mean they didn't see a specific higher personality who demanded worship and adoration. Rather they saw and experienced personality in every aspect of the universe and called it "Woniya" (Spirit), and looked to it for guidance, a lot like Socrates obeying his "daemon."

DJ: So Indians believe everything has spirit...

VD: No, not precisely. It's not something they believe. What happens in the different Indian religions is that people live so intimately with their environment that they enter into relationship to the spirits that live in particular places. Rather than an article of faith, it's part of human experience. And I think non-Indians sometimes experience this also when they spend a long time in one place.

Living in this universe, Indians believed that everything humans experience has value, and instructs us in some aspect of life. Because everything is alive and making choices that determine the future, the world is constantly creating itself, and because every moment brings something new, we need to always try to not classify things too quickly. All the data must be considered, and we need to try to find how the ordinary and the extraordinary come together, as they must, in one coherent, comprehensive, mysterious story line. With the wisdom and time for reflection that old age brings, we may discover unsuspected relationships that make themselves manifest in our consciousness and so come to be understood.

In this moral universe, all activities, events, and entities are related, and so it doesn't matter what kind of existence an entity enjoys—whether it is human or otter or star or rock—because the responsibility is always there for it to participate in the continuing creation of reality. Life is not a predatory jungle, "red in tooth and claw," as Westerners like to pretend, but is a symphony of mutual respect in which each player has a specific part to play. We must be in our proper place and we must play our role at the proper moment. So far as humans are concerned, because we came last, we are the "younger brothers" of the other life-forms, and therefore have to learn everything from these other creatures. The real interest of old Indians would then be not to discover the abstract structure of physical reality, but rather to find the proper road down which, for the duration of a person's life, that person is supposed to walk.

I would also say that one of the major differences between Western and indigenous religions is that aboriginal groups have never had any need for a Messiah. Not only is there no need, but in fact there really is no place for one in the cosmos.

DJ: Why is that?

VD: If the world is not a vale of tears, there's no need for salvation. Indians know nothing of a wholly different world—a heaven—compared to which this world is devoid of value. Indian religion is instead concerned with, as Bellah noted, "the maintenance of personal, social, and cosmic harmony and with attaining specific goods—rain, harvest, children, health—as men have always been."

A commonality among all civilized religions is that of transcendence. But what I'm trying to get at is that in the North American Indian tradition individuals do not transcend themselves, they simply learn additional things about the single reality that confronts them.

I think there are some very important questions we need to ask about religion in the dominant culture: Why do Western European peoples, and by extension before them the Near Eastern peoples, need a messiah? Why is their appraisal of the physical world a negative one? Why do their societies suffer such perennial and continuing crises? Why do they insist of believing that ultimate reality is contained in another, almost unimaginable realm beyond the senses and beyond the span of human life?

I don't understand it. Religion as I have experienced it isn't the recitation of beliefs but a way of helping us to understand our lives. It must, I think, have an intimate connection with the world in which we live, and any religion that promotes other places—heaven and so on—in favor of what we have in the physical world is a delusion, a mere control device to allow us to be manipulated.

DJ: What, then, in the Indian perspective, is the ultimate goal of life?

VD: Maturity…

DJ: …by which you mean…

VD: …the ability to reflect on the ordinary things of life and discover both their real meaning and the proper way to understand them when they appear in our lives.

Now, I know this sounds as abstract as anything ever said by a Western scientist or philosopher, but within the context of Indian experience, it isn't abstract at all. Maturity in this context is a reflective situation that suggests a lifetime of experience, as a person travels from information to knowledge to wisdom. A person gathers information, and as it accumulates and achieves a sort of critical mass, patterns of interpretation and explanation begin to appear. This is where Western science aborts the process to derive its "laws," and assumes that the products of its own mind are inherent to the structure of the universe. But American Indians allow the process to continue, because premature analysis gives incomplete understanding. When we reach a very old age, or have the capacity to reflect and meditate on our experiences, or more often have the goal revealed to us in visions, we begin to understand how the intensity of experience, the particularity of individuality, and the rationality of the cycles of nature all relate to each other. That state is maturity, and seems to produce wisdom.

Because Western society concentrates so heavily on information and theory, its product is youth, not maturity. The existence of thousands of plastic surgeons in America attests to the fact that we haven't crossed the emotional barriers that keep us from understanding and experiencing maturity.

DJ: I want to talk about dreams for a second. I have a friend who is an Okanagan Indian, from British Columbia. I once asked her where dreams come from, and she said, "Everybody knows the animals give them to us." I'd like to ask you the same question.

VD: Oh, this is very fascinating. Remember that the Indian relationship to the land is not abstract, but is very particular, tied to that piece of ground. Now, in high vegetation areas you have a different set of dreams than you do in the Southwest or the Plains. My people come from the Plains, and so we say dreams come from the spirits. If you look around the Great Plains you've got two or three really dominant creatures, and you don't run into them all the time. The buffalo, the bear, the wolf. On the other hand, you go up where she's from, Okanagan and the Pacific Northwest, and a lot of the traditional practices have to do with holding souls together, and keeping relationships firm, because there are so many live things in those areas that a person is always in danger of disappearing into the landscape. The Cherokee and Creek down in the Southeast faced this same reality, living as they did in these tremendous forests, as did the Iroquois up in New York.

So if she says that dreams come from animals, she's absolutely correct, for her area. If I say dreams come from spirits, I'm correct, but only for the Plains. If you've ever got the time, you ought to read some of the Iroquois dream theory. There's all this incredibly fascinating stuff that would be a tremendous help in psychology if only psychologists believed Indians knew anything. And look at it cross-culturally: if you check into loss of souls in the Northwest, then Cherokee dream therapy, and Iroquois dream therapy, suddenly the scales fall from your eyes, and you say, "Wait a minute, I see what these guys are doing."

DJ: Different subject: how do you see the endgame of the dominant culture playing itself out? It seems pretty clear to me that if it has its way, the dominant culture will destroy every living thing on the planet.

VD: No question about it.

DJ: What can we do about that?

VD: There's nothing we can do at this point, because the majority of the people in our society believe science can cure all problems. We can go to the moon! So long as we perceive science as the cure-all for everything, and so long as no one can conceive a situation in which science can't overcome nature, we're doomed.

For example, now that we're beginning to see the planet's response to industrialism, now that the weather is getting increasingly violent, our solution is to build cement safe houses so when tornadoes wipe things out we can go there. We're still adjusting ourselves to the system instead of abandoning it.

Now to move to the short term. You look at the stock market, and you look back to 1929, and you say, "Oh, my god, we're doing the same thing." In 1929 lots of people believed they could forever continue to buy on margins. Now you've got all these communications companies that have never made a profit, yet the guys who originated the companies are millionaires. At some point, as that thing slows, the stock market may just take a straight nosedive, in which case we're going to have one hell of a situation. All these mansions being built, and no one's going to be able to keep up the payments. All these suburbs with $400,000 houses are going to be rural slums. I really don't know what's going to happen. I don't know when it will end. But nothing goes up forever.

I think we're also reaching a stage where people are beginning to see the necessary end point of the global economy, which is that we will be down to one computer system, and one market system. It's all aiming toward a single unity, toward this horrendous economic dictatorship. When people finally realize that, and rebel against it, it will be impossible to predict what's going to happen.

DJ: Something I've fantasized about, but never before seen articulated, is the possibility—and god, this is such a beautiful hope—that extinction may not be forever, but instead that the creatures go away and do not come back until the location is once again being treated properly.

VD: Oh yeah. About ten years ago I went and spoke to the Society for Ecological Restoration. I said to them, "You know, I'm really glad to see you doing this. I have no complaints, although some of you look pretty yuppie." Then I said, "If you listen to traditional Indian knowledge, what they'll tell you is these beings never became extinct. They went underground. Or they went away. They have the power to do that."

I said, "In your restoration, you will find that if you're preparing the area right, suddenly plants you thought were extinct will begin coming back. Plants come back first, and then animals, and then birds. After four or five years you should see old species coming back without you planting them." Of course the audience response was that I was crazy. But the interesting thing was that after we finished the evening session I went to get a cup of coffee, and a whole bunch of people followed me. They said, "You're right. We're seven years into a swamp restoration in Wisconsin, and all the original plants are back."

I said, "Well, yeah, that's what the elders say."

This is not so extraordinary as it may sound. The elders tell us that the buffalo went back and forth between two worlds. During the summertime, people would find themselves in the middle of a big herd literally for weeks. Then in the wintertime they would look around and say, "Where the hell are all the buffalo?" There might be a few of them down in the riverbottoms, or up in the grasslands, but where were the huge herds? According to the Sioux, they were underground. There were about ten places where they went in or came back out. When I first heard that I didn't believe it, but I talked to some of the elders who said, "Oh, yeah. Of course." And they showed me the buttes where they used to come out in the springtime. So I scoured the literature, and I thought, "This is insane." I just couldn't find accounts of big buffalo herds in the wintertime. Then June came and the damn plains were covered with buffalo. Come October and they started disappearing. Next spring again there were animals like you couldn't believe. It's just part of the natural cycle.

I'm still working on this one. But that's what life is all about. You take disparate facts, bring them together, and say, "Now what's the real question? What are we really dealing with?" And so often you're amazed to find that the thing is much deeper than you ever imagined. But the point is to ask the questions, and keep asking them.

And then you'll find, when you've come out the other side, that you can go to some of these oldtimers, and ask them about it, and they'll just look at you, nod, and then say, "Yeah, that's what happened."

Jesse Wolf Hardin

Interview Conducted
Gila Wildlands, New Mexico
7.8.00

J esse Wolf Hardin's work and life are all about feeling. He has written that "we know that we live in order to feel—and feel in order to praise and celebrate that life. We sense and relate to the world through the complex symbiosis of emotion and instinct we call the heart, through the 'five senses,' and those unmeasured faculties like intuition and precognition that scientists have lumped together as the 'sixth sense.' While we can benefit by learning the 'facts' about any chosen bioregion or terrain, we can never really know a place by reading a book on the subject, or by thinking about it. We only come to know it like a baby, humbly and appreciatively touching and tasting the world we're a physical, integral part of… Our natural response to our being born is to pull the substance and meaning of the world closer to us, by grabbing a hold, to pull ourselves ever closer to it. In this way life 'makes sense,' and our senses make the experience of life."

These are not just words. Hardin lives in one of the most beautiful places on Earth. Part of its beauty is because of him. It is an eighty-acre inholding in the Gila National Forest. A hundred years of logging and grazing had devastated the canyon, and Wolf has put his life into restoring it. Cottonwoods rise up where none had been allowed to grow before. The stream has reemerged from underground, and fish have found their way back. He has helped to love the place back to health, with his love manifesting in sweat and patience.

Jesse Wolf Hardin, one of the founders of Earth First!, has written hundreds of magazine articles and several books and CDs, and has given thousands of talks over the past two decades. I know of no one who has received more praise from within the environmental movement. Pulitzer Prize winner Gary Snyder said that Wolf's work is "a surprising experience; archaic, fresh, future, wild, refined, all at once." John Davis, editor of *Wild Earth*, says that his "art, music, and words move people to action—to defending wild life." Alan Drengson, editor of *The Trumpeter Journal of Ecosophy*, says, "In terms of depth, personal commitment, and quality of performance, Wolf is peerless. Few others have all of his primal qualities. Except for some Aboriginal writers, there are few authors in North America who reflect such depth of being a native to its place." And finally, Terry Tempest Williams writes, "It is only through the power, strength, integrity, and courage of people such as Wolf Hardin that our society will be able to change its direction. Wolf's voice inspires our passion to take us further—seeing the world whole—even holy."

Wolf now leads workshops with his wife Loba at their home in the canyon.

I interviewed Wolf on a beautiful July day in 2000.

DJ: You've written: "To become native again is not to emulate Native American or any other past or existing cultures, but instead to recall and relearn our own connection to and responsibilities to the regions where we presently reside." What does that mean?

JH: We're native to the degree that we enter into reciprocal relationship with the living land we're each an integral part of. To the degree that we are not only in love with—but loyal to—the place that supports, nourishes, sustains, informs and inspires us. To be native is to give back our full sentient presence and artful acknowledgement, our protection and affection to repay the gifts of food, home and wisdom with personal activism and heartful prayer, with restoration and celebration; to repay with our fullest living of life, while we're alive…and with our bodies when we die.

What is essential is that we be open to the directives of the ecosystem. That we become conscious of its needs and troubles, character and flavor, integrity and health. Conscious of the essence and spirit of place.

DJ: Let's back up a second. It seems that before we can talk about inhabiting a place, we need to talk about home.

JH: To "lose our place" is to lose our way home. Home is the heart in deep relationship with the land. And it is the place that calls us most insistently, instructs us loudest and best. The place we inevitably miss when we leave, the partner to our pain, and reason for our joy. Home is not only where you want to live, but how you want to live. And it is the place where you want to be when death finally claims you.

Let me put it this way: the source of all psychological, social and environmental dis-ease is our illusion of separateness. And the first step in mending that artificial schism—that deep, damn wound—is to try to bring ourselves back to a place of engagement with our authentic beings, in the vital present moment.

DJ: I don't understand.

JH: The opening to the experience of the universe, is through intimacy with a living planet, Gaia. The doorway to the experience of Gaia is through our sentient animal bodies and our feeling hearts. And the journey—the work, the realization—can only happen in immediate present time. Reindigination begins with reinhabitation of our awakened bodies and roiling emotions, in the "now." Much of the natural world, and our own wild spirits, are dying as a direct result of our alienation and abstraction, from what I call our "great distancing." And perhaps most tragically of all, we are dying without having fully lived.

DJ: That reminds me of a quote you use from H. G. Wells: "One can go through contemporary life fudging and evading, indulging and slacking, never really frightened nor passionately stirred, your highest moment a mere sentimental orgasm, and your first real contact with primary and elemental necessities the sweat of your deathbed." What does this mean?

JH: It's all too easy to acquiesce to the status quo, to the latest trends, and to our habits and fears. To give up our dreams for a meaningless career. To seek distraction in the television set and salvation in the sky. To compromise on a mate, and to pretend we're a victim of something called fate. To reside in the busy mind, and thereby avoid the pain of the neglected body and the anguish of an untended heart. To flounder around in the superficial rather than risk the frightening depths. To accept and acquiesce rather than discern and confront. To settle for comfort and safety instead of sensation and response-ability. We civilized humans are as tourists in our animal bodies except during certain moments in the midst of the sex act...or when scared for our lives. All too often, it's only when we face mortal or psychological destruction that we come back to the body that feels, runs, retaliates or relieves. Back to ourselves, and back home.

Clearly social and environmental activism isn't enough, unless we can somehow change the way we as a species perceive and relate to the natural world, to land and place. We can claim all these small, short-term and small victories but the fact is that the world is being deforested ever faster as we speak. More toxic chemicals are being released into the ground and water than ever. We're changing the climate. And genetic engineering poses what is perhaps the single greatest threat to the health and integrity of life on Earth.

DJ: Are we losing?

JH: I'm afraid so, at least in the short term. But the trick to right relationship—and to really being worthy of this blessing called "consciousness"—is to do what is right, what matters most, regardless of the visible results. We seldom see the ramifications of all the good we do, but more importantly, we need to make the grand effort not because we imagine we'll succeed, but because it's right to do so. Because it really, deeply matters to us! And in a way, even discouragement and disgust are potentially good signs. They're evidence of an awareness of the odds stacked against us, and it is acting in spite of them that makes one's life heroic.

DJ: Are you saying results don't matter?

JH: Of course they matter. But we watch for results in order to figure out the best actions to take, not for a reason to act. And sometimes we're able to accomplish the impossible. When Crazy Horse saw his family and village under attack by the U.S. Army, he could see that the odds were stacked against him, and that any resistance could be futile. In spite of this he unsheathed his weapon and rode headlong into the fight, inspiring other braves to follow his example, and breaking the enemy ranks with the sheer intensity of his effort, his investment and risk, his life and love.

To keep from feeling discouraged it helps to look past the next two generations of getting kicked in the teeth again and again. What I live for is the realization of an epoch after technocivilization has met its ignoble end, blowing itself up, or slowly wasting away. For a time when wildlife takes back the ruins of our cities. When wild creatures stalk the shells of office buildings and malls, when the plants start growing up through the cracks in the pavement. We can't expect to see that.

DJ: But we do. You see it all around yourself. You got the cows off of this land, and the cottonwoods and willows have come back. It's beautiful.

JH: True. In a way I've been able to protect and restore more wilderness by working my butt off for it—by standing up to trespassers and developers and every other threat for all these years—than I ever did blocking logging roads. But even this single victory remains in jeopardy. I can't find a land trust willing to take on this special riparian refuge without an attendant bank account for monitoring it. I can't sign a conservation easement, if no one will accept it. It's protected for now, through sweat and threat, dumb luck or an assist from the spirits. And more than that, it's reveled in, honored, restored and resacramented…and yet there are no guarantees it can last. The best we can do is to wake up each and every day, giving thanks for being alive and aware in this enchanted place. Being who we really are, and doing everything we possibly can, for all the right reasons.

DJ: I'd like to go back to the notion of reinhabiting one's body.

JH: Your door to the entire world is located where your feeling body touches the giving ground. Your bare feet, your rear end, the few square inches of absolute contact are points of connectivity between yourself and millions of years of organic process. And the way to fully experience that connection is by disengaging our mental tape loops, our voice tracks, the constant commentary that keeps us perpetually anticipating the future or criticizing our self about the past rather than tasting the muffin we're eating right now. Then we can experience the world around us—as well as within us—like the awakened, hungering, feeling, responding, caring creature selves we really are.

DJ: So reinhabiting one's body is tied intimately to reinhabiting the present moment.

JH: We can't feel our connection to the sentient body, or participate in the processes of the natural world, anywhere but "here," and "now." And we can't really be either if we're forever residing in our brains, engrossed in the movies of our minds. All the while reality waves its arms and wings and cloud forms like flags trying to win back our attention, trying to give us back our lives. I mean, there's a reason why they call it a "present:" because it's a gift we're fools to miss.

Most of us have read that old science fiction classic where the professor departs his basement shop astride his "time machine," leaving nothing behind but a ring in the dust on the floor where it once stood. In the same way civilized humanity is often out of touch, absent, unreachable by a world of unfolding presence. Our bodies remain in place like that impression in the dust, while our minds orbit backwards and forwards through the years, inhabiting every period of time but now, and every place but here. Too often we dwell on our desires and worries, rather than dwelling in the present, in place. And meanwhile things like industrial development and environmental destruction are largely accomplished out of time, by future-looking planners and bureaucrats who are oblivious to the purrs and the pleas, the rewards and challenges of the beckoning present. What we need is a conscious, collective high-dive into the always decisive moment—reimmersing ourselves in the sensations and responsibilities of the real world—now!

DJ: How does one begin to do that?

JH: Reach out to what is real—a leaf, a chair, a friend—emissaries of the present glad to reconnect us to the now. If something exists for the senses, it exists in present time. Wake up from the nightmare of past events and far away places, peer into the gradations of black in the unlit bedroom, focus on the pressure of covers against skin, or give yourself over to identifying any smells making their way to you through the darkness. Try showers hotter and colder than you think you can stand, focus on the lover you're with until there are no others. And if all else fails, there's nothing like a loud boom, the sudden screeching of brakes, or a genuine near-death experience to bring us back into bodies ready to run or have fun.

There's so much distraction and obstruction we have to remain fiercely focused and totally insistent. Because almost everything in society calls you away from yourself. The clamor and bright lights, standing in lines or working in offices, going to movies or making small talk. For the unplaced few, our society can seem like a very lonely place. The average Joe doesn't seem to want to smell as deeply or love as much. Or to risk deeply caring, because it might mean he has to act on those things he sees and feels. Even the friends you've known forever might not affirm something that is a little bit heavier, a little deeper, than they may want to go. Maybe you becoming more of who you are mirrors something in themselves they don't want to deal with, and so they try to keep things light. Becoming yourself makes you momentarily the loneliest person on earth, but as you walk through that door you realize that you're a part of everything. And that in the end, it's impossible to be alone. That's the kind of assurance and wisdom that nature affords: intimate knowledge of this moment, this tree, this place, this home.

DJ: And it seems to me to take a long time. I've been living on the same land now for about three years...

JH: And you're just starting to get introduced.

DJ: Yes.

JH: This courting and bonding requires not only commitment but presence and attention, day after day after day. If we're only home seasonally, or if we're gone five days out of the week, it's not the same. Deepening relationship requires we get to see the sun come up in a slightly different place each and every day through each of the four seasons. I've got so many friends who live in cities, who work all day indoors, and some of them don't even know which way the sun sets. Until we're oriented, until we know where we are, until we know what direction is East, how can we know what direction to take our lives? And it takes time to recognize the ecological cycles, as many of them are long. There are seven-year cycles for different insects, and there are different flowers that come up only every four to eight years. Patterns of rain and drought. New species moving in or disappearing. Miss a single week in this enchanted canyon, and you could miss the bulk of the wild mulberry season. No single sunset will ever be repeated again, quite the way it shined today.

This intimacy of relationship, this narrowing down of focus actually expands what it means to belong and to be alive. Unfortunately, I'm not sure that such deep relating and reinhabiting will ever be compatible with making an income or covering one's medical insurance.

DJ: Why not?

JH: They require we do work that takes into account the integrity and needs of our bodies, our communities, other species, the air, water and land…and that's a hell of a way to try and make a living. The System rewards its citizens who acquiesce, compromise and conform. We're usually paid not only to do what we're told, but to "look the other way"—away from the effects of our tasks on our bodies, our families and our world. In fact, the more meaningless or destructive the position, the more money and benefits we can make. Corporate heads and politicians, geneticists and nuclear engineers, army generals and real estate developers are highly paid. Writers and dancers, preschool teachers and counselors, environmental activists and those who run food programs for the poor, wilderness restorationists and sage poets are lucky to be paid at all. Or else they're volunteers.

But there's an upside to this. Since the fields that require caring help pay so little, they tend to attract the most sincere people. People who are doing their service for the purest of reasons.

DJ: What's your story?

JH: There never really was a time when I felt like I fit in. There was never a moment I didn't feel alienated from the social agreement...

DJ: What social agreement?

JH: That only if we mind our "p's and q's" everything will be all right, medicine will find a cure for death, science will erect bubbles over our cities to purify the air, we'll meet Mr. or Ms. Right, the oil companies will come up with new forms of inexpensive energy, taking away our privacy is their way of protecting us, building more missile systems will make us safer, Social Security will really take care of us when we get old, and we can all have lots of babies with no serious effects on the environment or our quality of life. And in the end, if we play by the rules we'll all go to heaven where there are no endangered species or slaughtered Hutu tribesmen, nor wives being beaten by husbands with no self-respect.

The agreement is that we'll smile even if we don't like someone or something, and gather on Christmas and give presents even to those family members who happen to resent us the rest of the year. That we'll ignore the child abuse we know is going on across the street, and have secretive affairs rather than be honest with our spouse about our feelings and needs. That we won't talk about the effects of the pesticides we sprayed in our well trimmed yards this afternoon, the percentage of poor uneducated kids in the military, or the reasons for unwed mothers and chemically deformed babies.

Do you remember a magazine in dentists' offices when we were kids, called *Highlights*? Do you remember the page where they'd show a picture with something out of place, like a hammer hanging from a tree, and you were supposed to figure out what was "wrong with the picture?" From the time I was a toddler it's felt like that to me. It's like tapping on the rocks and discovering they're hollow; finding mold marks and seams once we look close enough at the local trees. It's like we're all living in a big theme park... and we have to pay to get out.

When I started running away from school at age fourteen, I found bouts of hunger more stimulating than daily doses of tasteless frozen dinners, and liked being lost better than always thinking I knew where I was going. Safety was a numbing straitjacket, so I embraced risk. I welcomed the pain, because I couldn't stomach denial anymore.

DJ: Are you talking emotional pain? Physical pain?

JH: Both. The pain of feeling isolated and misunderstood. Of empathy—for mumbling bag ladies on the streets, Hispanics jacked up by the police, the little kids that no one takes the time to listen to. Empathy for the forests cleared, for expatriate wildlife and seeds left crying beneath four inches of pavement. Even getting in fights or falling from a motorcycle had a certain refreshing honesty, functioning as calls to sensation, as adamant reminders that I was alive. Anything to know I'd escaped the paradigm of comfort, pretense and denial.

DJ: At what point did that process of cultivating pain turn over? When did you started reaping the benefits of being present?

JH: Immediately. It's clear that the more we're willing to feel our pain—and the agony of other people, other creatures—the greater our capacity for bliss, communion and love. The eyes that willingly look into the faces of the suffering are more likely to take notice the value of a smile, the shifting shapes in the clouds above, or the poetry of the falling leaf. Ears that find sirens unbearable, can better appreciate the whisperings of the river and the quiet squeaking of grandma's rocking chair. The heart that really knows the meaning of bliss has been sensitized by despair.

DJ: Let's talk about this place.

JH: The Sweet Medicine Sanctuary is a restored riparian wilderness, an eighty acre inholding surrounded by millions of acres of Aldo Leopold's Gila forest, in mountains that were one of the last refuges for free Apaches including Victorio and Geronimo. This particular bend in the river is place of power, and served the Mogollon pithouse dwellers as a site for ritual and worship for tens of thousands of years. Since the willows and cottonwood trees filled back in, we've seen the return of herons and ducks, owls and eagles, deer and elk, lion and bear.

When I first saw this land I fell helplessly in love with it. I sold the engine out of the school bus I lived in in order to get money, with no idea if I could get up the rest of the down payment that I'd offered.

DJ: How did you know this was the place you needed to be?

JH: Finding our home, like finding our destiny, is a matter of getting in touch with our intuition and instinct, and then learning to trust it and follow it. You can't pick a home by comparing the facts and maps in some atlas anymore than you can find your "medicine animals" by drawing cards from a deck. Home, like adventure, is something that becomes possible whenever we suspend our plans and criteria and feel our way to where we most belong. It's not only the place our souls need, but also the place that most needs us.

The events leading me to find, buy and preserve the Sanctuary have been nothing short of miraculous, convincing me without a doubt that I was meant to be here serving this place. And anyway, we can sense where we belong in the compass of our bones. Whenever we leave home we feel like we're going the wrong way. And when we turn back, we know in every cell of our being that we're headed in the direction of home.

As a youngster I preferred multiple affairs to lasting commitments, variety of experience over depth. I tried to love every place I traveled through in the same way, finding the "goddess" in each, promising to none. Coming here was the end to that, the moment of pledging allegiance, of marrying the land, entering into a reciprocal agreement that demands as much from me as it gives.

DJ: You've written that we can't own land, that land owns us. What is your contract with this canyon?

JH: How can we own that which contains us, predates us, and outlasts us? I didn't contract for this place so much as with it. We enter into a relationship sealed in blood and tears, sweat and semen, an equitable giving and taking that's clearly spelled out, and duly sworn to. The land is pledged to give wholly of its authentic self, to offer home and shelter, beautiful groves and stunning Mountains, the food and water we need, inspiration and instruction. We promise gifts in return, like our attention and presence. We promise to try and feel her needs, and meet them. To support her in her fullest flowering. To defend her integrity and honor from all threats including those that come from ourselves. To appreciate, and celebrate.

It is, as much as anything else, a marriage contract, bound by love rather than law. I've stood before these orange and purple cliffs many times and repeated my vows. That I'll do everything I can to restore her.

DJ: This may seem strange, but when I was walking down the canyon, before I came up here to do this interview, the one thing that was missing was a lover. Had I been here with a human lover, we would have had no choice but to make love.

JH: Of course! Everywhere we look we see the eroticized natural world both consuming itself and making love to itself through its constituent parts: pollen-laden flowers pierced by wild bees, the mating calls of the sex-addled elk, insect orgies and intertwining grape vines. We're drawn to participate in this lusting and cuddling, inspired to add our own variations of partnering and pairing. There exists what Terry Tempest Williams and I call an "erotics of place," the charged field we evolved from, and that we subconsciously long to penetrate again. My wife Loba lost a woman lover moving here to this paradise, but the canyon has become her femme paramour. You can see it in the way she touches each lichen padded rock on the way down to the trail. The hurt look on her face if she breaks the grasses she steps on. Her look of ecstasy as the shallow river carries her slowly downstream. And the way her voice rings out on a moonlit night...

DJ: When she asked what would be required of her if she stayed with you here, one of the things you said was, "Sing praise to the canyon."

JH: The land doesn't just need us defending it. It needs our hands-on care. Needs us to sing ritual and prayer, gratitude and celebration. From the time my sweetheart first got here, she'd stand above the river in front of a small wind cave, and sing out a cascade of trills and bars. I feel the whole canyon rising to take it in, the way a cat raises its back when you reach down to stroke it.

DJ: One of the things I love about your work is that activists generally do restoration, some new age types sing praises, but you do both. It's very evident how much work you've done here.

JH: You're a gentleman for saying so. Restoration and resistance can be arts, just like music and poetry—if we infuse them with passion and prayer.

The most adamant and beautiful work seems to emanate from the reptilian cortex, from caring souls and expectant flesh. From the Earth, and Spirit. The rational mind really only serves this work to the degree that it functions as an honest translator.

DJ: You said that people come here on quests...

JH: We offer resident internships, retreats with fasts and shelter, and wilderness quests: quests for a deeper experiencing of life and truth. For clarity. For ways of being, and doing. We don't call them "vision quests," partly out of respect for the cultural propriety of native peoples, and partly because the people who come here are already equipped with a vision, or they wouldn't have made it this many hundreds of miles from the nearest airport, and several river crossings from where they parked their car. The quest allows them to be away from the distractions of that other world. Out of this intentional experience, one hopes, comes a deeper recognition and acceptance of who they really are, their real feelings and useful intuition. If people can capture that here, hold on to that and take it with them, then the right path will be obvious, and their choices clear.

DJ: What do they physically do?

JH: Counsel. There is a day of purification, of slowing down the prattle of the mind, focusing on presence, gathering for the sweat lodge, infusing every rock, every piece of wood with our intentions and prayers. A night of tending the fire beneath the sacred cliffs, causing a sweat so hot it pushes us out of our minds and into body and earth. We get all the way into the cold river after each round. We stand in the first dawn light with the steam pouring off our skin. Then up to four days and four nights of fasting and opening in a favored spot near the water or up on a rocky peak. We suspend our disbelief, exceed our imagined limitations, and open up to the experience and instruction of the seamless whole.

DJ: You talked earlier about finding a "place of power." What does that mean?

JH: All of the Earth is sacred, with an accessible spirit and persona, and every place offers the same essential body of wisdom. But there have always been locations with a special ambiance, such as the confluences of rivers mountain peaks, landmarks where the energy seems more palpable, where our feelings, fears and hopes are reflected back to us. And where the lessons are harder to avoid. This canyon is like that, which is why it was a place of ceremony for the Sweet Medicine People for so many generations. These are places that need to be protected from encroachment, commercialization and misuse.

At the same time, by focusing on the Black Hills and Machu Pichu, Mesa Grande and Sedona, we risk missing out on the magic of the familiar and mundane, the miracle of outlaw dandelions pushing their sunny little heads up through the cracks in the pavement, and the living character of a neighborhood park.

DJ: In your book *Kindred Spirits* you write about learning from the land, and the lessons are far from the Disneyfied version where nothing or no one ever gets hurt.

JH: Wilderness is a largely benign and beneficial experience, but it has its dangers that force us to be fully awake, to be careful, full-of-care. Our strength is a product of those challenges we pull against. Our ancestor's speedy reaction time resulted not only from running after food, but running away from trouble. The experiences that are most unforgettable are intimations of death, and reminders to live. We were never more alive, never more fully present and aware as when we were stalked by cave bears and giant cats.

I've often stepped a few feet off a mountain trail, to let a noisy covey of hikers pass. I smile as they shuffle by staring at their feet, talking loudly about the next peak they're going to "bag," or the last woman they "had"—without them seeing me there, standing in plain sight. In grizzly country, they could end up lunch meat. It only takes one look at a grizzly's claw marks high up a tree to get us to pay a little more attention to our surroundings. Eyes alerted to spot bear tracks are more likely to notice the little flowers budding up through the clover, and the way the wind passes through the tall grass. Ears listening intently for the sound of the great bears, are more likely to hear the tinkling of a rain seep, and recognize the subtleties in a river's song.

DJ: How does death fit into this picture?

JH: Fear is a reason for increased awareness, and potentially, fuel for movement or change. In the same way, death is an ally that constantly reminds us of the real world around us, and of what's most important. If you think you only have a few weeks or months to live, you'll be unlikely to want to spend any of that time under fluorescent lights, quibbling or worrying. You'll try to spend time in your favorite places, or where you most belong. You'll revel in the moments you have with your loved ones, savor every scent and sound. But if you think you have several years left, you're likely to loiter in your mind, put off that trip to your beloved ocean or desert, suffer the cubicle lights to pull in a few more paychecks, miss precious hugs and giggles and winks with your kids and lovers. The more time you think you have, the more likely you'll postpone your spiritual work, your assignment, your purpose…the very living of life.

We already have a hard time being present and in-body—already treat the Earth as if it were a lifeless and limitless resource—knowing we're lucky if we have seventy years of relative good health. Just imagine how careless we'd be with our lives, and the lives of other species, if we could count on biomedicine to guarantee us fifty to a hundred years more. Sensitivity, compassion and gratitude are rooted in the awareness of mortality.

In this way, the big bears are our Buddhas. And even viruses are agents of humility and love.

DJ: We're not the top of the food chain.

JH: Dirt is at the top…because it gets to eat everybody! If we really want to feel like part of the endless cycles of life, we need to get used to thinking of ourselves as food. In this society people usually live their lives as though they were somehow separate from nature, and then they employ embalming fluids and metal lined coffins to try to keep nature out after death. Attempts to forestall decomposition, like science's search for immortality, signify our unwillingness to surrender to the very processes we arose from, extend out of…and all return to.

DJ: Facing death, like facing life, takes a lot of courage.

JH: Courage is being willing to feel, no matter what the costs. And doing the right thing—acting on those feelings—in the face of all obstacles. If we are courageous it is because we love something enough that we'd take risks to save it, help it, nourish it. The ultimate courage comes from the certain knowledge that we are an inseparable part of the Earth. We must learn to live lives that, like death, affirm the sacred connection between us and the land.

DJ: I've come to realize that there is no such thing as anything separate from land.

JH: There's no such thing as separate. That's the whole point. Every problem in the world, every social dis-ease, every environmental imbalance, every screwed up personal problem is because we're somehow able to imagine separation between our mind and our heart, between our mind and our body, between our body and this place, between ourselves and our loved ones, ourselves and our community. There is no original evil, only original imagined separation. The cure for that is love. And the way to manifest that love is through the courageous embodiment of our decisive responsible selves. Our natural selves, in partnership with what's natural in this world.

DJ: For the longest time I tried to define what is natural, and here is what I finally came up with: an institution or rule or artifact is natural to the degree that it reinforces our understanding of our embeddedness and participation in the natural world, and it's unnatural to the degree that it masks all of that.

JH: Exactly. And we're natural, to the degree that we embrace our embeddedness, and act out of that animal/spiritual sense of connectedness, interdependence, and inseparability.

DJ: When you say there's no separation, do you mean that everything is good? Do you mean that chainsaws and corporations are...

JH: I mean there is no separation between the physical and energetic bodies of the Earth destroyers and the Earth defenders, though we might wish there were! We will all be rejoined in fact, stirred and folded back into the great Gaian soup. Likewise the metals in the chainsaw will in time corrode back into seams of earthen ore, and even that abomination called plastic will break back down into native sediments and organic gases. That doesn't make the callous developer or arrogant geneticist any less accountable, or the Tupperware parties any less bizarre. But responsibility comes from the awareness of interdependency. In the long run, we'll need to make the corporate polluter and de-forester aware of their place in the web, and the results of their acts.

DJ: And you also, presumably, want to stop him.

JH: The moment we're aware of an injustice, we have a responsibility to do absolutely everything in our power, legal and extralegal, to prevent or rectify that wrong. But we shouldn't kill a plant or animal to eat without feeling empathy for its death, without feeling both intimacy and sadness, because you know you are connected to what you eat. By family. By flesh. And similarly, we shouldn't strike a blow against an enemy, no matter how egregious his acts, without recognizing the degree to which he is of us, and in us.

We do this work of activism, social change and wilderness restoration in the most compassionate, graceful and aesthetic ways possible.

DJ: What is the role of art in cultural transformation? Where does art come from?

JH: There's a spirit in all of us that likes to draw, handle a sharp pencil, splash water colors or get our hands into sculptor's clay. That longs to make a statement, and have an impact. It's rooted in the creative urges of a planet, imbued with the passion of evolution. One never really manufactures either adventure or art. We are confronted by it, consumed by it, and remade within it. It always has a purpose, and is willingly given away. Like mortal flesh. Like these golden cottonwood leaves. Like Hopi sand paintings intricately crafted, and then blown and blended by the wind. But then it's not in the completion of some project that we become fulfilled. It's in the making of our art, in the living of our lives that we're made whole.

Some art reflects what is, good and bad, and forces us to engage or confront both. Other arts are ways of living grace and balance, dancing them into the hearts and minds of an audience that has forgotten what it is to be Gaian respondents and participants in beauty. It's for us to make sure our arts are not only decorative but meaningful, contributing to greater awareness, sensitivity, understanding and response. And that our every act, from civil disobedience and litigation to the way we live or make love, be as artful and significant as we can make them. Deep art comes from deep seeing, and deep feeling. It becomes a deliberate mission to express our authenticity, our experience, our connectedness in a way that is as beautiful as possible. And then to give even our lives away. The result again is reconnection, as our art and practice weaves us back into the material of our experience. Together with the ritual efforts of others, we co-create the living fabric of culture, jointly paint on that fabric the story of our struggles and accomplishments, our love and our hope. And it's so important to recognize the art, beauty and meaning in the mundane, the simple, the plain. We're surrounded by art every day. And it's trying, like the rest of natural world, to communicate with us. What we need is not only the ability, but the willingness, to recognize it for what it is.

DJ: Walking up the canyon I took a friend to smell a ponderosa pine. At the base were some ant lion cones. He'd never seen one before. We hadn't noticed them as we were walking, until we stopped to pay attention. The patterns of their cones were so beautiful. Everything seemed so utterly alive. Lately it's seemed to me that even fires are just as alive as hummingbirds or humans. Have you ever thought about this?

JH: Everything that's a part of the living whole must in its own way be alive. Mute energies, unthinking rocks, all part and portion of a life: Gaian Earth. And in turn, that Earth is a part of a larger universe that must also be alive. I don't sense any awareness in fires, but I don't measure life by whether it's conscious or not. People have the capacity to be ultra-conscious, but we can be some of the least enlivened.

DJ: I'd like to change the subject. You've said that you live in one of the most famously anti-environmental counties in the country. What's that like?

JH: This is one of the few counties where folks have talked about seceding from the Union, and the Catron County Ordinance asserting local jurisdiction over federal agencies has been adopted by several other Western communities. Of the Mexican Gray wolves recently reintroduced into this area, a half dozen have been shot by locals afraid for their livestock and their livelihoods. The local saloon advertises Spotted Owl Stew.

It's been difficult, being the only self-confessed tree-hugger for miles around. I suppose if I'd been looking for alternative community I might have ended up in Cave Junction, Oregon, or Asheville, North Carolina instead. But I was looking for wilderness, adventure, magic… And in the end it wouldn't have mattered what I wanted, because I was being called here.

I had little respect for carpenters until I had to figure out how to build this cabin, or for mechanics until I tried to keep our old truck running. Then over the years I grew to see the value in a farmer's early morning schedule and the attention he pays to the rain. As upset as I get over the effects of public-lands grazing, I look up to the way the old-time ranchers ride the range everyday, do what they need to do without whining, and can fix almost anything with fencing pliers and a coil of bailing wire. In addition, these folks are quicker to express their true feelings. They're generally honest. They do what they say they're going to do, and they expect me to do the same. And there are ways that they're in touch with the land that my city environmentalist friends will never be. I would even support their resistance to being governed by a distant and out of touch elite, if only they wouldn't take advantage of their liberties to further strip the old growth forest, or kill off the native predators.

DJ: Freedom without responsibility is tremendously destructive.

JH: Teaching responsibility and inspiring stewardship is part of the assignment. And the only way to accomplish this is through an exploration of common ground.

The majority of the articles I write are in magazines for an audience that are already believers. Folks read *Talking Leaves* or *Earthlight* because they love the environment, or they're interested in spirit, or they're moved by personal and social change. It's more challenging to teach about sense of place in a piece for *Backpacker*, or sentience and sacrament in a food magazine. And the hardest pieces have been those written as a columnist for the local paper, trying to reach the hearts of my rural neighbors.

DJ: What kind of responses have you gotten?

JH: Mostly positive, oddly enough. I don't know how deeply I touch them, but I know how important it is to try. I call attention to our common threats, like condominiums and gentrification. I advocate wildness, by reminding readers of their respect for the unbreakable stallion, and explain the interdependency of nature by comparing it to the cooperative bonds of a healthy family. In one article I pointed out how easy it is to diss the old homestead as soon as they can afford a new doublewide—but then how much they'd miss it if the bank called in their loans, or if for some reason it burned down. Suddenly they'd recall the handrailings burnished smooth by their grandparents' hands, and remember the story behind every mark on the walls. I talk about how we may not fully appreciate a home until we've lost it, or a spouse until they've died or left us. And how it's the same with the loss of the last wild places.

DJ: Common ground is an interesting subject.

JH: I've always had a soft spot for honest confrontation because it polarizes things, and thus makes the choices clearer. But I've also come to see the advantage of focusing on those values and priorities that we share.

DJ: I think that before we can even talk about commonality we need to acknowledge polarities that already exist.

JH: I see common ground in terms of the actual land we share: our settings, ecosystems and environments. As a community we're all affected by what affects our watershed. We breathe the same clean or dirtied air. We face the same basic threats. We depend on the same sources of food. And we hopefully have a very similar love and affection for the place that we call home. It's this necessity, and this affection, that can bind us together.

DJ: I work a lot with independent loggers and farmers, and I'm always honest with them: we both want to take down the big corporations, and I want to take down civilization. So we work together in the short run, and in the long run maybe we don't.

JH: I have a vision of a world that is so wild that it can survive even our mistakes, even our insensitivities. We won't get that again until long after the fall, long after the population drop. Until then, we've got to individually make our lives a quest for reconnection, a quest for right livelihood and right living—even if we lose our credibility and careers, the support of our parents, the acceptance of our children, or the understanding of our mates—in the course of regaining our lives, our passions, our souls.

DJ: That's a hard sell.

JH: It will always be more popular to hand out "blessed" chocolates and get-into-heaven-free cards, and no call to sentience and responsibility can compete with selling prayers for angels that are willing to do all the karmic work for you. Hardly anyone wants to be told that they're in charge of their own lives, and that the fate of the natural world will largely depend on what we do or don't do.

I offer students and visitors nothing but truth, and their self: authentic and responsive, empowered and assigned, content and fulfilled. But they have to be willing to pay the price of admission to this, "the real world, muchacho!" The truth can seem to "cost us everything," but it gifts us with who we really are, and gives us back the fullest experiencing of the world we're a part of. This is insight with no borders, no convention, no pretense, no apologies. I don't ask for perfection or enlightenment from those I work with, only whole and heartful effort, a fierce focus and love. And a willingness to get up when you fall. We're a "no ropes" course: a chance to be aware and responsible, with nothing holding you down, and the knowledge there are no nets to soften our mistakes. It's supposed to hurt, so we know where and when we went wrong. Instead of "12 Steps," we've narrowed it down to two: Rebecome your most authentic, feeling self—and then manifest that self for the good of All. Therapists want you to have the "skills" to keep your traumas and unmet needs from interfering with your ability to "function productively" in society. I have no intention of making it easier for anyone to tolerate the hypocrisy and meaninglessness around them, or to ignore their needs and wounds. I try to give them back the will and power to resist what needs resisting, change what needs changing…and feel absolutely all.

If you come here as a student, I may not tell you want to hear. After all, there are schools happy to take your money year after year without graduating you. Priests will absolve you, and gurus give you a mantra to help you transcend. Counselors will process you endlessly, and never demand any major shifts. Not so with the teachings of the inspirited Earth, of primal instinct and intuition…and not so with us. Every "class" results in graduation, every lesson put to work for the good of not only one's self but other people, other species, and the sacred land. You can be redeemed and fulfilled, but not absolved, for the aware have a responsibility. We will ask you not to transcend but engage. And we will expect you to change—into becoming more who you really are: needy as well as giving, vulnerable as well as strong, physical as well as spiritual, angry as well as happy, determined as well as afraid. I will do my best to keep any politically correct timidity or New Age escapism from interfering with your fullest realization, even if it occasionally discomforts you, insults your sources, or threatens your preconceptions and plans. It's the least I can do.

DJ: What worries you most?

JH: The epidemic insecurity of our kind. We're in some kind of collective denial about the fact, but there is no single greater influence on our activities, no single greater factor in the repression of our native humanness and the distortion and destruction of nature. The drunk in the gutter, and the extrovert developer, are both responding to gut-wrenching self doubt. The building of absurd skyscrapers and the beating of wives, are attempts to compensate for a lack of self worth.

The world would be a saner, healthier place if only we could learn to really, truly love ourselves. But this self love can only come when we begin to recognize and experience our lives as truly, deeply significant. It grows proportionately with every challenge we rise to take on. It roots and strengthens with each difficult, selfless quest we see to completion. And it bears noble fruit, as we begin to fulfill our most meaningful purpose. Real self worth is determined by our capacity to share, not by how much we own—not by the amount of skills we have, but by the ways in which we employ them.

DJ: How do you define "secure"?

JH: One can't be secure "from" something, only "in" something. We're never truly secure from pain or poverty, hatred or harm, abandonment or libel, death or disease. We can be secure in who we truly are, in the reality of our weaknesses as well as the truth of our gifts. In the innocence of our hearts and the sanctity of our souls. We can be secure in the love we have available to give, if not always in the affections we hoped to receive. In our connection to all that is, to all that ever was, and to all that will ever be. In our blessings, our love, and our purpose.

DJ: What else scares you?

JH: The idea of a world robbed of wilderness. An end to the playground of evolution. The neglect or destruction of those places of magic and instruction that could lead us back to health and balance, self and home. We're rapidly losing the openings, the opportunities for personal reconnection and assignment. My fear is that the last natural places will be commercialized or destroyed, and that even the words reflecting and spreading this earthen wisdom will be lost. That there will no longer be a demand for things wild and real, in a culture of artificiality and control. And that we may soon lose the capacity to tell the difference. The coming generations will be starving not only from lack of food and space, but an absence of grounded advice... and the forgotten lessons of inspired place.

DJ: What about hope?

JH: I expect nothing...and hope for miracles. I find hope in Loba's unflagging compassion. In the faces of little children, the angst and anger of troubled teens, and in the determination of Zapatista women. In the efforts of Indian traditionalists, neodruids and radical pagans, spiritual activists and environmental ethicists. In small presses and regional zines. In urban gardens, and herbicide-resistant weeds. I find hope in the insistence of my students, and the concern of our resident interns. In my dear apprentice Scot, and the promise of a renewed lineage of protection and sacrament. And of course, I find it incredibly hopeful—that after the worst that technological civilization can do, life will spring back in all its diversity and glory for as long as the sun shall shine!

DJ: I've got a line in a book: "Every morning when I wake up I ask myself whether I should write or blow up a dam." That's because salmon are dying not from a lack of words, but from dams. Does writing help?

JH: It helps—at least to the degree we raise a reader's awareness of the pain and bliss of life, and help incite their honorable responses. If we remind them not to let any intermediary stand between them and God, or between them and direct experience. If they're more empathetic and grateful after reading our words, more likely to dance and less likely to "sit this one out." If they cry more, laugh more, feel more. If they never knew how to have fun, and they play more afterwards. If they were never serious about anything, and they end up dealing with the really heavy shit. If we can keep them from stubbing their toes on the same obstacles twice, and get them to chance new mistakes they can learn and grow from. If they read about all the things we learned from a certain mulberry tree, and then go out right away and eat berries! If they're a little less tolerant of evil and the artificial, and a little more willing to take risks. If we provoke or seduce them to go barefoot, taste their food, say "I love you" more often, or discover divine creation in even a single backyard flower.

It's an old metaphor, but we're all planting seeds. And this takes us back to the question of whether we can hope for results. A person putting out seeds can't stand around and wait and see what grows in every situation. Sometimes they might come up the first year. Others might take ten or fifteen generations, and come up when there is just enough sunshine, just enough moisture, just enough compost for the seed to sprout and bloom.

But these are just words. The essential thing is to re-become who we really are, opposing the destruction and lies, embracing the natural world, working and playing as if life itself depended on it. Once we do that, there will be no more quandaries, no more need to "process," no confusion about wrong or right, or wondering if we're on our path of heart. We'll feel, we'll care, we'll respond. We'll express this wholeness in acts of integrity, and beauty. We'll give everything…and that will be enough.

ABOUT DERRICK JENSEN

Hailed as the philosopher poet of the ecological movement, Derrick Jensen is the widely acclaimed author of *Endgame*, *A Language Older Than Words*, *The Culture of Make Believe* (a finalist for the 2003 J. Anthony Lukas Book Prize), and *Walking on Water*, among many others. Jensen's writing has been described as "breaking and mending the reader's heart" (*Publishers Weekly*). Author, teacher, activist, small farmer, and leading voice of uncompromising dissent, he regularly stirs auditoriums across the country with revolutionary spirit. Jensen holds a degree in creative writing from Eastern Washington University, a degree in mineral engineering physics from the Colorado School of Mines, and has taught at Eastern Washington University and Pelican Bay State Prison. He lives in Crescent City, California.

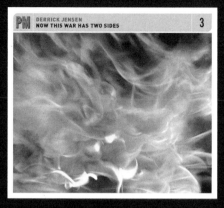

FRIENDS OF PM

These are indisputably momentous times – the financial system is melting down globally and the Empire is stumbling. Now more than ever there is a vital need for radical ideas.

In the year since its founding – and on a mere shoestring – PM Press has risen to the formidable challenge of publishing and distributing knowledge and entertainment for the struggles ahead. We have published an impressive and stimulating array of literature, art, music, politics, and culture. Using every available medium, we've succeeded in connecting those hungry for ideas and information to those putting them into practice.

Friends of PM allows you to directly help impact, amplify, and revitalize the discourse and actions of radical writers, filmmakers, and artists. It provides us with a stable foundation from which we can build upon our early successes and provides a much-needed subsidy for the materials that can't necessarily pay their own way.

It's a bargain for you too. For a minimum of $25 a month, you'll get all the audio and video (over a dozen CDs and DVDs in our first year) or all of the print releases (also over a dozen in our first year). For $40 you'll get everything that is published in hard copy. *Friends* also have the ability to purchase any/all items from our webstore at a 50% discount. And what could be better than the thrill of receiving a monthly package of cutting edge political theory, art, literature, ideas and practice delivered to your door?

Your card will be billed once a month, until you tell us to stop. Or until our efforts succeed in bringing the revolution around. Or the financial meltdown of Capital makes plastic redundant. Whichever comes first.

For more information on the *Friends of PM*, and about sponsoring particular projects, please go to www.pmpress.org, or contact us at info@pmpress.org.